GOODNESS NOT GRIEF

GOODNESS NOT GRIEF

Autobiography of **Yean Leng Lim** | *Australia, China, Singapore*

Published by

World Century Publishing Corporation

27 Warren Street, Suite 401-402, Hackensack, NJ 07601

Library of Congress Control Number: 2013923663

British Library Cataloguing-in-Publication Data
A catalogue record for this book is available from the British Library.

Goodness not Grief: Autobiography of Yean Leng LIM

Copyright © 2014 by World Century Publishing Corporation

All rights reserved. This book, or parts thereof, may not be reproduced in any form or by any means, electronic or mechanical, including photocopying, recording or any information storage and retrieval system now known or to be invented, without written permission from the publisher.

For photocopying of material in this volume, please pay a copying fee through the Copyright Clearance Center, Inc., 222 Rosewood Drive, Danvers, MA 01923, USA. In this case permission to photocopy is not required from the publisher.

In-house Editor: Darilyn Yap

ISBN 978-1-938134-41-8 (pbk)

Typeset by Stallion Press
Email: enquiries@stallionpress.com

Portrait of the Author
by Cheong Soo-Pieng

To God, creator of all things good

To my father and mother
For giving me life and education

To my wife, Wen Joy
My soul mate and love

And to my son, Iefan
My pride and joy

Preface

I became a doctor because my late father did not have a good doctor. He died after a brief illness at the age of 43 and I was grief stricken. The title of this book relates to this grief. I vowed after my father's death that my life would be dedicated to training good doctors. A good doctor should bring goodness, not grief, to his patients and their relatives. I hope to share with readers of this book, the journey to accomplish this goal.

I am an overseas Chinese who has lived most of my life in Australia. Born in Singapore and with my parents' foresight, I received a bilingual education from a young age. Later in life, I have the privilege to live and work in both the East and the West. Trained as a cardiologist, in many ways my life has actually turned out to be like a coronary bypass graft conduit. This conduit, however, does not connect two blood vessels, but two cultures, that of the East and the West. My photographic book, entitled *Eastern Eye Western Light*, also reflects the balance of eastern and western influences in my photographic art. Not only in art, but also in most endeavors of my life, I try to integrate and synergize western and Chinese views, culture and philosophy.

As a practising Christian, I know that God has carefully planned my life. He willed that I should be a doctor. In healing the sick and helping the weak, I have tried as much as I can to live a life in accordance to His will. I certainly hope my life journey as a doctor can inspire others, especially the younger generation in the same profession to bring goodness, not grief to their patients and relatives.

YLL

Preface by BG George Yeo

A great tide can be viewed from afar or it can be experienced afloat. From afar, the ebb and flow of China in the last two centuries can be read as history and current affairs. Afloat it is experienced in the drama of families and individual lives.

Yean Leng's autobiography records the voyage of one such life. The decline of the Qing Dynasty was followed by revolution and war in China. For over a hundred years, Chinese left China by the millions to Southeast Asia and beyond, creating modern Singapore. For many, Singapore became their new home. For others, the tide carried them further to America, Europe and Australia. As the tide gradually turned in China, it generated a return pull on these overseas Chinese. Some supported Dr Sun Yat-Sen in the 1911 Revolution. Many supported China in the war against Japan. A few went back to help Mao's China. After Deng Xiaoping reopened China to the world, overseas Chinese played a major role in China's modernization, building schools and hospitals, giving advice, teaching, trading, investing. Without losing their sense of Chineseness, they brought back to China western ideas, western methods, western values, western religion. In the very same process, these overseas Chinese became more Chinese again, rediscovering the civilization's ancient wisdom. In changing China, they also changed themselves.

Reading Yean Leng's story of his life, I see similarities with my own and with those of others who live in the Chinese diaspora. I was surprised that he asked me to write a preface for the English edition of his autobiography. It had been many years since we last met and many more years since we first met when I was Singapore's Health Minister. He was a well-known Singapore-born Australian cardiologist. We wanted him to help build up our heart centre in Singapore. He finally came after I had left the Ministry. Unfortunately for him, and for Singapore, our policies changed and the plan for the national heart centre that we had recruited him to establish was scrapped. Understandably, he left Singapore disappointed. But he left behind a legacy — in the patients he treated, in the doctors and nurses he taught, in the friends he made, in the field of the arts, in the way he lived his life as a Christian. For many years, an artistic photograph he took hung over my bedstead. There is much to learn from what he has written.

Preface by Richard Larkins

Goodness not Grief is a remarkable story of a remarkable life. Born into a poor family of an immigrant Chinese father in Singapore, Yean Leng Lims's autobiography shows how hard work and ability can combine to provide opportunities for talent to express itself for the benefit of people in three countries.

There are many important messages contained in this story and some wonderful insights gained from Yean Leng Lim's unique background and life experiences.

First, the insightful decision by Lim's paternal grandfather to instruct his fourth and youngest son to leave war ravaged Fujian province in southern China to seek out a distant uncle in Johor in the 1930s. Movingly, when Yean Leng visited his father's village in China many years later, all his relatives were illiterate peasants. As has so often been shown over the course of history in many lands, migrants and refugees can enrich the life of the countries that receive them.

Yean Leng Lim came to Australia to study medicine supported by the wonderful Colombo Plan scholarship scheme, one of the most effective aid programmes ever designed. Implemented in the 1950s and designed to help capacity development in South East Asia after the devastation of the Second World War, the scheme was extraordinarily effective. This success was not only through providing tertiary education opportunities in countries such as Australia for able students from the region but also for the host country through building enduring human links with the countries of origin of the students following their return.

Australia's generosity in providing the scholarship, has been repaid manyfold by Yean Leng Lim. His contributions to healthcare and education in Australia have been immense. He returned to Singapore to serve his country of birth many years later. His role in clinical care and training in that country as well as his tireless efforts at training young cardiologists from China and Singapore has certainly addressed the aims of capacity development to an unimaginable extent.

Yean Leng Lim's commitment to training cardiologists in China and his later recruitment as foundation Dean of the new medical school in Xiamen led to him spending significant periods in China and getting to know the country of his father's birth. His ability to straddle east and west gave him an ability to compare and contrast western and eastern styles of education, to contrast western and traditional Chinese medicine and to compare and contrast western and Chinese art and their evolution.

One of the privileges of consultant medical practice is to meet and learn about the lives of your patients. In Yean Leng Lim's case, his interests in art and music and his roles in medical research and medical politics as well as clinical practice in Australia, China and Singapore have led to friendships with an extraordinary array of people including senior politicians, artists, musicians, philanthropists and business people. All are described in this fascinating book.

But this is only part of the story. Yean Leng Lim was deeply moved by the poor communication and medical care received by his father leading to his death at the early age of 43. He has been motivated since that time to use his skill to ensure that the countless students and doctors he has influenced use their talents to treat the whole patient as an individual and not just as a technical challenge.

Preface by Richard Larkins xv

This is a human story about a good person, committed to his Christian faith, who has determined to use his ability to improve medical practice in three countries. It is the story of a multi-talented individual who combines his dedication to medicine with artistic talent expressing itself in painting and photography and a deep appreciation of music.

It is truly a story that bridges east and west, science and the humanities and faith and healing.

Emeritus Professor Richard Larkins AO
MDBS, PhD (Lond), LLD (Hon) (Melb), LLD (Hon) (Monash), FTSE, FRACP, FRCP, FRCPI, FAMSing, FAMMal

Foreword to Chinese Edition

(*Written in Chinese, translated by the author*)

At the time of the Chinese Spring Festival this year, Professor Lim or 'Lim', as we all affectionately call him, invited me to write a foreword for his thoughtfully written autobiography. I was initially burdened by this request because it is uncustomary in the Chinese tradition to write a foreword for a senior colleague. Twenty odd years ago, when I first encountered Professor Lim, he was to me, as a younger colleague, an outstanding and awe-inspiring doctor of Chinese descent. However, this awe gradually transformed into affection and respect over the years of professional contact and collaboration. For more than two decades, Professor Lim has selflessly shared his medical knowledge and expertise with countless Chinese doctors, travelling from far away Australia and Singapore. His reputation as a teacher from overseas is without peer in China.

After reading carefully his autobiography, I was deeply moved. He has blended three themes of his life into a single whole. *Goodness not Grief* describes his personal training and development to become an outstanding doctor; his deep conviction and societal mission to train better doctors; and finally his ambitious vision to improve interventional cardiology in the Asia Pacific region, in particular, China. Today, how a doctor can integrate the humanities and medical skills to benefit patients, especially Chinese patients, can be learnt from reading Professor Lim's autobiography.

It would be remiss to talk about Professor Lim without mentioning Mrs Lim. She is not only the indispensable partner in Professor Lim's professional work but also a great friend to many of us in China. As a wife supporting her husband, there can be no better role model. Her sincere and affectionate concern for anyone needing care, especially among Chinese fellows overseas, is legendary in China.

In addition to writing this preface, I would like to strongly recommend this book to a wide medical audience, in particular as essential reading for medical students and young doctors aspiring to become good doctors. This is also the wish of many venerable doctors in this country, who firmly believe that the humanities should not be neglected in medical education and training of doctors.

My initial burden of writing this foreword has been transformed into an opportunity to honour Professor Lim, for being a role model in teaching, learning and sharing and for his outstanding contribution to the growth and development of cardiovascular medicine in China.

I sincerely thank Professor Lim for this unusual honour of writing a foreword for his autobiography.

Huo Yong
President, Chinese Society of Cardiology
President, Chinese College of Cardiovascular Physicians
Director, Department of Cardiology &
Heart Centre, Peking University First Hospital

Preface to the Chinese Edition of Dr Lim's Autobiography
Goodness Not Grief

Brother Joseph Chang
Former Principal
Catholic High School, Singapore

This original English version of Dr Lim's autobiography, written in insightful but simple language and richly illustrated with accompanying photographs, complimented the already published Chinese edition that was eloquently translated by Mr Chong Wing Hong. I gladly consented to his invitation to write a Preface for the Chinese translation of this autobiography.

I still remember vividly a certain day in the 1960s when Yean Leng played for me one of Chopin's *Nocturnes*. Thereafter, like Leonardo da Vinci, he painted two large murals on elevated walls in two of the newly completed school halls. Everyone who saw the completed wall murals was amazed.

Most would agree that you are gifted, Yean Leng. The Chinese sage Meng-tze has warned that *before heaven will bestow a person with extraordinary gifts and large responsibilities, the person will need to be tested, his skin and bones labored and his body starved!*

Dr Lim lost his father at a young age. Physically, he is weak and sickly. However, his accomplishment later in life was great, in particular in benefiting the sick and in glorifying the word and work of God.

In the Chinese tradition, a teacher, though only for a brief period in the life of the student, will be treated as if a father for life. In this spirit, I celebrate with Yean Leng his life and praise the Lord for His abundant grace from now to eternity.

Brother Joseph Zhang
Handwritten in Chinese ink brush, aged 86
(Text translated from the original
Chinese script by the author)

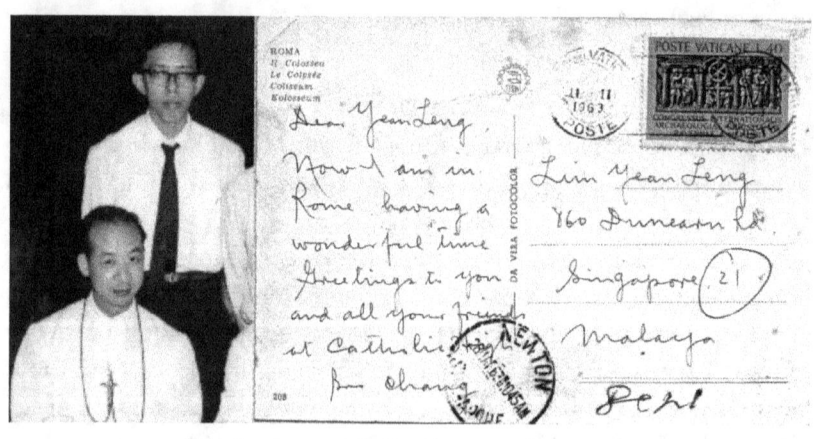

Acknowledgement

I wish to thank my parents for giving me life. I am grateful to Singapore for nurturing me when I was young, to Australia for my splendid education and to China for the unique opportunity to be part of its extraordinary growth and development, especially in its healthcare, over the past three decades. Without my soul mate Joy, this life story would not be possible. Without her love, sacrifice and strong positive spiritual influence, my story would not be worth telling. I am also indebted to my only child, Iefan, for his sacrifice and understanding of the precious little time that we have had together, a personal high price to pay for an active professional career.

Without my mentors, who have sculptured my intellect at various stages of my life, I would not have become the person that I am today. My high school principal Brother Joseph Dufreese and my university mentors, William Walters and the late Eric Glasgow, were my role models.

To my many friends who generously helped me to accomplish seemingly impossible tasks in China, I am grateful. In particular, the Singapore Lee Foundation, the late Mr Lie Siong Tay and Liem Sioe Leong for financially supporting the building of the Xiamen University Medical College. I acknowledge the generosity of Mr P S Lee and the donors of the ACIS Heart Foundation for funding the training programme of doctors from China to study in Singapore and Melbourne. My personal work in China would not have been possible without the financial and logistic support of the education teams of the multinational medical device companies in China.

To the former Minister for Health, the Arts and Information and Foreign Affairs of Singapore, BG George Yeo who recruited me back to serve Singapore and for writing a preface for this book, I am deeply grateful. I am also indebted to Professor Richard Larkins, the former Vice Chancellor of Monash University, who gave me invaluable advice in my career on numerous occasions and for his very kind and encouraging preface.

Last but not least, I am grateful to my schoolmate, Mr Chong Wing-hong, for the Chinese translation of my autobiography and Richard Pannell for proofreading this English version. Without their effort, this autobiography would never have been published.

Contents

Portrait of the Author by Cheong Soo-Pieng	v
Preface	ix
Preface by BG George Yeo	xi
Preface by Richard Larkins	xiii
Foreword to Chinese Edition	xvii
Preface to the Chinese Edition of Dr Lim's Autobiography	
Goodness Not Grief	xix
Acknowledgement	xxi
List of Figures	xxix
List of Tables	xxxvii

Chapter 1   Early Years — 1

Better Future in Nanyang	1
Extraordinary Parents from Ordinary Backgrounds	3
'Yean Leng'	5
Learning English from the King James Bible	8
Chinese Calligraphy and Medicine	11
Catholic High School's 'Sistine Chapel'	12
Boiled 'Phoenix' Flowers to Cure Asthma	14
Beautiful China	15

Youngest Art Graduate	16
'Memories of the Lovely Dreams of Youth'	18
Life's First Turning Point	21
The Vow to Train Better Doctors	23
Omega Watch, a Symbol of Love	24
Lim Koon Yaw Memorial Scholarship	25

Chapter 2   Vow to be a Doctor — 27

The 'Lucky Country' Down-Under	27
'Going to the Hospital to Die!'	29
Narrow Escape for a 'Singaporean Son'	30
My Singapore Story	32
Cultural Shocks	33
A Renaissance Man	35
Early Interest in Cardiovascular Physiology	36
Lesson in Scientific Writing	37
Violin and the National Heart Foundation Student Scholarship	40
The Three Queens of Queen Victoria Hospital	41
'Look After Miss Ma'	42
Marriage Proposal in Taipei	44
'Worthy of His Calling'	46
'I Think She's Dead'	47
'You've Tried Hard'	49
Joy in Australia	50
Iefan — 'Surpassing the Ordinary'	53
PhD Research in Pregnancy Hypertension	54
Training of a Cardiologist	55
From Nuclear Cardiology to PTCA	56
'I am a Butcher!'	59
Reviving Albert Tucker	62
First Private Cardiovascular Unit in Melbourne	63
Interventional Cardiology Training and the Epworth Connection	64

New Cardiac Centre in Melbourne's East	66
New Cardiovascular Centre in Melbourne's West	69
From HC to VIC to MVIC	71

Chapter 3 A Good Doctor — 75

Cushing's Four Portraits of a Good Doctor	75
Healing with Science and Humanism	77
Doctor, 'Docrat' or 'Dr Death'	80
Ethics — Cornerstone of a Doctor	82
Basic Healthcare Assurance	85
Inaccessible and Unaffordable Healthcare	86
Lim's Ward Round	88
'Treat Patients not Lesions'	89
The 'Alabama Student'	93
The 'Hudson-Taylor Spirit'	95
'How Would You Treat This Patient If She Were Your Mother?'	96

Chapter 4 Goodness not Grief — 99

Doctor Eyes China with Heart	99
First Visit to China	101
'This Foreigner Speaks Pu-tong Hua'	104
The Story of 'A Foolish Old Man Moving the Mountain'	106
Australia China Indonesia Singapore (ACIS) Heart Foundation	110
Hangzhou Fellows	113
First PTCAs in Hangzhou	114
'British Girl Chinese Wife'	115
'Duncan Main of Hangchow'	116
Hangzhou and Beyond	117
A 'Small' Hospital	121
Australian Steak Against Radiation Harm	123
Coronary Stenting without X-ray	126
The Wei-wei Story of Guangzhou	127

'I want to learn Interventional Cardiology from you' … 129
Hands-on Training in Coronary Interventional Cardiology
  for Overseas Doctors … 131
Unwitting Business Partner … 131
'To Live' but with Boomerang instead of Aeroplane … 132
Osler and the Peking Union Medical College … 134
Beijing Medical License for Foreign Doctors … 136
Returning to China When I Can Walk Again … 136
'Three Wise Men of Christmas' at Dunhuang … 139
'Goodness not Grief' … 141
'Tao Li Fen Fang' … 143
Following Father's Footseps (*Zi Chen Fu Yue*). … 145

Chapter 5   Xiamen University Medical College … 149

The Tallest House in Chen-chang … 149
Tan Kah Kee's 75 Year-old Dream Realised … 150
Birth of a New Medical School … 152
Doctors with Knowledge and Humanity … 157
Professors for Xiamen University Medical College … 160
Affiliated or Teaching Hospital … 161
Xiamen Heart Centre … 163
Top Surgeon or Pioneer Dean … 165
Big Party Secretary and Little Party Secretary … 167
One Pen … 168
Search for a Local Successor … 169
Loss of a Local Successor … 171
Dragon or Worm … 174

Chapter 6   Health Reform and Centres of Excellence … 175

I Left My Heart in Singapore … 175
Uniting the 'Cardiological Factions' … 177
Aussie Humor not Appreciated … 178

Professionalism for Nursing and Medical Technologist	180
First Asian Medical Technology Diploma Course	181
Role Model Leadership	182
Outpatient Clinic Bullying	184
Quantifying Academic Excellence	185
Pyramid of Excellence	188
Staff Appointment and the Electoral College System	189
'Kiasu-ism' — A Unique Singaporean Trait	190
'You Are On the Wrong Side'	193
'All-or-none'	195
Review of Medical Education in Singapore	197
NMRC, BRMC and A*STAR	198
'Mamas Always Come to Us'	200
'S' Stands for Singapore	202
Demise of the New National Heart Hospital	203
The Fateful Letter	206
Without Brain or Heart	208
'Idealists Must Suffer'	210
'How is He?'	212
'Where Exactly are We in Health?'	212
A New NAFA	214
Professor and the Beauty	217

Chapter 7   Asia Pacific — The Third Block   221

Live Demonstration Courses in Interventional Cardiology	221
Andreas Gruentzig Society 30th Anniversary Celebration	222
Singapore Live Course in Endovascular Therapy (SingLIVE)	226
Asia Pacific Society of Interventional Cardiology (APSIC)	228
Two Philosophies of APSIC Governance	230
China's Role in the Third Block	231
Coronary Intervention Salons of China (CISC)	233
China Interventional Therapeutics (CIT)	235

East West PCI — from 'Cross-Fire' to 'Co-Evolution'	238
Superimposition of the East West Pyramids	241
China's Contribution to the Treatment of Coronary Artery Disease	244
The Half-global Policy	246

Chapter 8 East and West, Science and God — 249

'Where Do You Really Come From?'	249
Rhythm of the East	251
'Wait and See'	252
Western and Eastern Learning	254
Traditional Chinese Medicine (TCM) and Western Medicine	256
Not 'Mainstream Science'	259
Between Painting and Poetry	262
Eastern Eye Western Light	265
Convergence of Chinese and Western Painting	268
Painting, Photography and Percutaneous Coronary Intervention	274
Emperor Qianlong's Mistake	276
Mao's Last Musicians	279
Chief Rabbi and the 'Wheat Kernel' Parable	282
God's Business and Your Profession	283
God's Words or Fairytales?	287
'What's the Difference Between Me and the Homeless Man On the Street?'	288
My Psalm 23	289
On Wings like Eagles	294
'God within You'	295
Rewards for Act of Love	296

Epilogue	299
Chronology	301
Index	309

List of Figures

Fig. 1.	New Year Resolution of my father in his 1940 diary.	2
Fig. 2.	Grandfather Lau Teck Jin (standing, 4th from left) with President Chai Yuan Pei (seated, middle), Peking University.	4
Fig. 3.	Family Portrait (Back: from left: Yean Chuan, YL, Yean Kai; Front: Yean Lian, Mother, Yean Teng, Father, Cheng Hwee).	6
Fig. 4.	Mural painting entitled *Fauna*, Science Laboratory, Catholic High School 1962.	13
Fig. 5.	Graduation class of 1961, Nanyang Academy of Fine Art (YL, back row, third from left).	17
Fig. 6.	Receiving the '*Special Prize for Drawing*' medal from the Queen of Malaysia, photograph taken by father, 1962.	20
Fig. 7.	'*Mountainous Landscape*', oil painting by Eugene von Guerard, 1840.	21
Fig. 8.	Father's grave soon after burial, 1965.	23
Fig. 9.	Mother presenting the *Lim Koon Yaw Memorial Scholarship* medal to Lee Hsien Loong, 1967.	26

Fig. 10.	My *Singapore Story*, painted in 1967, with SM Lee Kuan Yew, 1999.	33
Fig. 11.	My mentors at PhD graduation ceremony (from left: R Southby, WA Walters, YL, GF Glasgow).	38
Fig. 12.	Calligraphy of the biblical verse *Worthy of His calling* sent by Joy in celebration of MBBS graduation 1972.	48
Fig. 13.	Wedding at Swanston Street Church of Christ, Melbourne, Oct 20 1973.	52
Fig. 14.	Wen Joy and YL at MGH across Charles River, Boston, 1981.	58
Fig. 15.	With the Smorgons and Tuckers, South Yarra 1996 (From left: Iefan, Victor & Loti Smorgan, Barbara & Albert Tucker).	61
Fig. 16.	Founders of the Cardiovascular Unit, Epworth Hospital 1982 (from left: YL, E Manolas, G Sloman, R Dick).	65
Fig. 17.	Newspaper report in the *Herald Sun*, Nov 24 1994.	68
Fig. 18.	Four portraits representing the essential qualities of a good doctor (Clockwise from top left: Linacre, Harvey, Osler, Sydenham).	77
Fig. 19.	Excerpt from Sun Xi-miao's preface to the '*Treatise of the Thousand Golden Prescription*' (*Da yi Jin xheng*) representing the code of ethics for Chinese medicine doctors.	83
Fig. 20.	The 'Lim's Ward Round', Xiamen Heart Centre, Xiamen Medical College, Fujian 2011.	90
Fig. 21.	Lecture poster '*How to be a Good Doctor*', Beijing 2011.	92
Fig. 22.	My four role models (Clockwise from left top: Leonardo da Vinci, William Osler, James Hudson-Taylor, Albert Schweitzer).	94
Fig. 23.	James Hudson-Taylor's famous quotation in the church at Jenjiang, China where his tombstone is housed.	96

List of Figures xxxi

Fig. 24.	'Doctor eyes China with heart', *Whitehorse Gazette*, 1993.	100
Fig. 25.	Photograph of Pudong, taken from Weitan in Puxi, 1983.	102
Fig. 26.	Photograph of Pudong, taken from Weitan in Puxi, 2010.	103
Fig. 27.	With Professor Tao Shou-qi (third left) and Professor Fang Qi (third right), the Lim family (center), Beijing, 1986.	107
Fig. 28.	The 3rd Chinese Technical Cooperation and Training Centre of Cardiovascular Disease (CTCTCD), Fu Wai Hospital, Beijing.	108
Fig. 29.	Benefactors of the Australia China Indonesia Singapore (ACIS) Heart Foundation (from left: YL, Liem Sioe Leong, Mayor Zhu, Ng Eik Cheong, Lie Siong Tay).	112
Fig. 30.	Early PTCAs at the Zhejiang Provincial People's Hospital, Hangzhou 1992 (from left: Prof. Jin Fan, YL).	114
Fig. 31.	Planning the new Cardiac Unit at Run Run Shaw Hospital, Hangzhou, 1990 (from left: Fang JP, YL, Zheng Xu and two staff members).	118
Fig. 32.	Professor Wang Jian-an (first from right) and his team at the No. 2 Affiliated Hospital of Zhejiang University.	119
Fig. 33.	The Australian surgical team evaluating a patient before CABG surgery, Hangzhou 1992 (from left: Yan ZK, D Esmore, F Jin , YL, patient).	121
Fig. 34.	Teaching coronary angiography at the First Affiliated Hospital, Shaxi, 1990 (from left: JL Li and YL).	123
Fig. 35.	Portrait of Chairman Mao in the catheter laboratory of the Guangzhou People's Provincial Hospital.	125

Fig. 36.	Radiation protection headgear worn in the catheter laboratory of Guangzhou Provincial Hospital (from left: cardiac fellow, Chen Chuan-rong, YL).	126
Fig. 37.	The Great Wall International Symposium of Interventional Cardiology (GWISIC), Liangma Hotel, Beijing 1994.	133
Fig. 38.	Air-evacuated to Singapore General Hospital after Dalian car accident (from left: Joy, a friend, Rev. Steven Tong, YL, mother).	139
Fig. 39.	'*Three wise men*', photograph taken from a camel's back at Mingshasun, Dunhuang (from left: Liu Chao-zhong, YL, Joy).	140
Fig. 40.	The Cia Guo-liang couplet, calligraphy by YL.	142
Fig. 41.	Coronary painting by Lin X.X., containing the poem '*Goodness not Grief*'.	143
Fig. 42.	Calligraphy '*Tao Li Fen Fang*' with Fellows at my Erin Street Clinic in Richmond, Victoria 2006 (from left: Chen Ming, Zuo Luning, YL, Zhu Tie-bin)	144
Fig. 43.	Working with Iefan in the cardiac catheter laboratory at the Western Hospital, 2007.	146
Fig. 44.	Wedding photograph, Iefan and Krystal Lim, 5 December 2010.	147
Fig. 45.	A visit to the Lim clan at the village Chen-chang in Tong-an, Fujian 2000.	151
Fig. 46.	First batch of medical undergraduates of the new Xiamen University Medical College, 1996.	153
Fig. 47.	Meeting where the discussion of the new Xiamen University Medical College took place, Xiamen 1995 (from left: Lie Siong Tay, Wang Rong, Lim Zugeng, three government officals, Chou AT, YL, Wang LM).	155

Fig. 48.	Inaugural Dean appointment at the Opening Ceremony of the Xiamen University Medical College, 11 October 1996 (YL, Mayor Hong YS).	157
Fig. 49.	Teaching bedside clinical medicine at the Xiamen University Medical College, 1996.	159
Fig. 50.	The first Xiamen University Medical College Building, named after Li Wen Jen (Moktar Riardy), Chairman, Lippo Group.	162
Fig. 51.	The 'Three-in-one *Zhen-he building*' housing the Xiamen Heart Centre, Xiamen Emergency Centre and the XUMC Clinical Departments (left: Zhang Bei-mong, YL).	164
Fig. 52.	*Straits Times* article 'I left my heart in Singapore', 1997.	177
Fig. 53.	Meeting with vice-minister Huang Jiefu, Ministry for Health, Beijing 2009.	188
Fig. 54.	Pyramid of excellence in percutaneous coronary intervention.	189
Fig. 55.	Meeting of health ministers of Australia and Singapore to sign the DRG MOU (from left: Moses Lee, YL, Willie Tan, CT Yeoh, M. Woolridge).	194
Fig. 56.	Inter-ministerial executive advisory committee for life sciences, Singapore 2001.	201
Fig. 57.	Luncheon meeting with PM Goh Cheok Tong at the Istana 2002.	215
Fig. 58.	NAFA Graduation Ceremony 2002 (from left: Minister Ng Eng Hean, Principal Ho KL, Fu CA, clerk, YL).	216
Fig. 59.	30th anniversary of first PTCA in man performed by A. Gruentzig on 16 September 1977. University Hospital lecture theatre, Zurich 2007.	223
Fig. 60.	With Dolf Bachmann, the first man to receive PTCA treatment (left: YL, Dolf & Mrs Bachmann).	224

Fig. 61.	Calligraphic logo of the 'Singapore Live Intervention in Vascular Endotherapy', now part of EuroPCR-SingLIVE.	226
Fig. 62.	Live demonstration of coronary stenting by Dr A. Colombo at the Chaoyang Hospital, Beijing 1998.	232
Fig. 63.	Gala dinner of the First CIT at *Diao Yu Tai*, Beijing 2003.	237
Fig. 64.	Live transmission from Fu Wai Hospital to EuroPCR 2002 (left: Gao R, YL, M. Claude-Morice).	238
Fig. 65.	Differences (horns) and synergies (Hexagon) between East and West.	242
Fig. 66.	Singapore Ministry for Health TCM Taskforce at the Central Bureau of TCM, Beijing 2001.	259
Fig. 67.	'*Music to the Eye*', photographed at Westlake, Hangzhou; a tribute to P H Emerson.	264
Fig. 68.	Albert Tucker examining the book '*Music to the Eye*' at St. Kilda, 1995.	266
Fig. 69.	Photographic book *Eastern Eye Western Light*, published 1995.	267
Fig. 70.	Light introduced into Chinese painting (left: *Bamboo* by Xu Beihong; right: Watercolour *Melon* by P. Cezanne).	270
Fig. 71.	'Back-lit light' introduced into Chinese painting (*Li River, Kweilin* by Li Keran).	271
Fig. 72.	Title page for second photographic book, entitled *Window of the Heart* (to be published); calligraphy by Wu Guang-zhong.	273
Fig. 73.	At Zhang Da-chian's art studio '*Mo Ye Jing Se*', Taipei 1981 and couplet on the subjects of botany and zoology (From left back: YL, Joy, Mrs Zhang; seated: Zhang Dachian).	274

List of Figures xxxv

Fig. 74.	Photographs of a bird on branches of a tree (left images) when inverted (middle images) resemble human coronary artery angiogram (right images).	276
Fig. 75.	One volume of the *shi ku qian zu*, commissioned by Emperor Qian-long (left), and a page from D. Diderot's first edition encyclopedia (right).	278
Fig. 76.	Christmas caroling by the Combined Chinese Churches Choir, Melbourne, 1990.	290
Fig. 77.	Children of the Yi tribe, Da Liang Shan, Zhoujie, Sichuan, 2003.	291
Fig. 78.	Volunteer staff of the *Red Cross Pharmacy* (later renamed *Bethesda Clinic*), Hangzhou 1990.	292
Fig. 79.	Co-workers of the Chinese Christian Medical Mission, 1984 (from left: Wang RT, Joy, YL, Chai MT, Jian CM, Chai CR, Wang LT).	293
Fig. 80.	Reward of *work out of love* is Joy everlasting.	298

List of Tables

Table 1.	Essential qualities of a good doctor	79
Table 2.	Paradigm shift in culture needed to improve NHC	191
Table 3.	A comparison of western and traditional Chinese medicine	258
Table 4.	A comparison of western and Chinese painting	272
Table 5.	Science versus creation	286

Fig. 10. My *Singapore Story*, painted in 1967, with SM Lee Kuan Yew, 1999

Fig. 73. At Zhang Da-chian's art studio 'Mo Ye Jing Se', Taipei 1981 and couplet on the subjects of botany and zoology (From left back: YL, Joy, Mrs Zhang; seated: Zhang Dachian)

Fig. 46. First batch of medical undergraduates of the new Xiamen University Medical College, 1996

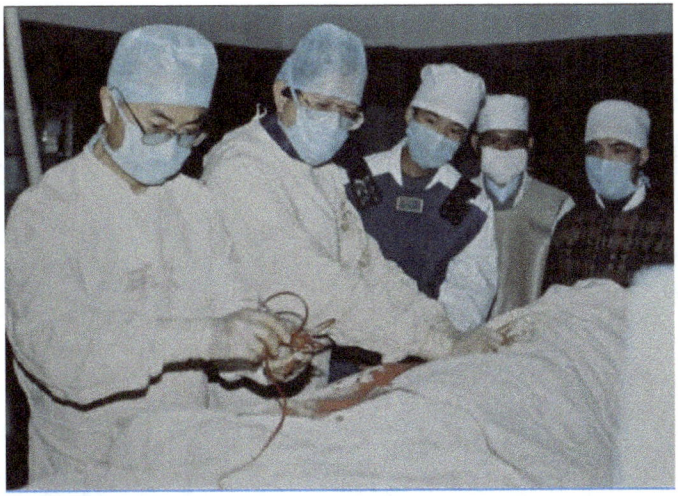

Fig. 30. Early PTCAs at the Zhejiang Provincial People's Hospital, Hangzhou 1992 (from left: Prof. Jin Fan, YL)

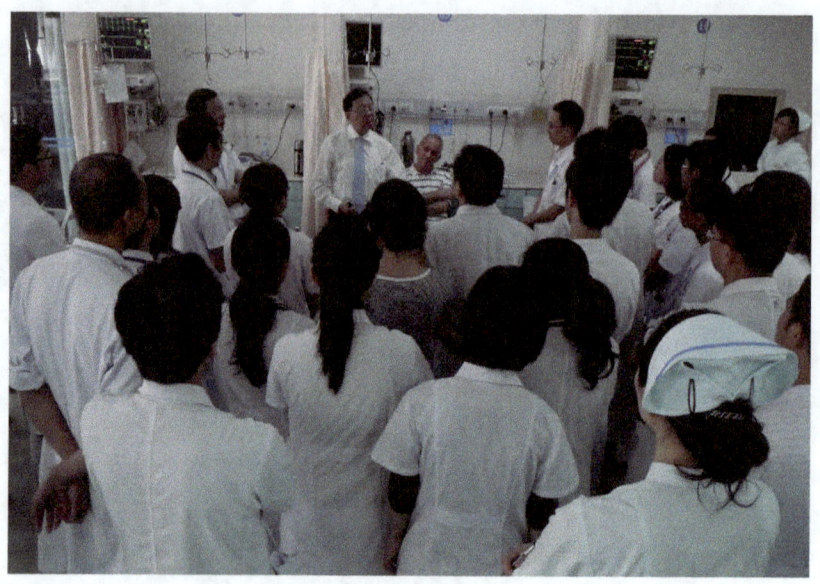

Fig. 20. The 'Lim Ward Round', Xiamen Heart Centre, Xiamen Medical College, Fujian 2011

Fig. 67. *Music to the Eye*, photographed at Westlake, Hangzhou; a tribute to P H Emerson

1

Early Years

Better Future in Nanyang

Southern China was ravaged by war when Japan invaded China in the 1930s. In a small commune of the Lim clan called Chen-chang, close to the village of Ma Xiang in the county of Tong-an, Fujian province, my paternal grandfather Lim Nan San told his fourth and youngest son, Lim Koon Yaw, to start a new life in a new country. He instructed my father, then 17 years old: *to go to Xiamen, the nearest sea port, get on a boat and go to Nanyang (Southern Ocean) to look for your distant uncle in Malaya, there you will have a better future.*

With only a toothbrush, my father did get onto a refugee boat, survived the sea journey and arrived in Singapore in 1938. Miraculously, he managed to track down this distant uncle in the state of Johor, adjacent to Singapore. This uncle gave him work in his rubber plantation. That was how my father started his new life in Nanyang. He had not quite completed his high school when he left home in Fujian. Two years later, on New Year's eve in 1940 at the age of 19 years, he entered the following New Year resolution in his diary:

> *The giant wheel of time will not halt for a moment. Time flies, and another year is coming to pass. Today is the first day of a new year.*

Looking back since arriving in Singapore 2 years ago, I asked myself what had I achieved. Still single, I have grown from adolescence to youth; and soon I'll be elderly. So while I am young, I must harness all my energies and battle all adversities. I must be independent in the society. I must train my body and mind, refine my behaviour, and refrain from all vices. I must work hard to achieve the ultimate victory. I must not fail this resolution.

Koon Yaw, written in Singapore, New Year day on the 29th year of the Republic of China, 1940 in the western calendar (Fig. 1).

My mother, Lau Eng Swan, showed me this page of my father's diary many years after he had passed away at the age of 43 years. It turned out that my father did not have a chance to become elderly, as he had hoped in 1940. At the time of his death, he probably thought that he had not achieved the success that he wished for in 1940.

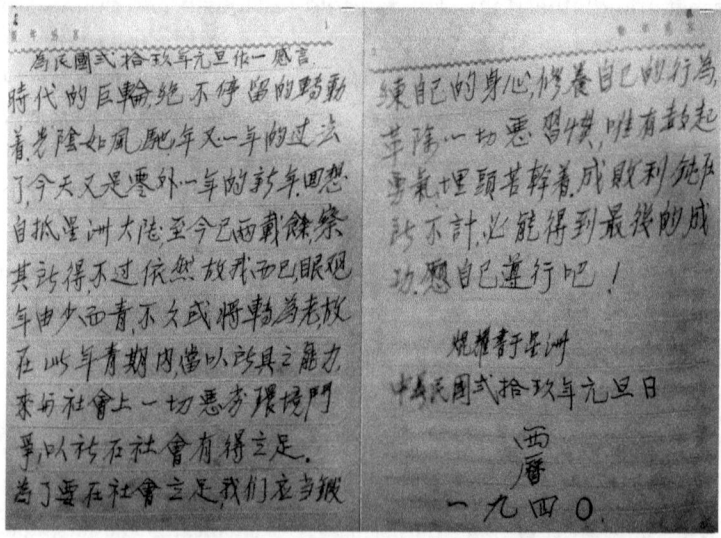

Fig. 1. New Year Resolution of my father in his 1940 diary.

My father and mother were married in 1944 and I was born in 1948, near the end of the Year of the Pig, the third of six siblings, five boys and one girl. My mother survived my father for another 41 years, and remained a widow until her death in 2006 at the ripe old age of 84. As a widow, she had attained what is considered the highest virtue of a traditional Chinese wife. Even though my father did not consider his life a success, to his children he had succeeded as he had hoped in his diary of 1940. My mother was more fortunate to have a full life with her children and grandchildren. She was both father and mother to us for most of our adult lives. My parents' success is reflected in the fact that they lived for their children, who have all turned out to be successful in one way or another, in their chosen lives.

Extraordinary Parents from Ordinary Backgrounds

After arriving in Nanyang, my father worked hard in the small plot of land given to him by his uncle in Johor, Malaya. He prospered with his labour but unfortunately lost everything he earned when the Japanese invaded Malaya and Singapore in 1942. He started afresh and worked as the most junior member of staff of the newly established Overseas Union Bank (OUB) in Singapore. He was one of the original 27 founding members of the bank. From the position of cleaner and office hand, he was eventually promoted to the rank of bank manager of the Tiong Bahru Branch of OUB three months before his untimely death at the age of 43 in 1965.

I knew little of my paternal relatives because most of them remained in Tong-an, Fujian province, in China. As a child, I grew up with my parents and maternal relatives who had all immigrated to Singapore, also in the late 1930s. My maternal grandfather, Lau Tek Jin, was one of the few western educated young scholars of his time in China, after the fall of the Qing Dynasty. He was appointed to the position of Secretary General of the Youth Male Chinese Association (YMCA) in Xiamen because of his proficiency in the English language.

He mixed with the literati of his time, among them the Founding President of Peking University, Chai Yuan Pei (Fig. 2) and the President of the Beijing Central Chinese Academy of Fine Art, the artist Xu Beihong. I attribute my love of art to the influence of my maternal grandfather, the only member of my extended family who was well-educated in the arts. Unfortunately, my maternal grandfather was not a family person. His life was ruined by opium addiction, the curse of many Chinese of the late 19th and early 20th century and the cause of the notorious Opium Wars in China towards the end of the Qing Dynasty. He had presenile dementia and was ineffective as the head of the Lau clan in his later years. After his death, I was the custodian of his art collection for many years. This probably laid the foundation for my life-long interest in Chinese painting and calligraphy.

Because of the mental incapacity of my maternal grandfather, my mother and her elder brother Hui Bu had to provide for most of what

Fig. 2. Grandfather Lau Teck Jin (standing, 4th from left) with President Chai Yuan Pei (seated, middle), Peking University.

his family needed. His youngest son, Tin Hua, whom we, the Lim siblings, called 'little uncle', was 12 years older than me. My maternal grandmother, Ngo So-Khim, although illiterate, was the matriarch of the Lau clan. My mother inherited some of her traits. My mother was an extravert and a vivacious lady. She lived for her children and her friends. She held three jobs simultaneously, working as a teacher, a private tutor and as head of the Hokkien department of Rediffusion Broadcasting Corporation. My mother was a God-fearing woman and a practising Christian. Together with my grand-aunt, they founded the Singapore Christian Home for the Aged. My mother was the Chairman of the Board of this Home for the Aged, from its inception until her death. She was also a deacon of the Chen-li (Truth) Church in Singapore for most of her life. From an ordinary origin, my mother was no ordinary woman. To her husband, children and grandchildren she will always be an extra-ordinary wife, mother and grandmother and a role model for all of us. She would endure all kinds of hardships to ensure the success of her offspring. In this regard, she was successful in her life the same way my father had succeeded in his life.

As for my paternal relatives, my father was the only one of five siblings who immigrated to Singapore. He had a distant nephew in Singapore who also died young. Two elder brothers of my father had immigrated to Indonesia. I have never met my paternal grandparents or uncles in China or overseas.

'Yean Leng'

My parents married in their early twenties and their first five children arrived in rapid succession, a year apart. The first four were boys and the fifth was the only girl, my sister Cheng Hwee. Ten years after my sister was born, my youngest brother Yean Teng arrived unexpectedly and the Lim family of eight was finalised (Fig. 3).

My eldest brother, the first child, was born in April of 1945 just before World War II ended. My parents named him Yean Peng. The

Fig. 3. Family Portrait (Back: from left: Yean Chuan, YL, Yean Kai; Front: Yean Lian, Mother, Yean Teng, Father, Cheng Hwee).

Chinese character for 'Peng' is the word 'peace' and 'Yean Peng' literally means 'prolong peace'. My parents, like everyone at that time, were hoping for peace and the end of the Japanese occupation of Singapore. Indeed, four months after he was born, the war miraculously ended after the dropping of the two atomic bombs in Japan. With victory over the Japanese occupation, he was renamed Yean Kai. 'Kai' is the Chinese word for 'victory'. The first name 'Yean' is common to all the male siblings in our family according to the Chinese naming protocol. The Chinese character for 'Yean' means 'prolong'. My second brother was named Yean Chuan, meaning 'endless stream' and I was given the name

Yean Leng. My middle name 'Leng' is the Chinese character for 'age'. My name, therefore, literally translated, means 'prolong age or life'. My name is often depicted in Chinese paintings in the form of cranes and pine trees, the symbols of longevity. My parents obviously wished that I would live a long life. As it turned out, I live a life mainly to prolong other people's lives! I have at least lived a longer life than my father.

I was born on 19th January 1948, in a small maternity hospital in Tiong Bahru, an older part of Singapore near the Singapore General Hospital. 'Tiong' is the Hokkien version of the Chinese word 'middle', as in 'middle kingdom', the original name of China. 'Bahru' however, is the Malay word for 'new'. With a name combining both Chinese and Malay words, one could already tell the multicultural nature of Singapore from the beginning. I was therefore destined to cross cultures!

Our first family home was a three-bedroom apartment at 53A Tiong Bahru Road, or the 'Street of new China'. In 1947, my parents made their first and only return visit to their hometowns of Tong-an and Xiamen, with me in mother's womb! Thus, I made my first visit to China *in utero*! This must have some bearing on my unexplained affinity for China in the years to come. Not long after my parents' return to Singapore, I was born. It was not until 2000, at the age of 52, that I visited the roots of my ancestors at Tong-an, Fujian.

There was a global epidemic of poliomyelitis in 1948–9. I was one of its victims. Fortunately, my disease was mild and it has only affected my right leg. A large part of the first few years of my life was spent attending physiotherapy and rehabilitation classes at the Singapore General Hospital (SGH) because of my polio-affected leg. This hospital is only a stone's throw away from where we lived in Tiong Bahru. SGH is also the hospital where my father later died. I still have vivid memories of my mischievous childhood, taking impossible short cuts, even with my right leg in steel calipers, to get to the hospital, much to the despair of my grandmother, who took me regularly to all my physiotherapy classes.

There was never a dull moment at home with four boys, each a year apart, growing up together in a small confined space. There were seven of us initially to share the three bedrooms before the arrival of our youngest brother. Competition for food, toys and space was intense. My father and mother had to spend a considerable amount of time each day settling disputes and dispensing punishments. My eldest brother was the big bully when he was young. One day he threw a dart that landed in my temple bone. The 'missile thrower' promptly removed it and told me to go to bed and not tell anyone. With total obedience, I followed his instructions to the letter! Fortunately for me, it missed the temporal artery and the wound did not get infected. My father had to set aside a special calendar for us to record our daily fights so that he could punish the offenders when he returned from work each day. My sister and I were the two least offenders. Years later, I still boast about the fact that I was the only boy in our family to avoid being locked in the toilet for misbehaviour.

There were also brighter memories of our childhood. My second brother and I shared a keen interest in chemistry during our high school days. We converted a very small storeroom at home into a chemistry laboratory. It was in the mid-seventies and the space race between America and Russia was at its peak, just before the landing of man on the moon. We were fascinated by the powerful rockets that were able to launch the space capsules and decided to make our own rockets at home. The necessary chemical ingredients were stolen from chemistry laboratory classes and we successfully produced a 'home-made' rocket ready to be launched in the back alleys of Tiong Bahru. The rocket launch was successful. Looking back, we were extremely naïve and irresponsible. It was by God's grace that no one was injured nor property destroyed with these dangerous rocket launchings!

Learning English from the King James Bible

Singapore was still a British colony in the early 1950s. It was and still is a multicultural society with three quarters of its population of Chinese origin. The education policy set by the Government for this small multicultural nation was to educate everyone in English, the working language plus one's mother tongue. Thus, a Chinese race Singaporean could choose to attend either a Chinese or an English school for education. English is compulsory in Chinese schools, whereas learning Chinese language is not essential in English schools. There were also a handful of Malay schools where Malay is the main teaching medium with English as a compulsory subject. Hoping to continue the traditional Chinese culture in Singapore, wealthy first generation immigrants from China donated generously to build numerous Chinese schools. Among these was Tan Kah Kee, a philanthropist who founded the Toa Nan Primary School and Chinese High School in Singapore and Chi Mei Primary and Secondary schools in Chi Mei and Xiamen University in Xiamen, China. Classic literature and texts, in ancient and modern Chinese language were part of the standard curriculum in all the Chinese schools in Singapore at that time. Many teachers in the Chinese schools were imported from China but some were trained locally. My primary school education started at the Toa Nan Primary School, founded by Tan Kah Kee, before I was transferred to Catholic High School, a school famous for its bilingual education. My connection with Tan Kah Kee was to be extended many years later when I helped to fulfill his dream of a medical school at the Xiamen University in China. Catholic High School was founded and run by the Marist Brothers, a sect of the Catholic Church renowned for its education mission. Catholic High School was the only bilingual school in Singapore at that time, using both Chinese and English languages in its teaching. Graduates from this unique school in Singapore could enrol in universities offering tertiary education in either the Chinese or English language.

Education is regarded as the most important attribute in a Chinese society. The ranking of professional esteem in a Chinese society in the Confucian order is scholars, followed by farmers, then workers and finally merchants. Scholars are revered whereas merchants less so. My parents subscribed totally to this traditional Confucian order and made education their top priority for our upbringing. They had the good foresight to channel all of us at an early age into this bilingual school run by the Catholic Marist Brothers. Without their wisdom and foresight, my life would be totally different today.

Singapore is situated near the equator. The weather is hot and humid all year round. One often jokes about the three seasons of Singapore, namely hot, hotter and hottest! Because of the intense heat, schooling was scheduled for about six hours each day, especially at the primary school level. In the fifties, most schools in Singapore were run as two full-time schools, one in the morning and the other in the afternoon. Morning school started at seven and finished at one o'clock in the afternoon. The afternoon school then followed immediately from one to seven o'clock in the evening. Our parents, wanting to take advantage of this dual school system, made us attend both the Chinese and English schools simultaneously in the beginning until we all got into the bilingual Catholic High School. We had to attend the Chinese Primary School at Tao Nan in the morning and then rush to the English school at Radin Mas Primary School in the afternoon. After I was transferred to the bilingual Catholic High School, my parents could not imagine giving us a free afternoon off. We were then sent to attend different classes, art institution for me, and music classes for the rest of my siblings. My parents managed to send me to an art academy, normally meant for full-time high school graduates when I was only an eleven-year-old primary school student. My brothers and sister had to go to their piano lessons after normal school. Life was indeed quite hectic for children of Chinese parents! Our parents had to work four jobs between them to give us the extraordinary childhood education that we all had. It was hard work for everyone in our family and everyone was busy. Looking back now, we can count our blessings and we could only be eternally grateful for the sacrifice and foresight of our hardworking parents.

When I was a secondary student at Catholic High School, an English missionary couple, Rev. and Mrs Frank Balchin, arrived as pastors at our

Chen-li Church in Singapore. They had spent more than 30 years as Christian missionaries in Xiamen and were fluent in Hokkien, my native dialect, as well as Mandarin. My mother immediately seized on this opportunity and managed to arrange free private English language tuition for all of us with Mrs Balchin. Even now, I have vivid memories of climbing the steep slope of Mount Sophia hill to reach the Balchins' residence at the Trinity Bible College. For one hour each week, I would learn the English language from the King James Bible! When the teaching got too difficult for me to understand in English, Mrs Balchin would switch to Hokkien or Mandarin to explain the English biblical passages! In this way, the missionary lady would teach me not only the English language but also the morals of the various stories in the bible simultaneously! The impact of this early learning was to have an immense influence in my life.

Chinese Calligraphy and Medicine

In the early 1960s, Catholic High School recruited many teachers from China to teach both the classical and modern Chinese language. Students were required to recite regularly in class, proses, poems and writings of famous authors of the Tang, Song, Ming and Qing dynasties. Daily homework included Chinese calligraphy written with the traditional Chinese brush and ink. The classical styles of Chinese calligraphy include the pictorial or heliographic *juan* script, the official or *li* script, the walking *xing* and the running *chao* scripts and the formal or standard *kai* script. A Chinese calligrapher would learn first the standard *kai*, followed by the *xing*, and eventually the *chao* scripts, much like a child learning to stand, then walk and run.

I liked calligraphy from an early age and my favourite is the *xing* script, especially in the style of Wang Xi-zhi, known to the Chinese as the 'Priest of calligraphy' since the fourth century. Chinese artists and calligraphers learn by copying old masters initially. I copied the *macro-script* (large script) or *da-kai* as well as the *micro-script* (small script) or *siao-kai* in the style of Liu Kong-qian, a famous Tang Dynasty calligrapher, from a young age. Catholic High School held annual calligraphic and art competitions and I would always come home with one or two prizes from fourth grade onwards. Tang and Song Dynasty poems are favourite calligraphic subjects for most Chinese calligraphers and I am no exception.

In order to write the micro-script or *xiao-kai* well, minute and exquisite hand and wrist control are necessary. This training of the hand movement to write small script or *xiao-kai* is the same technique necessary to perform complex coronary angioplasty operations. When training interventional cardiologists from China years later, I would ask them to write *xiao-kai* with a Chinese brush in order to refine their finger dexterity so that they can execute the exquisite fine movements necessary for performing successful cardiac intervention.

Catholic High School's 'Sistine Chapel'

Brother Joseph Dufresse or *Zhang Shi-dian* in Chinese, was the Principal of Catholic High School when I first enrolled at the school. He was a remarkable teacher and the most respected headmaster Catholic High School has ever had till this day. Brother Joseph was born in Beijing and was a graduate of Tsing-hua University. He was truly a Renaissance man: he was fluent in five languages (Chinese, English, Italian, French and Latin) and he played five musical instruments (violin, organ, piano, harmonica and trumpet). He was also the school's choirmaster and truly a gentleman and a scholar. One can confidently say that he influenced every student during his three decades of the stewardship of Catholic High School. He was my first mentor and role model and his influence on my intellectual development was profound. I was one of his favourite pupils at school, but I would never have known that he would also turn out to be my matchmaker later! My interest in music, especially singing and choir conducting must have germinated through contact with this extraordinary teacher.

Brother Joseph quickly recognised my painting talent. During the school vacation in 1962, he commissioned, or more accurately, ordered me to paint two murals in the science hall on the fourth floor of a newly completed wing of the school. This vacation job turned out to be a highlight of my early school life and I called it my 'Sistine Chapel' days. In two weeks, I had to complete two 'frescos', perched on a wooden scaffold, not unlike the way Michelangelo had to do when he painted the ceiling of the Sistine Chapel, except not as high up. However the most memorable part of the vacation job was the delicious western lunch provided by the principal each day. For a 14 year-old boy from a poor family who had never had a western meal, lunch break was definitely the highlight of the project. The subjects of the two back-to-back murals were *Fauna* and *Flora* of Asia. These two murals were unfortunately painted over and could not be found today (Fig. 4).

Fig. 4. Mural painting entitled *Fauna*, Science Laboratory, Catholic High School 1962.

Boiled 'Phoenix' Flowers to Cure Asthma

I was a sickly child. Apart from my polio-afflicted right leg, I also suffered from severe childhood bronchial asthma. I would miss school regularly, at least one day per week, because of severe asthmatic attacks. My parents tried every conceivable remedy to cure my asthma but to no avail. When standard western medicine failed, my father turned to traditional Chinese herbal remedies. One such Chinese prescription left me with a lasting scare and deep painful memories. A reputed herbalist from China was in town when I was about seven years old. His 'miraculous cures' were widely advertised in the local Chinese newspaper. My parents were desperate for a cure for my asthma at that time. They were impressed by what they read of this Chinese *sin-se* (the polite Chinese term for doctor) in the advertisement and I was taken to see this super *sin-se*. After a brief but expensive consultation, he gave my parents a herbal prescription consisting of petals of the flowers of a specific Phoenix shrub. The prescription specified that the flower petals of this Phoenix shrub must be wrapped in cloth and cooked in boiling water for one minute before applying it directly to the base of the back of the neck. This process had to be repeated several times until one could see blisters on the skin. Needless to say, it all sounded like a classic Chinese torture even to a young boy of seven. This species of Phoenix plant was not easy to obtain in Singapore. My parents had to comb many horticultural stores throughout the island before they could purchase enough flower petals required by the prescription. The image of their anguish and the dozens of pots of Phoenix plants they had to carry up the stairs to our first floor apartment is still vivid in my mind. After all their effort and expense and all the pain I had to suffer, the magic decoction made not one iota of difference to my asthma, except for a permanent burn scar at the back of my neck!

Miraculously, my bronchial asthma disappeared completely a year after I arrived in Australia to study medicine. I concluded that the clean air of Australia was much more effective than the Shamanistic prescription in trying to cure my asthma. This painful childhood experience left me with a very dim view of traditional Chinese medicine for many years to come.

Beautiful China

Among the fondest memories of my childhood were the visits to the home of the Yap family, after church on Sundays. The Yaps were close friends of my parents. They lived in a posh apartment in Serangoon, a middle-class district of Singapore. Mr Yap Toh Yan, many years my father's senior, was a traditional Chinese gentleman and scholar, a member of the literati circle that my maternal grandfather had belonged to. The well-educated Mr Yap had a good collection of books at home that fascinated me right from the beginning.

The Yaps had two daughters of our age group. Our family of seven would have lunch with them and stay the rest of the afternoon. Mrs Yap was an excellent cook and lunch at the Yaps was definitely a highlight of our childhood. The two Yap sisters had quite different characters. The elder sister, Ee-li, was quiet and reserved while the younger one, Ee-Na, was an absolute 'tom boy'. When the boyish Ee-na was wrestling with my equally extravert elder brothers, Ee-li and I would be reading quietly in a corner. Fortunately, my physical inactivity as a result of my polio forced me to spend a lot of my time reading and drawing. My favourite pastime at the Yaps was to read a large book that Mr Yap had in his library, entitled *Beautiful China*. This book completely enthralled me and I would spend the entire afternoon at the Yaps reading the book, oblivious to all that was happening around me. When it was time to go home, I would feel very sad to leave the book. At my next visit, I would resume reading the book from the page where I left off at the previous visit. The pictures in the book, consisting mainly of scenery from all parts of China, all in black and white, left permanent prints in my young mind till this day. The beautiful landscapes from this mysterious land called China were somewhat unreal to a boy who had grown up in Singapore. Seeing some of them today when I travel to various parts of China is like the realization of my childhood dreams. This book of China must have influenced me subconsciously from a young age and played a part in my unexplained fascination with China in my later life. Many years later, in Taiwan, I came across a new edition of this book and I now have my own copy of *Beautiful China*.

Youngest Art Graduate

Because of my poliomyelitis, I was exempted from attending physical education classes at both my Chinese and English primary schools. When the other students were out on the fields, the teacher would allow me to remain in the classroom and asked me to draw pictures, a task that I really enjoyed. When the teachers saw the drawings that I had made, they were impressed and one of them encouraged me to submit a work to an international children's art competition in India, advertised in the local papers. I was six years old at that time. To my surprise and that of my teacher and parents, a drawing of mine that the teacher submitted for me won third prize! Realising that I had some artistic talent, my parents, mother in particular, quickly decided that I should enrol at the Nanyang Academy of Fine Art (NAFA). NAFA was a tertiary educational institution and the only art academy in Singapore at that time. The year was 1959 and I was only eleven years old, in the sixth and final grade of primary school. The principal of NAFA then was Lim Hak Tai, an immigrant artist from Xiamen, China, who founded the Academy in 1938. Lim Hak Tai belonged to the same circle of literati as my maternal grandfather in Xiamen and my mother knew full well that she could take advantage of this connection. She was convinced that by the 'back door' approach, a typical way of getting things done in the Chinese culture, I could be enrolled at this tertiary institution even though I was still a primary school student then. My mother had a will that fits well into the traditional Chinese saying, *'when there is a will, there is a way'*. After several direct and indirect approaches made to the principal Lim Hak Tai, who supposedly had a Chinese sworn 'brotherly relationship' with my maternal grandfather, he eventually gave in to my mother's persuasions and accepted me as an informal student to the Academy. I was obviously too young to join the formal classes. He made me his *xue-tong* (pupil servant) in the classical tradition. My duties were to attend his art studio and prepare the Chinese ink, brushes and paper for the master's daily painting session. I actually learnt a great deal about Chinese ink brush painting purely from watching this master at work. I must have annoyed him sufficiently as he decided to send me off to join the formal Year 1 painting class after six months as a *xue-tong*. This was how I became a formal student of a tertiary academy at the age of eleven. There were 15 students altogether in my class, all high school graduates aged above 17 years (Fig. 5).

Fig. 5. Graduation class of 1961, Nanyang Academy of Fine Art (YL, back row, third from left).

My teachers at NAFA were pioneers of the school of 'Nanyang painting', a unique style of western painting that originated in South East Asia. Three of the teachers who taught me at NAFA, Georgette Chen, Cheong Soo Pieng and Chen Wen-xi were regarded as pioneers of this new art movement in Asia. Cheong Soo Pieng spent only a very short time at NAFA and I was fortunate to have been his pupil at the right time. Georgette Chen affectionately called me *xiao di-di* (little brother) because of my young age and to me she was more like a mother than a teacher in the classroom. Many artists of my generation were strongly influenced by the painting style of Cheong Soo Pieng, who was himself strongly influenced by fauvism and post-impressionism which was characteristic of Nanyang art at that time. In 1969, I had a rare opportunity to pay a visit to my teacher Cheong at his home in River Valley in Singapore during the summer vacation after my second year of medical study in Melbourne. He was very pleased to see me and sketched my portrait instantly (reproduced on the front page of this book). He passed away with cancer shortly after our meeting and I was so glad I had made the visit to see him for the last time. I am indebted to this great teacher and friend for my artistic development.

After a hectic three years both at the art academy and normal school, I finally graduated with a Diploma of Fine Art from NAFA in November 1961 at the age of 13. I remain the youngest graduate of the academy to date. Little did I know then that 40 years after graduation, I would become Chairman of the Board of Directors of my alma mater. I was also given the task of overseeing the construction of the new NAFA campus at Bencoolen Street, Singapore, now completed and a significant landmark of Singapore today.

'Memories of the Lovely Dreams of Youth'

Soon after my graduation from NAFA, I was awarded the Queen's Special Prize for Drawing in the National Art Competition of Malaysia in 1962. This award has a very special place in my heart not because of the prize but for the fact that it was the only time I spent two days alone with my father. Unfortunately, my mother could not afford the expenses to come along with us. Father and I traveled to Kuala Lumpur to receive the award by train. It was my first ever train ride. The beautiful kampong or countryside, the lush green paddy fields, the coconut and palm oil plantations, goats and cattle kept flashing past all the way. These were wonderful sights for a boy who grew up in Singapore, an island city-state. I could hardly contain my excitement, especially travelling with dad alone for the first and only time.

Being an employee of OUB and for this special proud occasion, my father was given the privilege of free accommodation at the suite reserved for important visitors of the bank, located on the top floor of the head office of OUB in the heart of Kuala Lumpur. Compared to our humble apartment at Tiong Bahru, it was paradise for a 14 year-old. The room was air-conditioned, enormous, luxuriously furnished and catered with all kinds of delicacies and drinks. I was especially fond of the preserved jerky beef, considered a delicacy by locals and something we just could not afford in our family. It was a real treat for me who normally had to fight with four other siblings for food. The two days spent there with my father alone were the best two days of my life. Imprinted deeply and forever in my mind was the quiet conversations I had with my father at night. The tranquil atmosphere was in stark contrast to the usual noisy quarrelling and yelling of my siblings and the unpleasant punishment that father had to dispense after work at home. I remembered that father was unusually happy and talkative during those two days and obviously very proud of my achievement. I rarely saw my father smile or laugh aloud but his joy at that time will live forever in my mind. He had borrowed a camera from a colleague for the occasion. With it, he captured the moment when I received the engraved silver medal from the Queen of Malaysia (Fig. 6).

Whenever I look at this photograph taken by my late father, memories of the two days we spent together would bring tears to my eyes. I recalled a similar emotional reminiscence by the German-Australian landscape

Fig. 6. Receiving the '*Special Prize for Drawing*' medal from the Queen of Malaysia, photograph taken by father, 1962.

artist, Eugene von Guerard, of his late father. Eugene's father, Bernard von Guerard, was also a landscape artist. He took Eugene on a painting tour to Italy when he was a teenager. They both sketched the beautiful countryside of southern Italy together. After looking at one of those sketchbooks when he was 80 years of age, Eugene von Guerard wrote the following on a particular page: '*Memories of the lovely dreams of youth when my beloved father was still alive and we saw these beautiful places together*'. I wanted and had an opportunity to acquire an original oil painting by Eugene von Guerard entitled 'Mountainous landscape', painted when he was in his thirties (Fig. 7), because of his reminiscence of the time spent with his

Fig. 7. '*Mountainous Landscape*', oil painting by Eugene von Guerard, 1840.

beloved father. I will pass on this painting to my son as an heirloom, hoping that he may have an equally fond reminiscence of his father in some way one day.

Life's First Turning Point

My parents' preoccupation with our education appeared to have paid off in the early sixties. My eldest brother Yean Kai had topped the Higher School Certificate examination in Singapore in 1963. He was awarded a Colombo Plan Scholarship by the Public Service Commission of Singapore funded by the Australian Government. The Colombo Plan was an international aid program funded by developed countries in the west to help developing countries in various technical and professional fields. Singapore was a recipient country and Australia a donor country of the Colombo Plan that lasted for nearly two decades.

My eldest brother was one of the first beneficiaries of the Colombo Plan to study Medicine at the University of Adelaide. A year later my second brother Yean Chuan followed in his footsteps and was awarded a Colombo Plan scholarship to study Medicine at Monash University. I had completed year ten at Catholic High School and had successfully switched to the Pre-university class at St. Andrew's School, an English stream school. In those days, switching from a Chinese to an English school was uncommon, and mostly achieved by students from the bilingual Catholic High School.

I was in my last year of Pre-university class in 1965 and the pressure was on for me to do the hat trick and win the third Colombo Plan Scholarship in Medicine for our family. The hat trick of winning three Colombo Plan scholarships in engineering, had been achieved by one family in Singapore, but not yet in medicine. When I graduated in Fine Art, I had tried to seek permission from my father to become an artist. His response was predictable: '*You cannot make a living as an artist*'! My father eventually agreed for me to be an architect. I thought architecture was the closest thing to fine art and gave ample opportunity to create and draw.

Just when our family's fortune appeared to have taken a good turn, disaster struck. One day in July 1965, I returned home from school to find my mother extremely anxious and agitated. She said father had been taken to SGH after he collapsed at work. Three months earlier he had been promoted to the position of manager of the new Tiong Bahru Branch of the OUB. His office was across the road, directly opposite to our apartment at 53A Tiong Bahru Road. This was his first and only serious illness in my memory. With my two elder brothers overseas, I was the oldest son at home. It was my duty to accompany mother to visit father in Ward 23, a surgical ward in the Boyer's Block of SGH. A young resident doctor told us that father had bled from a stomach ulcer. This was the initial working diagnosis. He was given a blood transfusion and needed an urgent operation. We were somewhat reassured when we found out that the surgeon in charge would be the Professor and Head of the Department of Surgery at SGH.

My father underwent a total of three major operations in the next three months at SGH. The second operation, to stop profuse bleeding from his esophagus, was called the *Tanner Operation* and it was performed by Professor Tanner himself, who happened to be in Singapore at that time as an external examiner for the Royal College of Surgeons. However, the operation was not successful and my father continued to bleed from various parts of his gastrointestinal tract. After three operations and a total of 55 units of blood transfusion, he passed away on 25th November 1965 (Fig. 8).

The Vow to Train Better Doctors

During the three long months of my father's hospital stay at SGH, my mother and I kept vigil at my father's bedside at Ward 23 each day. I was exempted from the internal final examination at St. Andrew's School

Fig. 8. Father's grave soon after burial, 1965.

but had to sit the compulsory Cambridge Higher Certificate examination, organized by the University of Cambridge and commissioned by the Singapore Government, to gain a place in a tertiary institution. Mother and I were agonized by the pains my father had to endure, with endless rounds of blood tests, intravenous cannulations, injections and blood transfusions. The lack of medical information from his treating doctor and the unsympathetic care of the Professor of Surgery added much sorrow and grief to all our family during the entire episode of my father's illness. My mother's command of English was poor and she had to rely on me to find out information regarding father's condition and treatment. The nurses were much more sympathetic and helpful than the doctors on the whole. We were told eventually that he died from cancer of the liver. Looking back now as a well-qualified doctor today, I am still uncertain of the actual cause of his death.

At my father's bedside in Ward 23 at SGH, I vowed that I would become a doctor one day and return to this hospital to train better doctors than the one who operated on my father. This was the turning point in my career choice. The vow that I made in 1965 was realised in 1997 when the Singapore Government headhunted me to direct the Singapore Heart Centre. The Singapore Heart Centre was located next to the Boyer's Block where my father passed away 32 years earlier. When I left Singapore in 2003, after five years as Director of the renamed National Heart Centre at SGH, I believed I had fulfilled my vow and improved the training of young doctors and specialists at the National Heart Centre and specialist training in Singapore in general. My father had not died in vain.

Omega Watch, a Symbol of Love

My father's dying wish was for me to follow in my two elder brothers' footsteps and win a Colombo Plan Scholarship to study medicine in Australia. He did not live to see his wish come true. After his death, as the oldest son at home, I thought I should remain in Singapore to look after mother and my younger siblings. Despite the catastrophic event of my father's illness and demise at the time of my matriculation examination, I still managed to win one of the seven Colombo Plan Scholarships offered in 1966 to study medicine in Australia. Against my wish, my mother insisted that I should follow father's last will and accept the Colombo Plan Scholarship. The hat trick of three Colombo Plan Scholarships in Medicine in one family was at last accomplished by the Lim family and never repeated.

Although not wealthy, my parents managed to save enough money to buy an Omega watch for each of my two brothers before their departure from Singapore to study in Australia. The Omega watch became a symbol of love and success in the Lim family. When my father was ill in hospital, my mother also decided to give to father from all of us, an Omega watch as a symbol of our deepest love for him. We went to the best watch store in Singapore, De Silva and Co., and purchased an Omega Constellation watch for father. The watch was engraved with the words '*DEAREST FATHER, from SONS & HWEE, 1965*'. He wore it each day for only a month before he passed away. After his death, my mother gave me father's Omega watch when it was my turn to go to Australia. I have worn no other watch except father's Omega watch with the original engraving done in 1965 to this day.

Lim Koon Yaw Memorial Scholarship

My father was an ordinary man from a humble background. Having emigrated as a refugee from southern China to Singapore, he dedicated his life to his family. He did not leave behind much material wealth but he did leave us many rich and tender memories. My mother and all of us wanted to do something to remember him permanently. Soon after his death, my mother approached the principal of Catholic High School Brother Zhang, and suggested a donation of 3000 dollars to set up a scholarship, named the *Lim Koon Yaw Memorial Scholarship*, in memory of father. The scholarship would be awarded annually to the Dux of

School, or the student who scored the highest aggregate in the graduating class of Catholic High School. The scholarship would serve to highlight father's belief in the importance of good education in one's life. His parents did not have the chance to give him a good education and he wanted to make sure that we did not miss out the way he did. It was the first academic scholarship to be established at the Catholic High School. The principal was very pleased with the idea and the scholarship was established immediately. The scholarship consists of an inscribed gold-plated medal, and the first such medal was awarded in 1966. The recipient of the third Lim Koon Yaw Memorial Scholarship was Lee Hsien Loong, the current Prime Minister of Singapore (Fig. 9). My mother was so thrilled with the winner that year that she ordered an extra replica medal to be made to keep for herself. This replica medal was subsequently passed on to me and remains with me in Melbourne today.

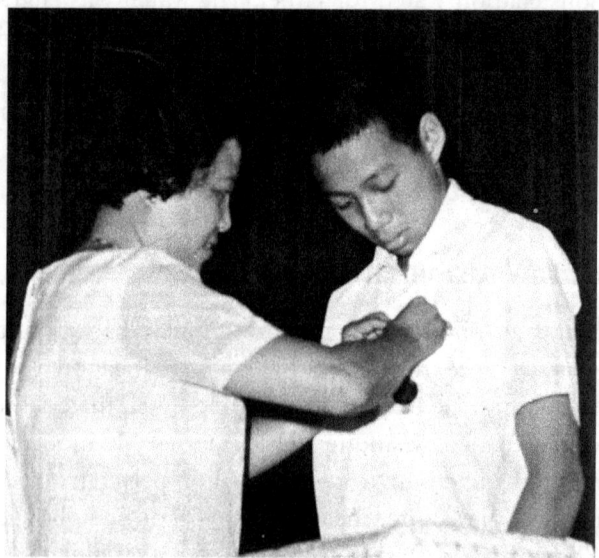

Fig. 9. Mother presenting the *Lim Koon Yaw Memorial Scholarship* medal to Lee Hsien Loong, 1967.

2

Vow to be a Doctor

The 'Lucky Country' Down-Under

I was one of the seven Singapore Colombo Plan students that arrived in Adelaide on 6th February 1966; the day Australia officially changed its currency from pounds to dollars. There was great confusion at the airport when I tried to change currency. My eldest brother, Yean Kai, was at the airport to welcome me. It was my first overseas trip and I was fortunate to have a brother to greet me on my arrival in a country totally new and strange to me. My brother had secured accommodation for me at Aquinas College in North Adelaide, within walking distance of the university. From my bedroom window, a statue of Colonel Light, founder of Adelaide, could be seen pointing at the cityscape of Adelaide. The view was magnificent. I was not accustomed to the tranquility of Adelaide having just arrived from the hustling and bustling surroundings of Tiong Bahru in Singapore. Colonel Light's vision was in stark contrast to the scene from my bedroom in Tiong Bahru, with a pedestrian crossing and the constant flashing amber light next to a bus stop with buses screeching to a halt constantly.

It was a Saturday morning when I first arrived in Adelaide and my very first programme in Australia was to attend the wedding of an

Aussie friend of my eldest brother. At the wedding, it was customary for the guests to line up to receive a kiss from the bride. This was a big cultural shock for a conservative young Chinese brought up strictly under the Confucius moral code! The prospect of waiting to be kissed by a stranger, a 'foreign devil' girl, really gave me tachycardia! This was my gentle introduction to western culture on the first day in Australia. They called Australia the 'lucky country' and my first experience of Australia did live up to its reputation! Little did I know then that I would call Australia home for the rest of my life.

The next day, my brother and I went to a Sunday church service and from there we went to lunch at the home of an Australian Christian lady named Grace Baker. Mrs Baker and her children are devout Christians but not her husband. A bible study group would be held at the Baker residence each Friday, for any Asian students in Adelaide who were Christian and who would like to attend. The Baker's house became a regular meeting place for many overseas students in Adelaide over the years. Mrs Grace Baker, barely five feet tall, is a giant of a Christian with endless love and bounding energy. Many Asian students in Adelaide were converted to Christianity because of her testimony and care for them in a land far away from home. To have the friendship of Grace Baker and her family has been a real blessing in my life.

After a month of waiting for medical undergraduate offers at Aquinas College in Adelaide, five of the seven Singapore Colombo Plan scholars were successfully placed at the University of Adelaide while I was offered a place in the Faculty of Medicine at Monash University in Melbourne. The last candidate was sent to the University of Queensland in Brisbane. I was quite happy to have a place at Monash University because my second brother, Yean Chuan, was also a medical undergraduate at Monash University. Unlike most overseas students, I was lucky not to be alone when I arrived in the 'lucky country' down-under.

'Going to the Hospital to Die!'

There was no vacancy at the Halls of Residence at Monash University where my second brother, Yean Chuan, was staying when I arrived in Melbourne. The Student Affairs Office of the university had arranged private accommodation for me with an Australian lady, Mrs M. Dalziel, in the suburb of Murrumbeena. This was the first Aboriginal word that I had come across in Australia. Many of the streets and places in Australia have names of Aboriginal origin. The famous Australian artist, Arthur Boyd, also grew up in Murrumbeena. I later found out that the Boyd family is one of the most distinguished families of artists in Australia. Murrumbeena was not a posh suburb and Mrs Dalziel's house was a single story average Australian home. My room, however, was not in the house itself, but a weatherboard extension at the rear end of the house, adjacent to the laundry. It was a small room, only about fifty square feet in size, spartanly furnished with a single bed, a dressing table and a chair. There was hardly any room to move around and I could fall back onto the bed from my stool at the dressing table desk after studying at night. It had a small window looking into an empty backyard. Coming from a room with Colonel Light's view of the skyline of Adelaide city, it was quite a disappointment.

From the Dalziel house, I had to walk ten minutes to the bus stop to catch a bus to Monash University and its teaching hospitals. One day while waiting for a bus at the bus stop, a friendly and talkative Aussie who was also waiting for the bus, decided to strike up a conversation with me. '*Good-die, mate, how are you to-die?*', he looked straight at me and asked. Not totally understanding what he was saying, I politely repeated the first word he said and replied: '*Good-die!*' '*Where are you going to-die?*', he quickly followed. I was shocked and thought how rude to ask someone where he was going to die! In the Chinese custom, to use words such as die or death in a conversation is considered a curse. I therefore ignored his second question completely. Thinking that I did not hear his question, he repeated it again. I thought I should not be rude having been in Australia only recently, and half guessing his question, I replied: '*I'm going to the hospital*'. '*So you're going to the hospital to die!*', he retorted. I said to myself, what sort of a country is this where people go to the hospital to die! Just as I was getting worried, the bus arrived and the strange conversation was interrupted. I was glad to hop quickly on the bus to avoid any more embarrassing questions from the 'friendly' Aussie. This was my very early experience in conversation involving the Aussie language.

Narrow Escape for a 'Singaporean Son'

A fellow Monash student, son of an Aussie farmer called Tom Love, was boarding at the same house with me at Murrumbeena. Tom was friendly and a *dinky-di* (genuine) Aussie and taught me many weird and wonderful Aussie words and slang. Tom confessed that he was a 'convict descendant' and was quite proud of being one. He arrived before me at the the place where we were boarding and scored the bedroom inside the house, while my room was a small weatherboard extension at the back of the house. Tom would go home to his dad's farm in Epping on the outskirts of Melbourne on weekends. Aussies, the abbreviation for 'Australians', have a unique sense of humor and it took me a while to get used to. They are peculiarly fond of 'knocking' (degrading) themselves, just for the fun of it. The term *Ocker the knocker* is used to describe this unique Australian culture of self-humiliation in a humorous manner. Tom and his two brothers, Robert and John, grew up 'on the land' and were 'fair-dinkum' (real) Aussie kids. Tom's father, also known as Tom Love, most confusing for a Chinese boy, was an Australian of Irish descent. In traditional Chinese culture, having the same name as one's father is unthinkable and considered ultimate disrespect.

The Love family owned a large farm, about 800 acres, in Epping, on the outskirts of Melbourne then but now a sprawling suburb.

I was often invited to the farm on weekends. Mr and Mrs Tom Love were an extremely kind and gentle couple, and my first impressions of an Australian family were very positive. Tom's aunt, the elder sister of Tom Love senior, was known to the Love boys as 'Auntie Georgie'. Georgie was an ultra-Monarchist. She lived in her own house at the other end of the property, opposite to that of her brother. The two houses in the Love farm were almost one kilometer apart. The Love family treated me like one of their own children and called me their 'Singaporean son'. From when we first met, initially on my own and later with my wife and son, we would visit the Love family at their farm at least once a year, either at Easter or Christmas. We remained life-long friends until the senior Loves and Auntie Georgie passed away in their eighties and nineties.

The Loves had a horse called Cindy. For a boy who had grown up in the city-state of Singapore, horse riding was learnt from watching Hollywood western movies. Riding a horse one day like John Wayne in the movie is a dream for an urban lad. This dream quickly turned into a reality at the Love's farm when I met Cindy! I asked Tom junior excitedly for a ride on Cindy. My request was instantly granted. Without any instruction or warning from Tom, I was literally hoisted onto the saddle. Before I could put my feet in the stirrups, Cindy took off! Without going through the walking and cantering sequences, she galloped the one-kilometer across the farm towards Auntie Georgie's house at full speed. She knew exactly where to go and how to get me off her back. God only knows how I managed to remain in the saddle without my feet in the stirrups. When we got to Auntie Georgie's front gate, Cindy took me under a low tree branch and wiped me clean off her back. The fact that my feet were not in the stirrup probably saved my life. I came off the saddle and landed squarely on my bum! Miraculously I only sustained a superficial cut in my neck and a torn shirt. Without a single bone broken, I picked myself up and staggered into Auntie Georgie's house. Her expression on seeing me I can still recall today. '*What on earth happened?*', she asked in her usual regal manner. I was too shocked to reply. My study in Australia could have been very brief. When I caught up with the Love boys after my maiden horse riding experience and accident, the two dinky-di Aussie boys just laughed their heads off! It was indeed a narrow escape for the Singaporean son. After this first riding experience, I have never mounted a horse since.

My Singapore Story

After a year of boarding at the Dalziel's residence, I moved into the Halls of Residence at Monash University, Clayton. In 1966, there were only three Halls in existence, namely Deakin, Farrer and Howitt and the latter had only six of the ten floors completed. My room was on the third floor of Howitt Hall. Compared to the little shed at the back of the Murrumbeena house, it was luxurious. I hung a calligraphic scroll with a verse from Meng-zi that I had written myself for self-edification, much like the new-year resolution my father wrote for himself when he was 19. The translated verse reads as follows:

> *Before giving someone huge responsibilities,*
> *Heaven will first labor his bones and starve his body!*

In other words, I should be mentally and physically prepared to endure all kinds of hardship and adversities during my years of study in Australia, far away from home. I stayed at Howitt Hall for the next two years during my pre-clinical training before moving to the hospital residential quarters for my clinical training.

One day when I was feeling homesick at Howitt Hall, I decided to paint a large oil painting of my homeland, Singapore from memory. With Smetana's *Ma Vlast* playing in the background, I completed the work depicting many of the landmarks of Singapore in the early sixties in three weeks.

Thirty years later, in 1997, when I returned to work at the National Heart Centre in Singapore, I had the painting hung in my office. The autobiography of the 'Father of Singapore', the then Senior Minister (SM) Lee Kuan Yew, had just been published in two volumes. The first volume was entitled *The Singapore Story*. As one of his personal physicians, I had the opportunity to tell him after a professional consultation one day that I too, have a *Singapore Story* in painting and asked him whether he would be agreeable to have a photograph taken with me and my *Singapore Story*. My wish was duly granted (Fig. 10).

Cultural Shocks

After completing my pre-clinical years of the medical course at the Monash Clayton campus, I moved once again to live in the student quarters of the hospitals for the various clinical training rotations. During vacation between the hospital residency rotations, I moved in

Fig. 10. My *Singapore Story*, painted in 1967, with SM Lee Kuan Yew, 1999.

with my brother who was boarding with an Australian couple, Ernest and Marjorie Roeder. Ernest Roeder immigrated to Australia from Germany after the Second World War. Majorie was born in Stawell, a country town in Victoria famous for its annual foot race, the Stawell Gift. The Roeders had no children of their own and treated my brother and his then girlfriend, Phaik Sim, and as if we were their own children. They had an Alsatian dog at all times, replacing one with another as soon as one passed on. The dog was treated like a son and would receive the same care and attention as all the boarders. We were all served the same food but the dog would get little extras such as electric blanket in winter, a pillow in the den and snacks at anytime!

Returning home to Singapore after completing their university studies, my brother and his girlfriend were married and their first child, a baby girl, was born. They called her Yin Yin. When the Roeders heard the news of the birth of my brother's baby girl, they were so thrilled and decided to call their newly acquired Alsatian dog *Yin Yin* as well, supposedly in honour of my newborn niece! When I broke this news to my brother and his wife, they were flabbergasted! The Roeders were extremely kind to all of us, and treated us and the dog truly like parents. We are forever grateful for the love and care that they gave us. After I qualified as a doctor, my wife and I would visit them regularly and I took care of all their medical needs when they were elderly until they both passed away in their seventies.

Another cultural surprise occurred when I attended my first biochemistry class at Monash University. The lectures were apparently delivered in the English language but I could hardly understand the lecturer who was a fair-dinkum Aussie! When I related this predicament to Mr Eric Chapman, an officer from the Department of Education whose job was to supervise all the Colombo Plan scholars at Monash University, he promptly arranged extra tuition in 'Australian language' for me. These are some of the cultural hurdles Asian students have to overcome when coming to be educated in Australia.

A Renaissance Man

Eric Ferguson Glasgow was a favourite teacher of many students at Monash University. He was our anatomy teacher, an all-rounder and truly a Renaissance man. He graduated in medicine from Belfast and his anatomical lectures were simply inspiring. Ambidextrous, he would draw with his left hand and write with his right hand on the black board, His drawings were beautiful and accurate, a wonderful sight to behold. He was an erudite lecturer not only in anatomy but also in the arts and his knowledge in many fields was profound. He once gave a public lecture on Leonardo da Vinci at the National Gallery of Victoria that I attended and it had a great impact on me in later years. His anatomy teaching was so inspiring that I decided to apply for a summer vacation prosector position at the Anatomy Department after my second year of medical undergraduate studies. I was given the job and my task was to dissect and display the twelve cranial nerves in a formalin-preserved human head. I worked on this human head daily for three weeks and eventually completed the challenging task. This specimen is still on display at the Monash University anatomical museum today.

Eric Glasgow was my second mentor. The Chinese believe in the concept that *a teacher even for just a day will be a parent for life.* Indeed we became life-long friends and I respect Eric as if he were my father. In the last years of his life, he held conjoint anatomy professorships at Monash University in Melbourne and Stanford University in the United States. He authored a textbook of virtual anatomy that has become a standard textbook for anatomy teaching worldwide. He adored the Orient and was appointed Visiting Professor of Anatomy at Hong Kong University. When I became the Foundation Dean of the Xiamen University Medical College in China in 1996, Eric gave me invaluable advice in planning the anatomy curriculum of the new medical school.

To everyone's dismay, he was diagnosed with acute leukemia while at Stanford in 1999. Typical of Eric, he agreed to participate in a double blind randomized clinical drug trial involving the use of a new aggressive chemotherapy protocol for the treatment of his condition. Within three months of the commencement of the trial, he was dead at the age of 70. Unmarried, Eric Glasgow devoted his entire life to education and his students and friends. He was a role model for me and I was fortunate to have such a teacher. He was the Guest-of-Honor who opened my first one-man art exhibition at Monash University Union Building in 1967.

Not long after Eric's passing, a large number of Monash Medical Alumni donated voluntarily to have a bronze sculpture of Eric Glasgow erected in the quadrangle of the Monash School of Anatomy. To my knowledge, no other teacher of Monash University has been so honoured by students.

Early Interest in Cardiovascular Physiology

Physiology practical classes in the third year of the medical course fascinated me immensely, especially experiments involving circulatory hemodynamics. I decided to pursue a year of research in cardiovascular physiology that would lead to a Bachelor of Medical Science degree. However, there was no suitable cardiovascular physiology research project in the department at that time. Research in the Department of Physiology at Monash University in the sixties was strongly orientated towards neurophysiology under the leadership of Professor Archibald McIntyre, an eminent neurophysiologist. Neurophysiology was attracting great attention in Australia around that time because another Australian neurophysiologist, Sir John Eccles, had just been awarded the Nobel Prize for Physiology.

Just as I was giving up hope of pursuing an honours degree in cardiovascular physiology towards the end of 1968, an obstetrician from the Queen Victoria Hospital Clinical School of Monash University came to present one of the weekly Clinico-Pathological Conferences at the Clayton campus. His name was William A.W. Walters. He dressed impeccably like a perfect English gentleman and spoke softly with an imperial English accent. That was my first impression of the man who was going to change my academic life. After his clinical case presentation, he proceeded to advertise for a research student to assist him in a project involving the study of uterine blood flow in pregnancy using an ultrasound probe. The words 'blood flow' immediately caught my attention. I had not done obstetrics and gynecology at that stage and the uterus was not my preferred target organ, as I would be happier if the heart was involved. However, this was my eagerly awaited chance to study hemodynamics and circulation and I responded to his call with great enthusiasm after the lecture was over. Within days of my positive response, he had arranged my Bachelor of Medical Science degree course under the joint-supervision of Professor Robert Porter, Head of the Physiology Department at that time and later Dean of Medical Faculty, and himself. My research project was later changed to a study of *the hemodynamic effects of combined oral contraceptive pill* due to the delay of the arrival of the ultrasound probe.

To my great relief, both the Australian and Singaporean Governments consented to extend my Colombo Plan scholarship in order for me to undertake this extra degree. Professor Walters promptly arranged accommodation for me at the student quarters of Queen Victoria Hospital, right in the central business district of Melbourne. This was the turning point in my medical career and both Professors Glasgow and Walters were key mentors (Fig. 11).

Lesson in Scientific Writing

Professor William Walters graduated from the University of Adelaide and did his obstetrics training in Aberdeen, United Kingdom. He obtained his doctorate at the University of London and his PhD thesis was entitled *Hemodynamic changes in normal pregnancy*. Using the dye-dilution technique based on the Fick Principle, his research on the various physiologic changes in blood pressure, plasma volume and

Fig. 11. My mentors at PhD graduation ceremony (from left: R Southby, WA Walters, YL, GF Glasgow).

cardiac output during the various stages of normal pregnancy was published in scientific journals and standard obstetric textbooks. His command of the English language is perfect and his handwriting is artwork. He taught me the importance of clear and simple English in scientific writing. Accurate expression, using clear and accurate short sentences without bombastic words, he said, was the essence in scientific writing. To improve my English, he gave me a copy of the newly published Simplified English Version of the Holy Bible. This brought back childhood memories of my English tuition with the Balchins using the Bible.

I spent the first term of my honours year of cardiovascular research in the Department of Physiology at Adelaide University, under the supervision of the world-renowned vascular physiologist, Professor Robert Whelan. His work on the peripheral circulation in the limbs using volumetric plethysmography was authoritative. I was sent there to learn the volumetric plethysmography technique. My research project there involved the study of the effect of the intra-arterial infusion of estrogen on forearm blood flow. Medical students at Adelaide were frequently asked to take part as 'volunteers' in his various research experiments. I am fortunate to have worked with Dr Eugenia Lumbers, a PhD student of Professor Whelan then, who became a famous scientist in her own right later. The short time spent in Adelaide was most fruitful with the publication of a peer reviewed journal paper.

After Adelaide, I returned to the Queen Victoria Hospital in Melbourne to conduct my own research under the supervision of Professor Walters. My research project then was to measure peripheral forearm blood flow as well as cardiac output in thirty young women before and after taking combined oral contraceptive pills for a month. Cardiac output was estimated using the photoelectric dye-dilution technique based on the Fick Principle, a technique well-known to my supervisor. Healthy young nurses at the Queen Victoria were recruited as volunteers for this particular research project. At the conclusion of a year of intense work, I was able to complete my thesis and publish a total of five scientific papers. I was over the moon when I successfully obtained my first university degree, with first class honours. Our work led to the publication of one of the first reports of the hypertensive effect of combined oral contraceptive pills, estrogen in particular, published in the *Lancet* in 1969 in the form of a preliminary communication. The finding was subsequently confirmed by other workers and had a great clinical impact on the subsequent use of combined oral contraceptive pills.

I learnt from Professor Walters the skill necessary for good British research, characterized by comprehensive literature survey, methodical experimental design, meticulous technique, accurate observation, honest interpretation, critical thinking and clear verbal and concise accurate writing. I am indebted to my third mentor, Professor Walters, who taught me not only research skills but showed me what scholarship, friendship and kindness really meant. This stood me in good stead and prepared me to lead a fruitful academic life in the years to come. When it was my turn to become a PhD supervisor, I tried to pass on as much as possible of what I had learnt from Professor Walters.

Violin and the National Heart Foundation Student Scholarship

For my research year as a student at the Queen Victoria Hospital, I was boarding with medical students two years my senior who were doing their obstetrics rotation. One of the students, John Jardine, was a very good violinist. I love classical music and, for reasons I cannot explain, I had a special love for the violin. Its aesthetics and the physics of its sound and tone had fascinated me since childhood. John owned and played a violin made by a Czechoslavakian luthier by the name of Frantisek Zivec. Zivec migrated to Australia after World War II. I was very fond of John's violin and he told me that the violinmaker had passed on but his widow was still alive and lived in the suburb of Brunswick in Melbourne at that time. One day, John told me Mrs Zivec was contemplating the sale of a violin made by her late husband. With great excitement, I went with John to inspect the violin. When we arrived at the Zivec home in Brunswick, I found out that there were three Zivec violins, one of which was for sale. The first belonged to the maker's daughter, a non-professional violinist. The second instrument belonged to the luthier's grandson, a teenager who was more interested in modern guitar than violin. The last was the instrument for sale. After listening to all three, I was most impressed by the one that belonged to the maker's grandson and asked Mrs Zivec to consider selling the instrument that belonged to the grandson. Recognising the violin as a work of art and giving due respect to the late luthier as a fellow artist, I offered to pay the full price of the violin plus one of my original Chinese paintings in exchange for the grandson's violin. The Zivecs were moved by my sincerity and eventually agreed to part with the grandson's violin with one additional condition. They wanted me to promise that I would never part with the violin without letting them know. I gladly agreed.

The price of the violin was exactly that of the National Heart Foundation of Australia's Student Research Scholarship that I had been awarded for the year's research. Without much hesitation, I had exchanged the scholarship for a violin. The Zivec violin is still in my collection today, with five other Australian instruments that I subsequently collected. Together, they represent a small collection of works by luthiers of the Australian school of violin making, considered the youngest school of violin making in the world today.

Of interest among my small collection are two Smith violins made by A.E. Smith, generally regarded as the Stradivarius of Australia, and her daughter Kitty Smith. I met Kitty Smith when she was in her eighties at her home in Brisbane. A viola made by Devereaux, the first European luthier that immigrated to Australia, together with his work book and original F-hole mould are items in my collection that were frequently on loan for exhibitions on Australian violins.

The Three Queens of Queen Victoria Hospital

After the research year, I resumed my medical undergraduate course and commenced bedside clinical training at the Alfred Hospital. Of all the clinical disciplines, I was most interested in internal medicine and made detailed notes on the various topics of general medicine. A few years later, after I passed my specialist examination, I edited these notes into a textbook designed to help young physicians pass their specialist examination in internal medicine.

From undergraduate days, my desire to become a cardiologist was clear. While doing my cardiovascular research at Queen Victoria Hospital, Professor Walters introduced me to Dr June Howqua, a lady cardiologist at the hospital, to learn the art of cardiac auscultation. Echocardiography was not invented then. Queen Victoria Hospital, previously called The Melbourne Hospital, was the oldest public hospital in Melbourne. Dr Howqua was one of the first female medical graduates of the University of Melbourne. She and two other female consultants, June Pash, an obstetrician, and Joyce Daws, a thoracic surgeon, were known as the 'three queens of the Queen Victoria Hospital'. The name Howqua came from two Chinese words, *hou-kuan*, meaning 'a good government official'. During the late Qing Dynasty, there was a very successful merchant in Guangzhou. He was a kind and generous boss and his staff affectionately called him 'hou-kuan', from which Howqua was derived. Dr June Pash later became my wife's obstetrician and delivered our son Iefan at the Queen Victoria Hospital. After a year of cardiology training, Dr Howqua, like Professor Walters, became a life-long friend and colleague. I will always remember her as my first teacher in cardiology and also the lady who gave my son, Iefan, the *black and yellow* baby suit.

My days at the Queen Victoria Hospital are filled with fond memories. I held my second one-man art exhibition at the Prahran Gallery for the Queen Victoria Hospital Appeal Fund. In appreciation of my effort, then President of the Queen Victoria Hospital, Dame Mabel Brookes, presented me with an engraved gold-plated stethoscope that I have treasured to this day.

I returned to Queen Victoria Hospital in 1971 to do my obstetrics term. After which, I returned home to Singapore for a brief holiday to visit my family. This trip proved to be the second important turning point in my life.

'Look After Miss Ma'

Whenever I returned to Singapore for holiday during my medical undergraduate course in Melbourne, I would visit my former high school principal, Brother Zhang or Joseph Dufresse, his Catholic priesthood name. It was Christmas of 1971 when I again visited him at the end of my fifth year of medicine. He was excited to see me and said to me in his usual commanding style: '*There is a young lady who is currently visiting Singapore from Taiwan. I would like you to look after her, her name is Miss Ma*'. Miss Ma was the chaperon for the Catholic Junior School Choir boys during their tour in Taipei to take part in an international childrens' choir festival a year earlier. Among the choirboys were my youngest brother Yean Teng and two of his cousins. Miss Ma made such an impact on the boys that on their return to Singapore as a group they persuaded their parents to invite Miss Ma to visit them in Singapore. While in Singapore, the plan was for Miss Ma to stay with each of the choirboy's families for a day or two each time. Miss Ma therefore was scheduled to spend some time at our home as well.

Miss Ma, whose original name was Ma Wen Jen, later changed to Ma Wen Joy or simply Joy, when she arrived in Australia. Taiwan citizens have no official English names on their birth certificates and Ms Ma could choose any English name she desired. Joy was a graduate of the Yang Ming Cultural College in Taipei, majoring in Chinese literature. Like many in Mainland China, Joy's parents went to Taiwan just before the fall of the Guomindang (Republic of China) Government in 1949. Joy was born in Taipei, the eldest and only girl of four children.

My first meeting with Joy took place when I had to chauffeur her from the home of another choirboy to the Christmas Sunday church service at our church. After the church service, she had lunch followed by a Christmas carol singing session at our home. My first impression of her was positive but not electric. Not long after the first meeting, it was my younger brother Yean Teng's turn to have Miss Ma at our home. I planned to impress her with the unique fruit of South East Asia called *durian* or the 'king of all fruits'. Durians emit a very offensive pungent, almost putrid, odor to the uninitiated. But to the initiated locals, the smell is irresistible and the taste heavenly! For durian lovers, the aftertaste is *like good music, lingering between the ceiling beams for three days*, as the Chinese would say. One either loves it or hates it and there is no in between. The strong odor makes durians impossible to hide and the fruit is banned in public areas and land transport vehicles in Singapore.

When I offered the 'king fruit' to Joy, a young lady from Taiwan with a sophisticated and impeccable upbringing, she politely sampled a small portion. '*How was it?*', I asked. '*Ok*', she replied. It was only after we were married that she confided to me that she retreated to the washroom and was violently sick soon after the durian tasting at our home. Her first impression of me could not have been positive, I gathered.

Her short visit to my home came to an end quickly and she returned home to Taipei after three weeks in Singapore. I too, returned to Melbourne not long after. Alone in Melbourne over the 12 months, her image and demeanor never left my mind. Unfortunately, there were no mobile phones, skype or facebook in the late sixties. International telephone calls were not affordable to scholarship students. For the next 12 months, our courtship was conducted entirely by letters and correspondence. I remember receiving an empty envelope addressed to me in her own hand-writing! I was too dumb to realise that it was her way of replying to an 'unacceptable' letter from me. I even wrote to chastise her for forgetting to include the letter in her latest correspondence!

I had secretly planned my visit to Taiwan to see her again as soon as I finished my graduation examination at Monash University. I was initially disheartened when I found out that the return airfare cost $700 Australian dollars. However, I found out that each year there were two clinical prizes, namely the Robert Power Scholarship for surgery and the Harriet Power Scholarship for medicine, open to competition for final year students at the Alfred Hospital Clinical School. The total prize money was exactly seven hundred dollars. The motivation to see Joy again in Taipai was inspirational and unexpectedly but not easily, I won both prizes for 1972. The Chinese saying that *Heaven will not disappoint longing hearts* was indeed fulfilled.

Marriage Proposal in Taipei

It was winter when I visited Joy for the first time in 1972. Although the weather was cold, I never felt cold in her company. Joy's family lived in a traditional Japanese style house in East Peace Road, Taipei. Unlike my parents who were of peasant origin, her father Ma Pu-yin came from a strong academic lineage. Her great grandfather was a Chinese scholar and physician. He was also a *Da Xue Shi* of the Qing Dynasty, the equivalent of a Fellow of the Royal Society. To become a *Da Xue Shi*, one had to pass many levels of official examinations set by the Imperial Qing Dynasty court. Her father, Ma Pu-yin, entered the first private high school in China, the Nankai High School, founded by the famous Chinese educationist Chang Bo-lin in Tianjin. Ma Pu-yin was the Dux of Nankai High School in Tianjin and a fellow-student of Chou En-lai at the school. He graduated in economics from the Nankai University School of Economics. World War II interrupted his postgraduate studies. He started work initially as the chief editor of a local newspaper before he became an accountant for the government-owned China Oil Company. He held the same post for more than thirty years before he retired at the age of seventy. He was an upright person, never use *kuan xi* or influence to his advantage and remained a humble civil servant all his life. He followed his wife's faith and was baptized a Christian late in his life and together they brought up the four children according to the teachings of the Bible. Miss Ma's mother was one of the few tertiary educated women of her time. Trained as a midwife, she attained the rank of matron of a maternity hospital in Tianjin at the peak of her nursing career. Joy has three younger brothers. They were all students at various colleges in Taipei when I first met them.

It was Joy's turn to take revenge for her durian tasting experience in Singapore. Our first outing together in Taipei was to watch a movie. Before entering the cinema, intentionally or not I am unaware to this day, she bought two pieces of Shanghai '*chou tofu*', or 'rotten tofu', a Shanghainese delicacy to the initiated. The stench of *chou tofu* to me must be what the odor of durian was to her. Throughout the entire screening of the movie, all I could recall was the smell of the rotten *tofu*! Happily, not all our outings ended up like the movie experience. The visit to the Taipei Imperial Palace Museum was a much more memorable occasion. Joy, being a graduate in Chinese literature, taught me a great deal about Chinese art, literature and culture during our tour of the Palace Museum.

It was clear to me after spending the two weeks in Taipei with Joy and her family that I had found my soul mate. According to the Chinese tradition, the marriage proposal has to be approved by the bride's father. It is more like asking for permission from the father than proposing to the bride-to-be. On the night of seeking such permission at the home of Joy's parents, Joy's mother, a superb cook, had prepared a sumptuous dinner for the occasion. I had prepared carefully the marriage proposal or more accurately the 'permission speech' I thought worthy of a potential son-in-law! I delivered the speech in great trepidation. In spite of my uncommon memorizing feats and numerous rehearsals, when the time came, I had forgotten half my prepared speech! The message, however, appeared to have gone through and to my great relief, Joy's father's response was positive. I was ecstatic and so was Joy. My Catholic High School headmaster, Brother Zhang, the unintentional match-maker, would be proud to know that I have carried out his command to '*look after Miss Ma*' for as long as I live!

'Worthy of His Calling'

My final examination for the medical degree at Monash University consisted of a multiple-choice questions (MCQ) paper and an oral clinical examination. Given a choice in general in life, I seldom have much luck and would more often than not make the wrong choice. For example, when unsure of turning left or right at a traffic junction, nine times out of ten I would pick the wrong turn! Similarly, when faced with a question in a MCQ examination that I did not know the answer to, I would invariably pick the wrong answer. My special ability to consistently pick the wrong choice is astounding and could prove to be costly in a MCQ examination. I really had to positively score with solid knowledge. Many years after our wedding and knowing my unique skill in making the wrong choice whenever there was a need, my wife calmly asked me whether I had made the right or wrong choice when choosing her as my soul mate. Fortunately there were no others to choose from in my case!

As for the oral clinical examination, again I did not have much luck when I scored an obstetric long case despite wishing for a general medical case after years of meticulous preparation in internal medicine! Nevertheless, I graduated in Medicine with Honours and was extremely relieved and happy to be a doctor at last. When I broke the good news to Joy, only my girlfriend at that time, she sent me a congraulatory letter with the following biblical verse to guide me for the rest of my professional life:

> *That our God would count you worthy of this calling, and that by His power he may fulfill every good purpose of yours and every act prompted by your faith so that the name of Lord Jesus may be glorified in you. 2 Thessalonians 1:11* (Fig. 12).

'I Think She's Dead'

I was offered an internship back at my own Clinical School, the Alfred Hospital. As for clinical postings, I was immediately thrown straight into the deep end with a country rotation as my first intern rotation. As a fledgling new baby doctor, I was sent to the Central Gippsland Hospital in a country town called Traralgon, 200 miles from Melbourne. As the only major hospital in the area, it was a very busy hospital and the resident doctors there have to deal with every kind of illness, from colds to major traumas and accidents. Half a dozen local general practitioners, a general physician and two general surgeons who visited the hospital supported the resident doctors. One could not rely on senior colleagues for supervision most of the times, only occasionally when needed. The clinical skill of one of the two general surgeons at the country hospital was impressive and totally incredible. He could perform all kinds of surgery, from appendicectomy to neurosurgery.

Fig. 12. Calligraphy of the biblical verse *Worthy of His calling* sent by Joy in celebration of MBBS graduation 1972.

Major motor accident traumas were frequent and he was one of the most competent orthopedic surgeons that I have come across as well. In general medicine, we were entertained and taught by a 'true blue' Aussie general physician who would not start a ward round if there was no beer in the refrigerator! My fellow intern at Traralgon was Dr Rowan Walker, a graduate from the opposition, University of Melbourne. We got on extremely well and helped each other to cope with the unsually heavy responsibilities at the busy country hospital. Having to be on call every alternate night and weekend, we would often clock more than 200 working hours in a fortnight.

On a particularly busy Sunday afternoon, I was frantic with sick patients strewn all over the Emergency Department. A man pacing up and down in front of me incessantly was distracting and annoying me. I had to stop him in his track and asked whether I could help him. He replied without a whiff of excitement: '*My wife has gone out like a light*'! When I asked him where his wife was, he calmly said, '*In the car at the carpark outside*'. I rushed out immediately with him leading the way and found his wife slumped motionless on the backseat. With the help of a porter and a trolley, we transported her back to the resuscitation bay. Fortunately, at that very moment, Rowan Walker walked into the Emergency Department, having returned from Melbourne after his weekend off. I asked for his help immediately to intubate the patient while I attempted to cannulate the patient. A few minutes into our resuscitation effort, Rowan whispered into my ear, '*Limmy, I think she's dead*'. I promptly made a careful and thorough clinical assessment to determine whether Rowan was correct. I concluded that there was no carotid pulse nor respiration and no audible heart sound on auscultation. All the clinical criteria to pronounce death were present and whispered back to Rowan, '*I think you're right!*' It took a good few minutes of combined effort by medical graduates of two great universities in Melbourne to make the profound diagnosis of death! We then instantly activated the 'Code Blue' alert to call for help. Happily, the patient was successfully resuscitated and recovered completely after gastric surgery, having bled from an ulcer. Fresh medical graduates today should be encouraged to know that the two young interns went on to become professors and directors of their respective chosen specialties in cardiology and nephrology.

'You've Tried Hard'

My first medical posting at the Alfred Hospital was in the Clinical Research Unit (CRU) of the Baker Medical Research Institute at the Alfred Hospital. The CRU would provide rare training in clinical research for junior medical staff as well as providing for clinicians to pursue some of their clinical research interests. Dr Alf Barnett was the Director when I was posted to CRU as the intern. Alf was a kind and gentle physician and a leader in scleroderma research. I learnt from his methodical approach and critical analysis of patients' clinical problems. His influence on my clinical training and my interest in clinical research was lifelong.

To finish off my internship, I was posted to the Monash University Department of Surgery unit, headed then by the newly appointed Professor of Surgery, Sir ESR Hughes, or ESR as he was affectionately called. ESR was a renowned colorectal surgeon who pioneered the 'pull-through procedure' to treat rectal cancer. However, Australia and the world would remember him more for the introduction of compulsory seat-belt legislation for motor vehicle drivers than for his surgical prowess. An absolute workaholic, he often commenced his ward rounds at six o'clock in the morning. To prepare for his early-bird ward rounds, interns would have to start at 5 am. The Monash University Department of Surgery at the Alfred Hospital also ran the Burns Unit for the State of Victoria, a service headed by a delightful Scottish surgeon, John Masterton. During my surgical term, with every Friday and alternate nights and weekends on call, and the round-the-clock care of burns patients, an eighteen-hour working day was routine! At the end of the hectic surgical term, ESR would usually reward his hard-working interns, residents and registrars with a farewell and 'thank you' party at his home. When it was time to leave, ESR shook my hand and said to me, '*Lim, you've tried hard*'! This personal 'end-of-term assessment' from the boss confirmed my thought that I was not cut out to be a surgeon, despite having won the surgical prize at the Alfred Hospital a year earlier.

Joy in Australia

1972 was an important year in Australian politics. A General Election held that year saw a change of government with the defeat of the

Liberal Party by the Australian Labor Party, led by Gough Whitlam. Before the election, as a final year medical student at Monash University, I followed very carefully all the newspaper reports of the election campaign and sensed that a change of government was likely. Whitlam had promised diplomatic recognition of the People's Republic of China if elected, in contrast to the Liberal Party's official support of Taiwan's Republic of China. An official visit by President Nixon to China had already taken place before the election in Australia. This change of foreign policy towards China by the Labor Party would of course have a great impact on Joy's coming to Australia, something that I had already started to plan after my visit to her home the year before. Never in my wildest imagination did I guess that Australian politics would play a role in my personal love affair! I surmised Joy's chances of coming to Australia from Taiwan would be made more difficult should the Labor Party win the election. There was not much time left before the election and for Joy to apply for a visitor's visa to come to Australia. Rather anxious, I went to see my superior, Associate Professor John Masterton, the kind and sympathetic Scottish surgeon whom I knew I could trust for help. I confided to him my secret plan and my anxiety caused by the political scene at that time. John was both moved and amused by our love story, especially the courtship by correspondence. He was impressed by my rational and clinical approach to matters pertaining to the heart! As I had predicted, the Labor Party won the general election later that year and Australia established a formal diplomatic relationship with China. The seat at the United Nations held by the Republic of China or Taiwan since the inception of the United Nations was replaced by the People's Republic of China after Nixon's visit to China, supported by Australia.

Politics aside, the most important thing for me was that Joy's application for a visitor's visa to Australia was granted before Labor's election victory. Joy arrived in Australia in the beginning of 1973. After a short engagement, we were married on the day of the official opening of the Sydney Opera House on 20th October 1973 (Fig. 13).

Fig. 13. Wedding at Swanston Street Church of Christ, Melbourne, Oct 20 1973.

Regrettably, none of Joy's family could attend the wedding from Taiwan because of visa reasons. Professor Walters kindly played the role of the bride's father at the wedding. The simple but solemn wedding was held at the Swanston Street Church of Christ in downtown Melbourne. I was on duty at the hospital doing my anesthetic rotation on the morning of my wedding day and my registrar allowed me to go home early so that I would get to my wedding at 4 pm in the afternoon on time! The song 'Get me to the church on time' from Lerner and Loewe's musical *My Fair Lady* became very real on my wedding day. The wedding was held on a Saturday; the weather was not friendly, drizzling on and off all day. After the wedding reception, we headed off to Phillip Island in the best man's relatively new red VW Beetle for a short one-day honeymoon. I had to return to the Alfred Hospital on Monday morning to resume my normal intern anesthetic duties. At the completion of my internship, Joy and I had a belated honeymoon in beautiful Tasmania, the southernmost island State of Australia.

Iefan — 'Surpassing the Ordinary'

Our first home in Melbourne was a small two-bedroom unit at Caroline Street, South Yarra, close to the Alfred Hospital. Joy had a sad miscarriage at 22 weeks of her first pregnancy and we were both devastated. The sadness turned to joy with the birth of a son in 1976 two years after the miscarriage. Joy's second pregnancy was not plain sailing either. The child was born prematurely at 36 weeks by urgent Caesarean section after a difficult and obstructed labour. When delivered, the baby had an Apgar score of only 2. He remained in the neonatal intensive care for premature infants for two weeks. We were overjoyed when he was eventually strong enough to return home.

When naming our newborn son, Joy and I wanted a name that is firstly Chinese, secondly biblical and thirdly preferably Caucasian sounding so that it will be easy for him to live in Australia. I was determined that he should not have the same difficulty as his father when people wish to address him in Australia. Joy had chosen his Chinese name, with two Chinese characters 逸凡 (pronounced *Ee Fun*), meaning 'surpassing the ordinary'. It was my duty to find the English name with all the prerequisites mentioned above. I eventually found an ancient Welsh name, *Iefan*, that sounded close to his Chinese name in pronunciation. In fact other versions of *Iefan*, such as *Ivan* and *Evan*, are the biblical name *John*. We are confident that Iefan will have an easier life in Australia than I have had, as far as names go.

When Iefan was six months old, I was writing up my PhD thesis. I loved to hold him in one arm while typing my thesis, using an old-fashioned ribbon and paper typewriter. To my dismay, Iefan would occasionally screw up some of the typed pages close to him. He was too young and precious to be reprimanded. Computer word processing to reprint the missing pages were not invented at that time and I just had to retype the pages.

One night, my thesis typing was interrupted by an agitated knock on the front door by our next-door neighbor. When I opened the door, he asked anxiously: '*Are you a real doctor?*' '*Do you mean someone who can treat patients and not a PhD?*', I replied. '*Yes*', he said. He wanted to find a doctor in a hurry because his wife was unwell with a high fever and he knew that there was a 'Dr Lim' next door. I went immediately to attend to his wife's medical needs and did not have the time to explain to him that a PhD doctor is the real doctor, not the one who can treat patients. It is a pity that PhD doctors are not as highly regarded by society as medical doctors. The incident reminded me of a favourite newspaper cartoon that I had cut out to stick on the board above my desk in my laboratory office when I was pursuing my PhD. The cartoon depicted a scruffy old man lying on a bench in a park under a street lamp. Beer cans and bottles were strewn on the ground next to him. Sitting next to him was a young man neatly dressed in coat and tie reading the 'Job Vacancy' page. The caption of the cartoon reads: '*Was it wine, women or PhD?*'

PhD Research in Pregnancy Hypertension

The recipients of Colombo Plan Scholarships were bonded to return to serve their country after completion of their undergraduate studies. However, after the fruitful year of research with Professor Walters, he made a personal plea to the Singaporean Government for me to complete a doctorate degree under his supervision. The Singaporean Government acceded to his request and I was allowed to remain in Melbourne to complete my PhD degree. This time the research project involved the study of hemodynamics and left ventricular function of hypertensive pregnant women. A delicate balance of complex neurohumoral adaptation maintains blood pressure during normal pregnancy. Hypertension in pregnancy occurs as a result of imbalance in these changes. My doctoral research findings supported a hypothesis that sympathetic overactivity played a key role in the establishment of hypertension in pregnancy. If this hypothesis is correct, blocking the sympathetic overactivity would correct the abnormal blood pressure elevation during pregnancy. Beta-adrenergic receptor blocking drugs, commonly known as beta-blockers, are standard agents used to treat hypertension. However, at the time of my research their use was relatively contraindicated in pregnancy because of possible adverse effects on the fetus. If sympathetic overactivity were a key factor in pregnancy hypertension, then beta-blockers should be the anti-hypertensive drug of choice for treating this condition. Until then, alpha-methyl-dopa was the standard drug used to treat pregnancy hypertension. Around the time of my doctoral study, various large-scale clinical trials involving the use of beta-blockers to treat pregnancy hypertension were undertaken, and the results of these trials were positive. Beta-blockers are standard therapy for pregnancy-induced hypertension today. I was awarded the degree of Doctor of Philosophy in Medicine from Monash University in May 1977.

Training of a Cardiologist

I was supposed to return to Singapore after the completion of my PhD. However, the Chairman of the Cardiology Sub-specialty Committee of the Royal Australasian College of Physicians (RACP), Professor Paul Korner, strongly advised and supported me to complete my cardiology specialist training after my PhD. I could complete the specialist training in 18 months instead of the normal three years. This was possible because the RACP would credit me for the 18 months of advanced training for the cardiovascular research that I had already done. This was great news until the Singaporean Public Service Commission refused to extend my time in Australia any further. The only way to resolve this impasse was to legally dissolve my contract with the Public Service Commission of Singapore signed at the time of my acceptance of the Colombo Plan Scholarship. With some difficulty, my bond with the Singapore Public Commission was nullified by a financial settlement with my mother's help. The Australian Government promptly granted us citizenship and my wife and I became naturalized Australians in March 1976.

I resumed my clinical programme and physician training at the Alfred Hospital in 1977. After two years as resident medical officer, I passed the Part I FRACP examination. While studying for the RACP examination, I edited the notes that I had previously made while an undergraduate and upgraded the notes into a textbook entitled *Revision Notes in Clinical Medicine* in 1981. The book was designed for candidates preparing for the clinical examination in General Medicine of the RACP. The book was initially published in 1981 by Churchill & Livingstone and then reprinted by Pitman Medical Press. I had much positive feedback on the book from young doctors who used the book to prepare for their clinical examination.

The first year of advanced training in cardiology as a registrar at the Alfred Hospital was followed by the second year as a research fellow with a National Heart Foundation grant to conduct research in the new discipline of nuclear cardiology. As promised by RACP, I was awarded a Fellowship (FRACP) after 18 months of advanced training. I have been registered as a legal practitioner as a General Physician and as a Specialist in Cardiology and Nuclear Medicine in Australia since 1980.

From Nuclear Cardiology to PTCA

Nuclear cardiology was a new branch of cardiology in the late 1970s. It involves the imaging of the heart using photon-emitting radioactive pharmaceuticals. It was pioneered in the United States, with Boston and

New Haven as the leading centres. An Australian colleague, Dr Michael Kelly, had gone to Yale University and brought the technique of 'radionuclide gated blood pool scan' back to the Alfred Hospital in Melbourne in 1979. Apart from Melbourne, Prince Alfred Hospital in Sydney was the only other centre with nuclear cardiology expertise then. My supervisor and Director of Cardiac Services at the Alfred Hospital, Dr Aubrey Pitt, was keen to add this new technology to his unit, known then as the Cardiac Diagnostic Service or CDS in brief. His application for a National Heart Foundation of Australia (NHF) Research Grant for a research project using radionuclide gated blood pool scan to evaluate the improvement in cardiac function after coronary artery bypass graft surgery in man was successful. A joint research programme in nuclear cardiology at the Alfred Hospital was started in which I was the Research Fellow, working with my two other colleagues, Dr Michael Kelly and Dr Victor Kalff, in the Nuclear Medicine Department.

The NHF research project was duly completed over the next 12 months with the publication of a landmark paper in the peer reviewed journal *Circulation*, demonstrating the improvement of left ventricular function after coronary bypass graft surgery in man with severe coronary artery disease.

Following this work I was awarded a National Heart Foundation Overseas Research Fellowship to do post-doctoral research and clinical training at the Massachusetts General Hospital (MGH) of Harvard University in Boston (Fig. 14).

At MGH, I worked with a veterinary surgeon to create an infarct dog model to measure the infarct size using a thallium imaging technique under the supervision of Dr Gerald Pohost, a leader in thallium cardiac imaging at the Cardiac Unit of MGH. This research required the input of a physicist from Massachussets Institute of Technology (MIT), Dr David Chesler. I am fortunate to have worked with David because he showed me the importance of precision and team effort in research. The year of research resulted in the establishment of a novel

Fig. 14. Wen Joy and YL at MGH across Charles River, Boston, 1981.

quantitation of thallium cardiac imaging, now widely used clinically and known as the *MGH-UAB thallium quantitation program*. This early collaboration between clinicians at MGH and basic scientists at the MIT would in time evolve into the Center for Integration of Medicine and Innovative Technology (CIMIT) of Harvard University.

A year at MGH had greatly widened my research horizon. It made me understand the meaning of an old Chinese saying, *the sky is small to a frog at the bottom of a well.* At the Alfred Hospital, one was like the frog at the bottom of a well in evaluating the significance of one's own research. I was the only research fellow at the Alfred Hospital while MGH had 45 research and clinical fellows from all over the world and I was only one of the forty five! Although my clinical research project at MGH was similar to that at the Alfred Hospital, I learnt the importance of being competent in Phase 1 basic animal research before one could be competent in carrying out Phase 2 and 3 human clinical research.

My clinical research project involved a very new clinical therapeutic modality for coronary revascularization known as Percutaneous Transluminal Coronary Angioplasty (PTCA) at that time. This would become a new and major disruptive technology to treat blocked coronary arteries under local anesthesia in time. A cardiologist named Andreas Gruentzig performed the first PTCA in man at Zurich in 1977. My research project at MGH was to show the improvement in myocardial perfusion after PTCA in twenty patients with a critically blocked coronary artery. The impact of PTCA on coronary artery disease treatment was not apparent at that stage, but I was fortunate and privileged to have witnessed and learnt PTCA at a very early stage of its development. Within a few years, this revolutionary technique would start the third medical therapeutic modality known as 'percutaneous interventional therapy', in addition to the two well-established pharmacologic and surgical therapies in medicine. This therapy not only revolutionized medicine, it also changed my career and life as a doctor.

'I am a Butcher!'

After the sojurn in Boston, I returned to Australia in 1982 and commenced medical practice as a cardiologist. I was appointed Associate Director of the first private cardiovascular unit in Melbourne at the Epworth Hospital, under the leadership of Dr Graeme Sloman. At the same time, I was appointed Visiting Cardiologist and Outpatient Consultant Physician in the Department of Cardiology and General Medical Unit 4 at the Alfred Hospital respectively.

My private practice was located at the Epworth Medical Centre, adjacent to the hospital. On a busy outpatient afternoon, my waiting room was full of patients. When I called for the next new patient, an ordinary looking elderly gentleman by the name of Victor Smorgon walked in. I started the consultation in the usual manner, by asking his personal details. *'What do you do for a living, Mr. Smorgon?'* 'I am a butcher', he replied. I then took his clinical history and was told that he had recently been investigated for his heart condition in New York. I was a little surprised and thought that he must be a well-off butcher to be able to afford medical treatment in New York. Out of curiosity, I asked him: *'Where did you have your heart investigations?'* *'Cornell University Medical Centre,'* he replied. *'What's the name of the doctor who treated you?'*, I probed further. *'Dr Jeffrey Borer'*, he answered. With this answer, I stopped writing and looked up to ask the next question: *'What investigations did you have at Cornell?'* *'A nuclear scan of the heart'*, he recalled. My fascination with this butcher was now maximal because Jeffrey Borer was a world-leading specialist in nuclear cardiology, the field of my research for the past three years. He was the father of 'gated blood pools scan', a novel and most accurate way of assessing left ventricular function using radionuclides tagged to red blood cells. I had read most of Borer's publications during my research at Harvard. Noting my fascination, Mr Smorgon volunteered to have the reports of his investigations 'faxed' to me from New York. I did not fully understand the meaning of the word 'fax' at that time. In 1982 the fax machine had just become available and was not a routine office equipment, even for sophisticated cardiologists!

I duly finished my consultation with Mr Smorgon and called for the next patient, Mr L. Glotzer, a Jewish old patient of mine. Before he even sat down, he looked at me with a joyous expression and said to me, *'My my, Dr Lim, you have certainly moved up in your world!'* Not understanding what he was talking about, I asked him, *'What do you mean?'* *'Wasn't that Victor Smorgon who just walked out?'*, he asked. *'Yes, do you know him'*, I replied. *'Everyone knows Victor Smorgon. Don't you know who he is?'* *'He told me he is a butcher'*, I quipped. *'Some butcher!'*, my patient laughed. *'He is one of the richest men in Australia and head of the Smorgon Empire'*, my patient informed me. Mr Smorgon certainly did not exude the air of a very wealthy man but that would have explained his medical check-ups in New York. Simply dressed and humble in his manner, he could easily pass as an ordinary butcher.

The next day, nearly 30 pages of medical reports on Mr Victor Smorgon appeared on my desk. I looked at them and wondered how all these photocopied documents could be delivered to me from New York in less than 24 hours? Couriering them by express post would take more than a day! The secret was of course the fax machine, which Mr Smorgon probably had in his car! After the first consultation, Mr Smorgon became not only a patient but also a good friend until his death at the age of 96.

Soon after his death, the Smorgon family made a substantial donation to the Epworth Medical Foundation to create three Victor Smorgon Chairs for Monash University and the University of Melbourne at the Epworth Hospital. Three inaugural Victor Smorgon Fellowships were also created for young training doctors at Epworth Healthcare to further their studies overseas. My son, Iefan, was the recipient of the first Victor Smorgon Fellowship in Cardiology, much to the delight of the Smorgon family (Fig. 15).

Fig. 15. With the Smorgons and Tuckers, South Yarra 1996 (From left: Iefan, Victor & Loti Smorgan, Barbara & Albert Tucker).

Reviving Albert Tucker

Treating Albert Tucker, the famous Australian artist, was another highlight in my medical career. Tucker was admitted to the Coronary Care Unit of the Alfred Hospital when I was a junior cardiology resident. When I saw the name of the new patient I had to clerk, Mr Albert Tucker, I was wondering whether it was *the* Albert Tucker, a name that I was familiar with, unlike the name Smorgon. Rushing to his cubicle, I saw a distinguished bearded gentleman and quickly asked, 'Are you Albert Tucker the artist?' 'Yes', he answered in a very gentle voice. I was excited and introduced myself saying, '*I am a student of art and it's a great honour to meet you, Mr Tucker*'. Instead of taking the medical history as I should have done, we talked about art, Australian art in particular. He told me in a nutshell the history of modern Australian art in our hour-long conversation. He spoke about the Great Depression, the beginnings of the social realist movement and the origin of the 'Ugly Penguins', his friendship with Sidney Nolan and Arthur Boyd, and the time with the Reeds at Heide. I was privileged to hear the story of modern Australian art from the horse's mouth as it were. I considered this a real privilege, a rare honour and one of the highlights of my artistic career.

We then got on to the reason for his hospital admission and he told me how a fellow artist, Clifton Pugh, who had just had a bypass operation, had advised him to go to the Alfred Hospital to have his chest pain checked out. Tucker took his colleague's advice and turned up at the Emergency Department. He was promptly admitted to the Coronary Care Unit with the diagnosis of unstable angina where I first met him. The next day, with most of his tests showing negative results, he was transferred out of Coronary Care to a normal ward bed. Shortly after his transfer, Tucker suffered an unexpected cardiac arrest from which he was successfully resuscitated. I was a member of the resuscitation team that brought Tucker back to life! His heart condition was promptly treated and the famous Australian artist went on to live and paint for another 22 years! I was fortunate indeed when Albert Tucker agreed to write the foreword for my photographic book *Eastern Eye Western Light* that was published in 1995. Our friendship continued until he passed away in 1999 at the age of 85.

First Private Cardiovascular Unit in Melbourne

Dr Graeme Sloman, an Australian pioneer cardiologist, was famous for his invention of the Mobile Intensive Care Unit (MICA) in Australia. In 1981, after his retirement as head of cardiology at the Royal Melbourne Hospital, he was invited by the Epworth Medical Foundation of the Uniting Church in Melbourne to start the first private cardiac unit in Melbourne at the Epworth Hospital in Richmond. Dr E. Manolas, his protégé at the Royal Melbourne Hospital, was recruited before I returned to Melbourne from Boston to join his team. Dr Manolas, a Greek cardiologist, was one of the first coronary interventionists in Australia, having trained with Andreas Gruentzig at Emory University, Atlanta. Andreas Gruentzig was headhunted by Dr Spencer King III to go to the United States from Zurich, Switzerland.

At the American College of Cardiology meeting in Atlanta in 1981, Dr Sloman had asked me to consider joining his new team at the Epworth Hospital. I was very grateful and excited by the prospect and impressed by his vision of a centre of excellence in cardiovascular medicine in the private sector, a novel concept for Melbourne at that time. Dr Sloman was very innovative, extremely energetic and a superb administrator. My first encounter with this great man was at my interview with him for an Australian National Heart Foundation Overseas Research Fellowship. Graeme was a forthright person, direct in his approach, sincere in his belief and brilliant in his organization. I learnt from him most of my administrative skills. The Cardiovascular Unit that he had created was the first of its kind in Australia to combine cardiology and cardiac surgery into a cohesive functional unit. Brian Buxton, a brilliant surgeon from the Austin Hospital, was recruited to head the cardiac surgical services. With the arrival of Buxton and many other Melbourne cardiac surgeons, the Epworth Cardiovascular Unit at the Epworth Hospital in Richmond was established and it was the first private hospital to perform cardiac surgery in Australia. Melbourne, however has other more conservative cardiac surgeons who did not believe that cardiac surgery could or should be done in the private sector in 1981. Among them, George Stirling, then head of the C J Officer-Brown Cardiothoracic Unit at the Alfred Hospital, was a strong opponent. A few years later, when the success of the Epworth Cardiovascular Unit was beyond doubt, George Stirling was gracious enough to publicly retract his initial opposition and became a member of the cardiac surgical team at the Epworth Hospital himself.

Interventional Cardiology Training and the Epworth Connection

At the Epworth Hospital, Dr Manolas and I were the first two cardiologists to perform percutaneous transluminal coronary angioplasty (PTCA) in Melbourne. Peter Valentine at the Royal Melbourne Hospital was the first doctor in Australia to perform PTCA in 1980. For many years after its establishment in 1981, the Cardiovascular Unit at Epworth was the busiest coronary intervention unit in Australia. A few years after my arrival, Dr Ronald Dick was also recruited by Dr Sloman to join the Cardiovascular Unit and trained to become an interventional cardiologist (Fig. 16). The success of the Epworth Cardiovascular Unit was undoubtedly due to the great leadership and vision of Graeme Sloman, who inspired all who worked with him.

Achieving academic excellence has been the priority in my medical career, both in the private and public sectors. With a very busy private practice at the Epworth Hospital, a hospital active in interventional cardiology, the opportunity to train many coronary interventionists from the Asia Pacific region was utilized to the full. Thus, Dr Sloman and I recruited overseas interventional cardiology and pacing cardiac fellows from India and China to train at the Epworth Hospital. In the eighties,

Fig. 16. Founders of the Cardiovascular Unit, Epworth Hospital 1982 (from left: YL, E Manolas, G Sloman, R Dick).

overseas fellows were allowed to have hands-on practical experience during their training in Australia. This training was unique, especially for a private hospital where patients expect personal service from their private cardiologists. It is remarkable that in two decades of such hands-on PTCA training, no major adverse events or litigation have occurred. I constantly remind my trainees of the sacrifice my private patients have to make in order for them to have hands-on training. To compensate for their sacrifice, future patients of the trainees in their own country must benefit from their hands-on learning experience in learning this new life-saving treatment technique. This training was meant to help their patients and not to equip them with skills for financial gains or academic rewards. Many years later when I saw the rapid growth and development of interventional cardiology in China and India and the vast number of patients that have benefited from this training programme, I knew that this worthy goal had indeed been achieved.

The training of cardiologists and surgeons from China and India was not only confined to hospitals that I worked with in Melbourne. I led various teams of cardiac surgeons, anesthetists, theatre nurses, medical technologists and perfusionists from the Epworth, Alfred and Austin Hospitals in Melbourne as well as the National Heart Centre in Singapore to help develop coronary artery bypass graft surgery and coronary angioplasty in many cities throughout China. Looking back over three decades, the end results are heartening.

New Cardiac Centre in Melbourne's East

In 1993, my ambition of becoming a professor after eight misses was realised when I was appointed the founding Director and Associate Professor of the newly created Department of Cardiology at Box Hill Hospital, a teaching hospital of Monash University, my alma mater in Melbourne. To commemorate the occasion, my wife gave me a first edition copy of William Osler's famous textbook *Principle and Practice of Medicine*, published in 1892. This was the book that I wanted but could not afford to buy when I came across it in an antiquarian bookstore while I was an overseas fellow in Boston. My wife inscribed the following words of encouragement in her own hand: '*He who upholds God shall prevail*'.

Being in a university teaching hospital in the public sector, the new department provided an ideal platform to train cardiologists, both local and from overseas, China in particular. At Box Hill Hospital and Epworth Hospital, my life goal of training better doctors, both for Australia and Asia, was greatly enhanced.

From Box Hill, I started to make frequent training trips to China. Box Hill has a special significance in the history of Australian art. It was the cradle of the Australian impressionists, the so-called Heidelberg School. The first Australian impressionists frequently painted around Box Hill and Heidelberg, in open air. Because of this, they were called the *plein air* artists. On my arrival at Box Hill Hospital to start the

Cardiology Department, I hoped to transform Box Hill Hospital into a centre for 'heart', much the same way as the Heidelberg impressionists turned Box Hill into a centre for 'art' in Australia. The 'Box Hill heart school' indeed was to become the centre of learning for many cardiologists from China while I was there. I also gave Box Hill its Chinese name 博士山, literally translated means '*Hill of PhDs*'. This Chinese name for Box Hill was first used on my business card and later by the local Chinese newspaper when they published a feature article for the new cardiology services at the Box Hill Hospital. It is now the officially adopted Chinese name of Box Hill in Melbourne.

During my term at Box Hill Hospital, I unintentionally made headline news when the then Health Minister of Victoria, Ms Marie Tehan, visited the hospital as Guest of Honour for the official opening of the newly renovated hospital entrance and main foyer. I was part of the official welcome party. Prior to the Minister's arrival, I had asked the Chairperson of the Board to hand a letter to the Minister during her morning tea break with the Minister. In the letter I humbly asked for increased funding for the busy new cardiac unit at the Box Hill Hospital. The Minister duly arrived. Accompanied by the Board Chairperson, she was being officially introduced to each member of the official welcome party. When my turn came, the Chairperson suddenly handed my letter back to me and said: '*You can give it to the Minister yourself*'. I did as she instructed and said to the Minister: '*honoured to meet you, Minister. I have a personal letter for you*' and handed the letter directly to her. She accepted my letter graciously and handed it to her personal assistant next to her. I thought that's that but in the local *Herald Sun* newspaper the next day, my encounter with the Health Minister appeared as front-page news, with the headline '*Patients Die waiting — Doctor's claim*'! An accompanying photograph on the next page (Fig. 17) and an editorial followed the headline in subsequent pages of the newspaper. In the editorial, the newspaper chief editor was telling the story of how the Professor of Cardiology at Box Hill Hospital had protested in writing to the Health Minister concerning patients

Appeal: *Prof Yean Lim (left) tells Mrs Tehan of equipment shortages. Picture: GENEVIEVE EDWARDS.*

Patients die waiting — claim

Fig. 17. Newspaper report in the *Herald Sun*, Nov 24 1994.

dying while awaiting for their operations due to the lack of government funding! I was flabbergasted as this was not the content of the letter that I had handed to the Health Minister. My strong objection to the Chief Editor fell on deaf ears. Over the next two days, even the then Premier of the State of Victoria, Jeff Kennett, waded in to criticize the '*Professor who thought he knew best*'. At that time, health was a hot public issue as the ambulance service was on strike and emergency departments of public hospitals were closing down due to lack of government funding. The media was aggressively attacking the Government over the chaotic health scene in Melbourne and the photo of me handing a letter to the Health Minister provided a perfect story for the media. In fact, the reporter who concocted the front-page story actually rang to apologize to me and to say that he '*just had to use me*'! My confidence with reporters was at an all time low.

During the five years at Box Hill Hospital, I also championed the idea of a co-located private hospital at Box Hill, initially to be funded by an Asian consortium. Negotiations for such a hospital continued even after I left Box Hill for Singapore. This vision eventually came to fruition with the establishment of the Epworth Eastern Hospital, funded by a different source and operated by the Epworth Healthcare Group.

New Cardiovascular Centre in Melbourne's West

Just before I left Singapore in 2003, Dr John Balla contacted me. He was previously the Medical Director of Box Hill Hospital and had worked closely with me there. He was then the Chief Medical Officer at the Western Hospital in the western suburbs of Melbourne. Knowing that I was planning to return to Melbourne from Singapore, he head-hunted me to come to the Western Hospital to develop the Centre for Cardiovascular Therapeutics there, similar to the one that I had created at Box Hill Hospital. Having worked for many years in Hong Kong, John Balla was one of the few Australians who could call me by my full Chinese name, *Yean Leng*. We met at his house in Toorak and he said to me in his usual direct manner, '*Yean Leng, you are a builder, and we would like you to build a new cardiac service for us at the Western Hospital in Melbourne's west*'.

The Western Hospital is the largest teaching hospital of the University of Melbourne in western Melbourne. It was affiliated with the Royal Melbourne Hospital Clinical School at that time. Today, it has become the fourth independent Clinical School of the University of Melbourne. The population of the western suburbs of Melbourne consists predominantly of working-class families and these suburbs of Melbourne boast the highest heart disease burden in the State of Victoria. John Balla was confident that I could improve the cardiac services of the Western Health cluster in the same way I did for Eastern

Health. I was duly appointed as the inaugural Professor and Director of the new Centre for Cardiovascular Therapeutics, a conjoint appointment of Western Health and the University of Melbourne. With this new role, I returned to Melbourne after five years of productive services to Singapore, my country of birth.

With very limited resources from the hospital and health department, I had to create new visiting cardiologist positions by sacrificing my own salary. However, the Centre thrived and quickly became one of the busiest interventional cardiac services of Victoria. Within three years, the Centre was fully accredited by the Royal Australasian College of Physicians for advanced cardiology training with three advanced trainee positions.

Unlike Box Hill in the east, the productive partnership between John Balla and I could not be repeated because of sudden leadership changes in the management of Western Health for the worse. My uncompromising leadership in the reform of the cardiology senior medical staff structure and my insistence on academic excellence at Western Health was also met with strong resistance by a small group of mediocre senior staff who wished to maintain status quo. This group persisted in undermining my leadership with a series of false and defamatory allegations. They also complained to the administration about my constant absence from my job due to my heavy and important commitments in China, even though I had fulfilled and exceeded all my tasks as set out my employment contract. The administration unfortunately chose to support my antagonistic colleagues and together eventually gave me an unexpected heart attack. I was forced to retire after this incident but fully remunerated to the end of my contract with Western Health at the age of 65 years.

It was indeed ironic that an interventional cardiologist would eventually need coronary intervention himself, brought on by extreme stress at work. My own coronary angioplasty was successfully carried out by two trusted colleagues, Dr E Manolas and Dr A Walton, who attended to my acute illness at the Epworth Hospital. The cardiac catheter laboratory staff, who are all colleagues at work, were amused by the exchange of treatment strategies that went on between the doctors and the patient on the table! I was glad when the procedure was successfully completed and I live to tell the story. I now use my own coronary intervention experience to teach the appropriateness of staged percutaneous coronary intervention and the minimization of stent usage in China and elsewhere.

Despite the unexpected and unjustified way that my association with Western Health was abruptly terminated, the management saw fit to establish an annual interventional cardiology fellowship training position, named the *Y L Lim Interventional Cardiology Fellowship*, to recognise my significant and positive contributions at the Western Hospital. The first YL Lim Fellowship was formally awarded in September 2013.

I am privileged to have the opportunity to help establish modern cardiovascular services in Eastern and Western Healthcare. I am glad that I have been able to maintain the balance of the East and West, even in the important delivery of cardiac care for the State of Victoria over two decades.

From HC to VIC to MVIC

The modern concept of the 'hospital' started in the West in the 18th century. It was introduced to the East in the mid-19th century. The modern hospital as we know it today, rather than the earlier 'house of charity', had its origins in the 'Age of Enlightenment' in the 18th century when the earlier charitable healing places evolved to become what we now know as 'general hospitals'. With the rapid progress made in science, medicine and engineering, the accuracy of clinical diagnosis has been enhanced and treatment options have also improved with the advent of new technologies, especially in the latter half of the 20th century. As a result, specialized diagnostic departments and centres gradually evolved within general hospitals. The first sub-specialty departments and centres that evolved within a large general hospital were that of heart and cancer centres because of their high disease prevalence. Single specialty stand-alone hospitals have their strengths and weaknesses. When heart or cancer patients become critically ill or when multi-organ failure occurs, these patients will need intensive care and support from other medical disciplines. Thus life-supporting expertise of intensivists, nephrologists, neurologists, gastroenterologists, endocrinilogists and surgeons are often required to provide optimal and total care of very sick patients. A heart or cancer hospital should therefore, ideally be located in the vicinity of a general hospital where such support could be easily available. Fu Wai Cardiovascular Institute in China and M. D. Anderson and Sloan-Kettering Cancer Centres, in America are existing examples of stand-alone specialty hospitals.

Atherosclerotic diseases of the blood vessels will affect many target organs, most important of which are heart, brain, kidney and limbs. Some of them are more life threatening than others. Cerebrovascular mortality remains the number one or two killer in the world, developed or developing. Modern imaging technology can now pinpoint diseases of the blood vessels to allow accurate percutaneous intervention of the diseased 'culprit' vessel. Prior to the advent of endovascular therapy, radical surgery, such as limb amputation, bypass graft surgery or neurosurgery were the only available treatment options. Mortality rates of atherosclerotic vascular diseases have dropped significantly as a result of interventional therapeutic advances. Percutaneous endovascular therapy under local anesthesia can now be applied to treat patients with acute coronary syndrome, stroke, refractory hypertension and many other structural and valvular heart diseases. In the field of electrical heart disease, percutaneous ablative and occlusive device therapies have also replaced invasive traumatic open-heart surgical procedures. These novel interventional therapies have brought together many previously independent medical disciplines such as cardiology, radiology, nephrology, neurology, endocrinology and vascular surgery.

Sharing of common facilities such as diagnostic, therapeutic laboratories by all the various specialties is both efficacious and cost-effective from the health economic point of view. Expensive duplications of machine cost and labour can be avoided and inter-desciplinary synergism can be enhanced. The labeling of a target organ such as the heart, brain and kidney often encourages territorial ownership disputes that are detrimental to good and efficient services. Since vessels are the common link between vital organs such as the heart, brain, kidneys and limbs, the concept of individual organ centres such as heart centres (HC) and brain centres should be discouraged. These specialist centres should assume names such as vascular intervention centres (VIC) to promote the concept of global vascular intervention for these specialty treatment centres.

Of all the major risk factors associated with the development of atherosclerotic vascular diseases that affect the heart, the brain and elsewhere, the two most common risk factors for vascular diseases are diabetes mellitus and its precursor, the metabolic syndrome of hypertension, hyperlipidemia and obesity. By 2050, a quarter of the human population will develop metabolic and diabetic vascular disease and cerebral-vascular mortality will be the number one killer in the world. It makes good prophylactic sense to plan metabolic vascular intervention centres (MVIC) that incorporate the concept of VIC plus the prevention and treatment of metabolic diseases. The expertise of endocrinologists, dietitians and sports medicine practitioners are essential to develop successful MVICs.

Whether in the East or the West, the evolution of a comprehensive metabolic vascular intervention centre (MVIC) from the current target-organ centres will be a major breakthrough in the reduction of mortality rates from vascular diseases. This should be the direction of planning and development of future specialized hospitals.

3

A Good Doctor

Cushing's Four Portraits of a Good Doctor

To many, Boston is a modern Renaissance city. It is a city remarkable for its intellectual and spiritual ambience. During our time in Boston, God prepared for us a spiritual home at the Chinese Christian Church of Greater Boston. My wife and I regularly attended the Bible study group led by a Harvard Professor of Dentistry, Yan Kai-ran, a good role model for young Christians. Boston was also the cradle of the American War of Independence. I loved to walk the Freedom Trail, starting at the statue of the midnight ride of Paul Revere near Faneuil Hall. There were numerous quaint old antiquarian bookshops scattered along the Freedom Trail. I would spend many weekends hunting for old books in those antiquarian bookstores. I was fortunate to acquire a first edition copy of Harvey Cushing's *The Life of Sir William Osler*, published in 1925 in two volumes. This copy carried the bookplate of Edward Revere, the great grandson of Paul Revere and brother of Grace Revere, who later became Mrs William Osler after the death of her first husband. Harvey Cushing, after whom Cushing's Disease was named, was a famous student of William Osler. Cushing's biography of Osler won him a coveted Pulitzer Prize in 1926. The life story and writings of William Osler, especially his literary works, were to have a profound impact on my medical career, especially as a teacher. Years later, when I had a chance to start a new western-style medical school in Xiamen, China, the Johns Hopkins School of Medicine co-founded by Osler and his colleagues would be the model that I aspired to replicate. In William Osler I jelled my idea of a good and great doctor.

Osler's last academic appointment was the Regius Professor of Medicine at Oxford University. At the house of Clifford Albutt, his friend and counterpart at Cambridge University, he saw three portrait paintings, those of Thomas Linacre, Thomas Sydenham and William Harvey which together were meant to represent the essential qualities of a good doctor; namely humanism, literary, scientific and bedside clinical skills (Fig. 18). Osler had the portraits duplicated and the three replicas now hang in the Osler Library at McGill University Medical School, Montreal. In Harvey Cushing's biography of Osler, Cushing added his commentary to Osler's acquisition of the three portraits. Cushing opined that there should be a fourth portrait, that of Osler himself, to represent humanism to complete the essential qualities of a good doctor. I concurred thoroughly with his addition of the fourth portrait, and agreed with Cushing that the fourth is probably the most important. Osler was not only a superb clinician and scientist, but also a compassionate doctor, loved and revered by his patients, students and colleagues. He is my role model of a good doctor. To quote Osler himself, *'a physician may possess the science of Harvey and the Art of Sydenham, and yet lacking those finer qualities of heart and head which count for so much in life'.*

Today, Osler's philosophical essays are more treasured than his scientific publications. Whilst a Professor of Medicine, he was elected President of the British Classical Society in 1919, the only medical practitioner to be so honoured in the entire history of the Society.

Fig. 18. Four portraits representing the essential qualities of a good doctor (Clockwise from top left: Linacre, Harvey, Osler, Sydenham).

Healing with Science and Humanism

At the time of my father's final illness, I was young and angry with his doctor. I had decided that his principal doctor was not a good doctor because he did not show the expected care or concern for his patient and relatives. Not knowing exactly what a good doctor should be like as a teenager, I expected a good doctor to be kind and show compassion and care to his patient. Humanism and humility, represented by William Osler, the fourth portrait of a good doctor, is as essential as good clinical skill and knowledge. Healing without science is superstition. Healing without humanism is technology. Only healing with science and humanism is medicine. The Chinese sages praised a great physician or *Da-yi* as '*one who possesses a magnanimous heart and extraordinary skill*'. But how does a doctor cultivate this desirable combination of '*heart and skill*'?

To achieve this noble combination, one must have what Osler described as both extrinsic and intrinsic education. *Extrinsic education* provides one with the knowledge of disease and its cure. It involves training of the head and the hand. In contrast, *intrinsic education* pertains to the study of humanities or training of the heart. Of this two-fold education, Osler had the following to say:

> Special Education is the knowledge of disease and its cure, a knowledge that will make you practitioners of medicine; extrinsic, accomplished by text, teachers and tongue. Inner education is the knowledge of oneself, a knowledge that may make you a truly good man; intrinsic, mental salvation wrought out by each one for himself, and achieved through personal contact with men of high purpose and character. The first without the second, an active practitioner, but through life you have been a fool; the second without the first, you may have the endowments of heart and head that make the little of what you possess go very far. The desire is to have a due proportion of each.

A good doctor is like an artist. The work of an artist, be it in painting, calligraphy, music, poetry or literature, is evident by the presence of life or *Qi*, in Chinese. Work lacking in *Qi* is regarded as craft, accomplished by artisans rather than artists. Crafts are decorative and often fail to evoke sustaining emotional response from viewers, readers or audience. The viewer's interest in craft works thus wanes quickly.

Therefore, a real doctor should be like an artist rather than an artisan. His medical practice must be an art and not a craft, a calling and not a business. During medieval times in the West, the title 'doctor' was bestowed upon those who have the knowledge and ability to heal. The modern dictionary definition of 'doctor' is 'a learned person'. Doctor is an honorary title conferred to graduates of the medical faculty when in fact they possess only a bachelor degree. This does not apply to any other bachelor degrees except medicine. A medical doctor, although learned, should heed the following quotation of William Osler: *'Bookworms (doctors) sometime fail not because they have not studied books, but because they have not studied men'*.

I have attempted to summarize the essential qualities of a good doctor from several of Osler's occasional addresses in the following table (Table 1):

Table 1. Essential qualities of a good doctor.

Competence	Art of Detachment
Knowledge	Virtue of Method
Wisdom	Thoroughness
Compassion	Humility
Integrity	Equanimity
Leadership	

At the official opening ceremony of the new Xiamen University Medical College, I addressed the first batch of 25 students in my capacity as Dean with a speech entitled 'Wise and Humanistic Doctor'. The gist of the lecture is summarized as follows:

A doctor must not be satisfied with mere scientific knowledge and clinical skill, more importantly he must have a heart filled with compassion and care. A real student will pursue knowledge with zest, sagacity and humility, thirst for the ability to be able to differentiate between right and wrong, good and evil. He must possess not only knowledge, but also wisdom. A skilled and knowledgeable doctor may not be wise. Knowledge can be obtained from books, but wisdom comes from life experience and contact with sages and great men. A wise doctor operates like an artist, not like an artisan. The distinction between the two is the possession of the quality of life or 'Qi', present in the former but not the latter. A good doctor should possess the qualities represented by the four portraits described by Cushing, including that of Osler himself, and not only the three that Osler had collected. A good doctor, thus, must have bedside clinical skill, sound scientific knowledge, good communicative skill and above all a humanistic heart.

Doctor, 'Docrat' or 'Dr Death'

Great doctors or *Da-yi* in Chinese, are highly revered in traditional Chinese society. The two Chinese characters for doctor are 醫生 (*yi-shen*). These two characters literally translated mean *heal and live*. The wisdom of the Chinese name for a doctor tells us that after the healing work of a doctor, the patient will be alive! The Chinese characters for *patient* also consists of two characters, 病人 (*bing-ren*). If one follows the classical format of a Chinese couplet or the art of pairing a phrase or a sentence, doctors or *yi-shen* written in two characters should treat patients or *bing-ren*, also two characters. He should not just treat disease or *bing*, only a single character. However, the average doctor today like craftsmen treats only diseases and not patients. A good doctor must never be a mere artisan, or *yi-jiang* (醫匠) who treats only a patient's disease, he must be a good and complete doctor or *yi shen* (醫生), and treat the patient as a person with disease.

To emphasize this important concept, I have created an imaginary word '*docrat*' (a hybrid of doctor and technocrat) to describe a doctor who is a craftsman or artisan. A docrat is a doctor who does not have the art of healing but only the craft of healing. Finally, doctors of the worst kind can be light-heartedly called *yi-shi* (醫死), which literally translated means Doctor Death or '*heal to death*'. Such *Doctor Deaths* must never be allowed to practice! I therefore jokingly classify doctors into the first class, *Doctors*; second class, *Docrats* and the bottom of the class, *Doctor Deaths*.

In the computer age today, many doctors are unable to practise medicine or make a diagnosis without using machines, tests or investigations. This group of doctors are slaves to modern diagnostic machines or 'machine doctors' as I call them. A competent doctor or clinician should be able to make a reasonably accurate *clinical diagnosis* based on detailed history and a thorough physical examination of the patient. A good doctor will then order relevant investigations after making the clinical diagnosis to confirm a final *definitive diagnosis* of the patient. The prescription of the best treatment options will be based on the *definitive* rather than the *clinical* diagnosis. The role of machines is therefore to help doctors make more objective and accurate diagnoses of patients. The use of any diagnostic machine should add value to the clinical diagnosis made without it. Thus, a good doctor is a *master* of the machines he uses whereas a docrat is a *slave* of the machines that others have invented. Today the widespread use and dependency on machines by doctors, or rather docrats has made them mentally dull and regressed their thinking and analytical abilities. In this computerized age, we need more *thinking* and less *testing* doctors. A century ago, before diagnostic machines were available, Osler described two sorts of doctors, *'those who practice with their brain and those who practice with their tongues'*. Furthermore, his observation that *'it is astonishing with how little reading (knowledge) a doctor can practice medicine but it is not astonishing how badly he may do it'*, is still *very* relevant today.

A doctor, therefore, can easily be differentiated from a docrat in my classification of doctors. The former, a doctor, treats *patients with disease*; the latter, a docrat, treats *diseases* and not human beings. Docrats or craftsman doctors will not be able to practise without investigations. They have little genuine interest in their patients and rarely talk or interact with their patients as fellow human beings. Modern medicine has become heavily reliant on machines and this is the root cause of escalating healthcare costs all over the world today, especially in the developed countries. The vast majority of sick patients in both the developed as well as the developing nations in the world today will not be able to afford this kind of machine-dependent healthcare.

Ethics — Cornerstone of a Doctor

In western nomenclature, British in particular, an experienced, well-qualified and highly respected doctor is accorded an honorary title, a *Consultant doctor*. The eastern equivalent of a Consultant doctor is simply called a *Great doctor* or *Da-yi* (大医). The necessary qualities associated with this honorary title of *Da-yi* were carefully documented in the preface to the ancient traditional Chinese medical classic, entitled *qian jin yao fang* or the *Treatise of the Thousand Golden Prescriptions*, written by Sun Xi-miao during the Tang Dynasty. I presented a calligraphic summary of this well-known preface, the 'Da-yi Jin chen' (大醫精誠) preface, as a graduation gift for my son when he became a doctor (Fig. 19). The following is the English translation of the summarized preface:

To become a Da-yi, one must be a master of clinical skills, delivered with impeccable ethics. One must be familiar with the classics of Zhou, Yi, Lao-tze and mathematics. One must read widely, know all the different prescriptions and medical texts. One must have a big heart, refrain from distractions, and treat all patients with sagacity and sincerity.

Only doctors who have demonstrated these qualities are to be considered *da-yi* or *great doctors*, in the same manner the honorary title of 'Doctor' is bestowed upon a learned person. A *da-yi* or great doctor is a first-rate physician who has read widely, possesses superb clinical skills, high morals, and extensive knowledge but, just as importantly, is also caring and compassionate. Of all the qualities listed, that of impeccable ethics is probably the most essential for a *Da-yi* or Consultant, both in the East and the West. Ethics is also the cornerstone of the Hippocratic Oath which establishes the moral guidelines of western

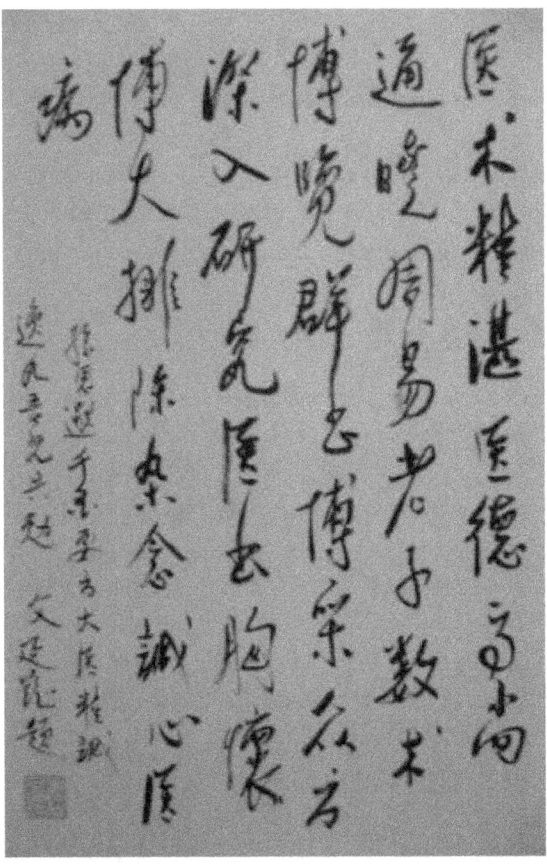

Fig. 19. Excerpt from Sun Xi-miao's preface to the '*Treatise of the Thousand Golden Prescription*' *(Da yi Jin xheng)* representing the code of ethics for Chinese medicine doctors.

medical practice. A great Doctor or *Da-yi* will treat his patients as human beings and not diseased states. He is deeply interested in the welfare of his patients, concerned not only for their physical illness but their entire well-being and that of their families and loved ones. Doctors of this caliber are rare today.

Osler, in his philosophical writings, also describes three classes of consultant doctors and four classes of professors and I concur. The three eminent consultants of worldwide repute are:

Firstly, a good physician and no humbug; secondly, no physician but a great humbug; thirdly, a great physician and a great humbug. The first achieves great success, professional, social possibly, but not financial.

Teachers, he also rated:

a mediocre teacher tells, a good teacher explains, a superior teacher demonstrates but a great teacher inspires.

Professors he classified into four classes:

one who can think, but who has neither tongue nor teaching, is a Thinking Professor. One who can talk, but who can neither think nor work, is a Phonographic Professor. One who has technique, but who can neither talk nor think, is a Technical Professor and finally, the Professor who can do all three, is a Rare Professor.

The 'last but not least' quality of a good doctor is leadership. A doctor is usually the leader in the healing team. Leadership qualities are required of any good doctor. I subscribe to the following classification of leaders:

The wicked leader is one who people despise; the good leader is one who people revere; the great leader is one when people say eventually, we did it ourselves.

To be able to inspire, to make a difference and achieve something great for others to continue and improve, is the hallmark of a great leader, a doctor not to be excepted.

Basic Healthcare Assurance

According to the former President of China, Hu Jingtao, the goal of healthcare is to ensure the provision of basic healthcare to the vast population of China, both in the rural and the urban areas. To achieve this goal, one needs to define the term *basic*. The standard of basic healthcare is closely related to the state of economic development of a nation and it varies from country to country. It takes into account the size of the population and whether the country is developed or developing according to the Organization for Economic Cooperation (OECD) criteria. The criteria for *basic healthcare* delivery can only be defined by some internationally accepted guidelines drafted according to expert medical consensus. Only medical experts with detailed knowledge and experience in the treatment of diseases can define what basic healthcare in each common disease is morally acceptable. The following true case history of a patient with coronary heart disease that I had encountered, can be used to illustrate the concept of basic healthcare that a government should provide. The case occurred in a rural China town as follows:

An elderly farmer awoke one morning with epigastric pain and coughing. He was anorexic and unable to work as usual. He sat for two hours before seeking medical attention from a local doctor in the village where he lived. The doctor prescribed him two pills and instructed him to seek further help at the Emergency Department of the closest large city tertiary teaching hospital, an hour by car, if the pills did not give him relief. Feeling no better an hour after taking the two pills, the patient and his wife travelled by bus to the nearest Emergency Department. Two hours after they registered at the Emergency Department, he was warded in a respiratory unit, presumably because of his coughing symptom. A routine electrocardiogram performed two hours after admission alerted his doctors to the fact that he had suffered an acute anterior myocardial infarction. He was rushed to the cardiac catheter laboratory and coronary stenting was perfomed successfully to his blocked anterior descending artery. He was effectively treated and discharged home well.

This case illustrated that basic healthcare could be suboptimally provided and a correct diagnosis made with the aid of a machine even though the doctors at both the rural and city levels were not competent to make the right clinical diagnosis. This case highlighted the fact that patients in rural or urban China could not be assured of basic healthcare. Machines capable of making accurate diagnosis are not always available in primary healthcare clinics in rural areas in China or other similar developing nations. In this case, if the primary care doctor had the basic clinical knowledge that acute left ventricular failure with lung congestion following a significant myocardial infarction could account for the patient's coughing, and epigastric pain could arise from infarction of the inferior aspect of the heart, the clinical suspicion of a heart attack might have been made and intervention performed sooner to the patient's advantage. The basic knowledge and physical examination skill of the doctors involved was lacking and healthcare assurance at two levels of healthcare had failed. The lack of basic bedside clinical skill is the root cause of expensive investigative medicine in both developed and developing countries in the world today. Basic healthcare reform therefore needs to start from changes in basic physician training as well as healthcare policies and governance.

Inaccessible and Unaffordable Healthcare

Until recently, healthcare has been the number one social issue in China. China may not be the only nation facing healthcare challenges. 'Inaccessible and unaffordable healthcare' is still the slogan used by citizens in many developed nations when describing their plight in trying to obtain basic healthcare. One reason for expensive healthcare is the current training of machine or tests orientated doctors instead of thinking doctors. Careful analytical and logical thinking has been replaced by results obtained from a multitude of tests and investigations, the feature of current medical practice. Investigations are costly, and the cause of 'inaccessible and unaffordable healthcare'. To reform healthcare, it is fundamental to improve bedside clinical training of doctors. The training of a doctor should emphasize more *thinking* and less *testing*, to solve patients' problems. 'The Cost Conundrum — What a Texas town can teach us about health care, the "Annals of Medicine"', a feature article in the June 1 2009 issue of *The New Yorker* by Atul Gawande highlighted this important conclusion.

The author of this important report analyzed the cost-benefits of healthcare in America. The findings were most instructive and applicable to countries struggling with healthcare costs in both developed and developing countries alike. The article contrasted the worst healthcare practice, based on standard Key Performance Indicators (KPIs) of healthcare outcomes, at a private hospital in McAllen, Texas to the best practice at the Mayo Clinic in Rochester, Minnesota. At McAllen Hospital, a for-profit private hospital, the average cost to treat a disease was almost three times that of the Mayo Clinic. This inverse relationship of quality to cost is also reflected in a survey of 20 developed countries undertaken by the World Health Organization in 2008. The United States of America, with the highest healthcare expenditure, almost 18% of GDP, was ranked 19th in terms of quality of care in the group of twenty developed countries. The features of the expensive McAllen healthcare was profit-driven, fragmented, doctor-centered *more testing less thinking* medicine. In contrast, the coordinated patient-centered, not-for-profit *more thinking less testing* medical practice of Mayo Clinic was cheaper and yielded better results. The reliance on tests and procedures, sometimes unnecessary, is the hallmark of high cost and low quality healthcare seen in most developed countries in the world today. The 'Cost Conundrum' article concluded that the Mayo Clinic healthcare model must be the norm and not the exception in all healthcare services. Unfortunately, in most countries in the world today and developed countries especially, the McAllen model continues to be the norm and the Mayo Clinic model the exception.

Healthcare delivery is unlike any other industry. The consumers are in fact the doctors and not the patients. In the healthcare industry, the doctors are the service providers who determine the cost. They decide which tests to order and prescribe what drugs and therapeutic procedures the patients need. A basic good therapy for a disease must be one that is accessible to and affordable by all patients afflicted with the disease. If a very effective therapy is only available for a small proportion of patients, then it cannot be really good for the disease. Myocardial revascularization by Percutaneous Coronary Intervention (PCI) is an effective but expensive therapy for coronary heart disease. If this basic life-saving therapy can be made affordable to all patients who need it, then PCI will truly be a good therapeutic modality that will benefit millions of patients with coronary insufficiency in both developed and developing countries.

Lim's Ward Round

Traditional bedside clinical training in China was severely disrupted by the Cultural Revolution in the 1960s. A whole generation of clinical teachers was lost during this period. However, the rapid economic growth in China over the last three decades has allowed China to catch up with western developed countries, especially in the healthcare industry. I was privileged to be given a role in the development of coronary intervention in China at a critical time. In the process of introducing this novel therapy, traditional clinical bedside training was also reintroduced in many hospitals that I visited. My clinical bedside methods were fondly given a brand name, the 'Lim's Ward Round'. There is really nothing unique about the Lim's Ward Round and it follows the traditional bedside methods initiated by William Osler a century ago. However, I strongly emphasize treating the patient as a person and not just a disease. This necessitates taking a detailed social and clinical history and a careful physical examination of the patient and critically analyzing the information gathered from the history and examination before subjecting the patients to a multitude of investigations. A *working* or *clinical diagnosis* must be made based on careful history and positive physical examination findings. Appropriate investigations can then be ordered. Careful analysis of the history and physical findings, together with correct interpretation of investigation results, will allow a doctor to arrive at an accurate and *definitive diagnosis* of the patient's illness. Treatment options will then be based on this *definitive diagnosis*. This was what Osler did routinely at Johns Hopkins Hospital a century ago but rarely now by doctors both in the West and the East. With technological advances and proliferation of machines, this art of clinical medicine has now been lost in the training of doctors in many countries. Clinical medicine has become investigative medicine today and the thinking doctor is a rare breed.

Without proper diagnosis and clinical indications, myocardial revascularization by percutaneous coronary intervention, is sometimes inappropriate and may not benefit the patient in the long run. The training of coronary intervention to date has focused more on the technical aspects of *how* to perform the procedure at the expense of the more important reason of *why* the treatment is necessary or *when* the procedure should be done. This paradigm shift from *how* to *why and when* is urgently needed in the training of coronary interventionists today and perhaps the 'unique' feature of the Lim's Ward Round (Fig. 20).

'Treat Patients not Lesions'

Interventionists use telescopes, catheters and other minimally invasive devices to probe, remove or repair diseased parts of the body. This group of minimally invasive interventionists is prone to turn themselves into technocrats or *Yi jiang*, as described previously. Of all the minimally invasive operators, interventional cardiologists are by far the largest group because of the prevalence of atherosclerotic coronary

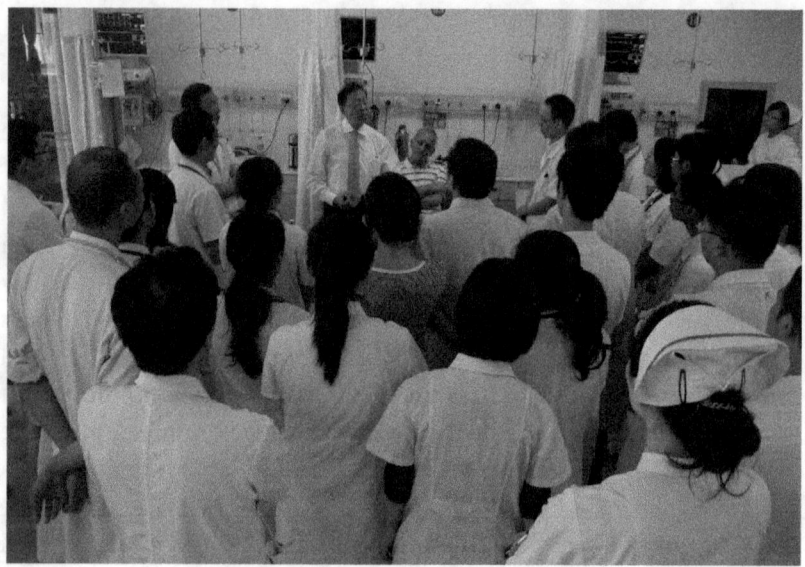

Fig. 20. The 'Lim's Ward Round', Xiamen Heart Centre, Xiamen Medical College, Fujian 2011.

heart disease. Today coronary stenting done under local anesthesia has significantly replaced the very traumatic open-heart coronary bypass graft surgery in the treatment of severe obstructive coronary artery disease. The relative ease of percutaneous coronary intervention (PCI), its effectiveness coupled with the high incidence of coronary disease has made coronary stenting the most commonly performed operation in the world today. Coronary interventionists have mushroomed worldwide, especially in China. The growth of PCI in China is phenomenal. From 500 cases per annum in 1995, it is now in excess of 400,000 at the last estimate. In absolute numbers, the volume of PCI in China is second only to USA in the world today. However, quantity does not always correlate with quality. The widespread practice of treating coronary 'lesions' rather than 'patients' can be seen worldwide.

Decisions to alleviate any obstruction in the coronary anatomy of a patient are often based on X-ray images rather than consideration of the patients' clinical conditions. The term *oculo-stenotic reflex* is used to describe thoughtless intervention to improve angiographic lesions rather than treating the patient. '*Treat Patients not Lesions*' was and is a slogan I most often used in teaching PCI throughout China over the decades.

The importance of treating a patient as a person and not a pathologic lesion found in his or her coronary angiogram cannot be overemphasized. I also think that interventionists, like doctors, can be grouped into three classes, a *doctor interventionist* who treats a patient; an *artisan interventionist* who treats a disease and a *lesion interventionist* who treats only angiographic lesions. The action of the last group could be potentially fatal when judgment is poor and skill lacking. A *lesion interventionalist* can do serious harm to his patient like the class of *Yi-shi* or killer doctors!

A good interventionist should have hand, head and heart, similar to that of a good doctor. *Hand* represents the technical dexterity required to perform complex operations. *Head* refers to the scientific and evidence-based knowledge necessary for recommending any interventional therapy. Most importantly, *Heart* defines the essential quality of care, compassion and humanism of an interventionist. Before offering any intervention therapy, an interventionist must be certain that the benefit of the procedure contemplated will outweigh the harm or risks. Doctors who care for their patients will always try to do the right thing for their patients. They will always follow the principle of 'first do no harm' and give their patients the best therapeutic recommendations and services.

A first-class *doctor interventionist* must first be a good doctor. He must strive to be a doctor, not a docrat and definitely not a Dr Death, as defined previously. Interventionists with 'oculo-stenotic reflex' are good examples of docrats and rarely serve their patients well. To be a

Fig. 21. Lecture poster '*How to be a Good D*octor', Beijing 2011.

good interventionist, therefore, one must first and foremost be a good doctor. During my clinical teaching circuit throughout China over the years, my lecture entitled 'How to be a good doctor' has been in most demand (Fig. 21).

A good interventionist must firstly *know the patient*. Without this, he will not understand the reason for the treatment. Secondly, he must *know the evidence* for recommending the treatment. Finally he must *know thyself*, that is one's own technical competency and limitations. I call these the *three knows* of a good interventionist.

Once skilled, a good interventionist must also be able to pass on skills and knowledge to the next generation. This is the hallmark of any great doctor. He or she must not only be a good healer but a great teacher.

The 'Alabama Student'

William Osler possessed all the necessary qualities of a good doctor. He was regarded as the father of modern medicine in the western world today. Osler started his tertiary education at a theological college, but that lasted for only a year. His father was the parish priest at Bond Head, the small Canadian town where he was born. His first mentor, a priest named Father Johnson, was a keen naturalist. His mentor's interest in science and nature may have influenced his switch to a medical career. Throughout his life, Osler was a practising Christian and his Christian values came across strongly in his work, writings and medical practice. One particular essay by Osler entitled 'The Alabama Student' tells the story of a general practitioner who went from Birmingham, Alabama to study medicine in Paris, the Mecca for western medicine at that time. This young doctor left his wife in Birmingham and travelled alone to far away Paris with the goal of learning the best clinical practice so that he could better care for his patients in Alabama. Osler was so impressed by the motive and learning spirit of this young American doctor that he later chose *The Alabama Student* to be the title of one of his books of biographical essays, published by Oxford University Press in 1908.

The young Alabama doctor's name was Bassett. While studying in Paris, he wrote to his wife in Alabama regularly, telling her of all his learning experiences in Paris. In one of his letters, he wrote: '*I am glad I know what great men are. I am glad I know of what they are made and how they made themselves great*'. Unfortunately, Dr Bassett did not live long enough for his patients to benefit from what he had learnt from the great medical center in Europe, for he died of tuberculosis soon after his return to Alabama. Osler intended to help perpetuate Dr Basset's learning spirit with his book *The Alabama Student*, I guessed.

Like Basset, I too am glad to know what great men are made of and how they made themselves great. Osler is one of the great men

Fig. 22. My four role models (Clockwise from left top: Leonardo da Vinci, William Osler, James Hudson-Taylor, Albert Schweitzer).

in my life. Four great men have inspired me. They are William Osler, father of modern clinical medicine; Leonardo da Vinci, the Renaissance artist and scientist; Albert Schweitzer, the humanitarian musician doctor and James Hudson-Taylor who brought Christianity to China in the mid-nineteenth century (Fig. 22).

The 'Hudson-Taylor Spirit'

James Hudson-Taylor was born in England in 1832. He died and was buried in Jenjiang, a small city in the province of Zhejiang, near Hangzhou in China in 1905. After graduating as a doctor, he became a Christian missionary and left England for China. Arriving in 1865, he established the China Inland Mission (CIM). When China became a Communist country in 1949, CIM was renamed the Overseas Missionary Fellowship (OMF) in 1951 at a crucial meeting in Kalorama, a small township in the Dandenong Ranges in Melbourne. The headquarter of CIM was then moved from China to Singapore. The name Hudson-Taylor is well-known to most Chinese Christians in China because five generations of Hudson-Taylors had devoted their lives to missionary work in China and Taiwan. Today, the surviving fifth generation Hudson-Taylor, whose Chinese name Dai Ji-zhong means 'following his ancestors', is based in Taiwan and still devotes his life to the Christian mission among the Chinese. I was privileged to have known and worked with the fourth generation Hudson-Taylor, James Hudson-Taylor III, when he visited some Chinese churches in Melbourne in the 1990s. James Hudson-Taylor III founded the Medical Services International (MSI) in 1991 in Hong Kong. James Hudson-Taylor III returned to Szechuan and Yunnan region in southwest China to work among the Yi minority tribe. The remains of James-Hudson Taylor were discovered only recently in Jenjiang. When I was invited as one of the guests of honour to the 5th Interventional Cardiology Symposium at Jenjiang in April 2012, I paid special tribute to James Hudson-Taylor in a speech at the opening ceremony of the meeting. I introduced the Hudson-Taylor spirit, reflected in the following famous quotation of James Hudson-Taylor, a calligraphic copy of which is now on display at the church that housed his tombstone (Fig. 23):

> *If I have a thousand pounds, China can access them all,*
> *If I have a thousand lives, I will not withhold one from China…*

Fig. 23. James Hudson-Taylor's famous quotation in the church at Jenjiang, China where his tombstone is housed.

Five generations of Hudson-Taylors have served the Chinese people selflessly for more than a hundred years. This spirit of the Hudson-Taylors can inspire the doctors of China today to better serve their own people. Almost all Chinese doctors will be familiar with the spirit of Norman Bethune, the Canadian surgeon who died while on duty after three years of medical service at the frontline of Mao's red army. In contrast, few Chinese doctors would be aware of the sacrifice that the five generations of Hudson-Taylors have made in China for well over a century.

'How Would You Treat This Patient If She Were Your Mother?'

A good doctor will treat his patients as if they were his own relatives. I wish to end the discussion of the concept of a good doctor by paying a special tribute to my mother who reared four doctors in her family, while remaining a widow for 41 years. Alone for all these years as a widow, she attained the highest virtue a Chinese woman can achieve in the Confucian code of ethics. As a practising Christian, her life as a widow was far from being lonely. Instead, her life was filled with love, compassion and joy. She was constantly surrounded by her many friends and travelled extensively with them. Her life was dedicated to her children and her role as a mother had greatly impacted her children and their offspring in turn. Her devotion to and care of my father during his final illness would influence profoundly my later role as a doctor. I learnt from her what it meant to care for someone who is sick.

Until her death, she served as the inaugural Chairperson of the Board of the Singapore Christian Home for the Aged. This home was designed to look after poor and lonely elderly Singaporeans, many without a home or family to look after them. It was the first of its kind in Singapore. Until the government took over its running soon after her passing, this charitable Christian nursing home for the aged was operated by a handful of voluntary and dedicated Christians, among them my younger brother Yean Lian and his wife Siew Yen. After my mother's death, my youngest brother Yean Teng, also a leading cardiologist in Singapore, succeeded my mother as Chairman of the Board.

Grief has followed me all my life after the loss of my father at a young age. One important factor of this grief was the lack of compassion shown by the senior doctor treating him. Because of this, throughout my medical career as a senior doctor, I have tried to be a good role model to my junior medical staff. I encourage them whenever I have a chance to care for their patients as if they were their own father or mother. When a patient unfortunately succumbs, most young doctors who care for their patients would feel genuinely sad. However, the sadness is usually transient and the sorrow dissipates quickly with time because he or she is just another patient. To the relatives of the deceased, the loss of a loved one, especially one's parent, is forever and usually catastrophic. I have first-hand experience of this grief and know intimately this grief would follow one for the rest of one's life.

During my routine ward rounds, whenever a management decision of a patient is needed, I ask the junior doctor treating the patient this question: '*If this was your mother or father, how would you treat her or him?*' This very question would come back to haunt me when my mother became critically ill with a heart attack. She was warded at the National University Hospital in Singapore where my youngest brother, Yean Teng, was Head of the Cardiac Unit of the hospital. My brother and I agonized for a long time over the best treatment strategy for our mother. Although my mother had left clear instruction to do nothing should she become critically ill on life-support, her management had indeed become a real dilemma for both of us. We eventually went against her will and successfully resuscitated her. When she came round and realised what had happened, she chastised us severely for what we had done. We explained that although she wanted to go, we, her children, were not ready to let her go. This decision, rightly or wrongly made, gave my mother a few more happy months until she passed away suddenly and peacefully in her sleep one day. From this very personal experience, I now empathize completely with the young doctors when I ask them: '*How would you treat this patient if she were your mother?*'

4

Goodness not Grief

Doctor Eyes China with Heart

Paul Morawetz, an Australian Jewish leader and philanthropist, was my patient and friend. He was born in Austria and lived his childhood in the Czech Republic before immigrating to Melbourne during the Second World War. He presented me with a copy of his autobiography entitled: *What a Life*, and autographed the book as follows:

> *Going to China is like going to Box Hill. Music, painting, photography, Christianity — all a full activity, each of them. How can one find time to deal with cardiology? No man I know is as gifted as you. I salute you. Joy, true companion, warm and full of care. A wonderful person. Love to you three, Paul.*

I lost a great friend with his passing in 2000. He was a true music lover and played a significant role in supporting the Musica Viva of Australia. He endowed and created the Hephzibah Menuhin Scholarship of the Musical Society of Victoria as well as the Hephzibah Menuhin Chair of Music at Hadaza University in Jerusalem. Through him, I had the privilege of knowing the great violinist, Sir Yehudi Menuhin.

A feature article was published in the local newspaper of Box Hill City, the *Whitehorse Gazette*, with the heading 'Doctor eyes China with Heart' (Fig. 24), reporting on the training programme of Chinese cardiologists at the new Department of Cardiology at Box Hill Hospital.

The training of doctors from China to perform the relatively new percutaneous transluminal coronary angioplasty had been ongoing for 10 years at the Epworth Hospital prior to my appointment to Box Hill Hospital. The new cardiology unit at Box Hill gave me a broader base to continue this important work. Starting on a small scale in 1986, I did not envisage that it would become the most rewarding part of my medical career. Today, almost thirty years later, more than 100 interventional cardiologists from all over China have benefited from this programme in Australia, Singapore and within China itself. They have in turn trained, locally, the next one or two generations of interventional cardiologists. The impact of this training programme on the development of coronary intervention services in China and the benefits

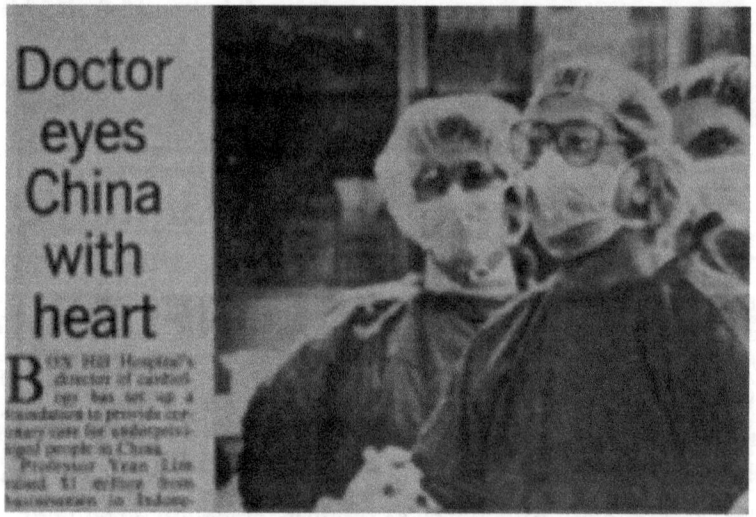

Fig. 24. 'Doctor eyes China with heart', *Whitehorse Gazette*, 1993.

brought to coronary heart disease patients is the most rewarding, professionally but not financially, aspect of my entire medical career.

First Visit to China

My first visit to China was in 1983, visiting Beijing, Shanghai and Kweilin, some of the few cities open to tourists at that time. The moment when my plane landed and I saw the two large Chinese characters *Shang Hai* on top of the roof of the airport terminal building, tears welled uncontrollably in my eyes. For an overseas Chinese, descendent of the Chinese diaspora, I had at last returned to the land of my ancestors. The moment of returning to one's roots or *Ju-guo* (land of origin) is emotionally overwhelming indeed. From Shanghai I travelled to Suzhou and Wuxi by taxi, costing me 240-yuan return, equivalent to four months average salary for a worker in China at that time. Suzhou and Hangzhou were dubbed the *heaven-on-earth* cities of China, whereas Wuxi was known as the cultural *eye area* of ancient China. These two cities in *Jiang-nan*, or 'South of Yang-tze River', are famous for producing many well-known artists, poets and writers from the Tang Dynasty to the present.

Shanghai in the 1980s could be represented by the image of Pudong taken from Puxi, on the west bank of Huangpo River, during my first visit to the city (Fig. 25).

One could see the junks that were commonly used in those days to transport goods or sailors. Pudong was still predominantly farmland then. My first impression of Shanghai was that of an extremely crowded city, with commuters, workers, hawkers and people from all walks of life carrying their goods, some in baskets strung across the two ends of a bamboo stick straddled across their shoulders. As soon as I disembarked from the ferry, I was besieged by an army of hawkers, all screaming to change their local currency, *Renminbi* (people's money) for my *wei hui juan* or Foreign Exchange Notes (FEN). The two-currency system was still enforced in China at that time to limit the purchase of

Fig. 25. Photograph of Pudong, taken from Weitan in Puxi, 1983.

goods that were in short supply. Three essential household items, namely bicycles, washing and sewing machines, nicknamed 'the three cycles', were most sought after by locals. Possession of these items would elevate one into the 'wealthy' class in society at that time. These 'luxurious' household items could only be purchased with *wei hui juan* or FENs at the local Friendship Stores, designed primarily for foreign tourists.

Almost thirty years later, I returned to the same spot to take another photograph of Pudong from Weitan in Puxi. The contrast between the two images taken 30 years apart is breathtaking. The once empty skyline over Pudong is now filled with shiny skyscrapers, including some of the tallest buildings in the world (Fig. 26). This incredible transformation of China, however, has come at a huge cost of indiscriminate destruction of heritage buildings and mindless environmental pollution.

The cityscape is even more spectacular at night now, with the nocturnal sky lit up with multi-colored dancing neon lights and laser beams. These two chronological images of Pudong show the results of

Fig. 26. Photograph of Pudong, taken from Weitan in Puxi, 2010.

Deng Xiao-peng's economic reform program and the modernization of China at a truly neck-breaking pace. Seventy years ago, my father left his homeland and immigrated to Singapore to seek a better life. Today, many south Chinese Singaporeans are returning to retire in China. The Chinese diaspora is turning a full circle.

After Shanghai, I took a day trip by taxi to visit two other famous *Jiang-nan* cities, Suzhou and Wuxi. I departed from Shanghai before sunrise and the car journey was unforgettable. The never-ending stream of cyclists, pedestrians, occasional pigs, chickens, dogs and ducks darted constantly in front of our car. Drivers on the road would hoot incessantly at anything. To make things worse, in order to save batteries, drivers in China do not routinely turn on their car headlights at night. Instead they would flash their headlights at each other from opposite directions as signals of communication. This stroboscopic style of driving would precipitate a fit in any foreigners with epilepsy travelling by car at night. As mentioned above, the cost of the return trip was only 234 yuan (40 Australian dollars) and I was very impressed when the driver flatly refused to be tipped.

While Wuxi, located on the northern bank of Lake Tai, was home to famous poets, painters, writers and philosophers, Suzhou is petite and sophisticated. After Marco Polo's sojourn in China, westerners knew Suzhou as 'the Venice of the East' because of its famous waterways or canals. To the Chinese, however, Suzhou, together with its neighboring Hangzhou, were given the elegant title of the two *heaven-on-earth* cities. This distinctive honour was bestowed on them because of their beautiful landscape, exquisite traditional Chinese or *Suzhou* gardens, cultural nobility, peace and tranquility. The trip to these two heavenly cities was unforgettable for a first time visitor.

'This Foreigner Speaks Pu-tong Hua'

From the crowded and disorderly Shanghai, I took a domestic flight to the 'northern capital' or Beijing. The abbreviation of the name of the official national airline in China in those days was CAAC. Because of its unreliability and the frequent unexpected cancellations of their flights, the locals gave it an unofficial name, calling it *China Airline Always Cancel*. Boarding time was always a stampede and some flights did not have allocated seating. I was amazed to hear an air stewardess yelling out to boarding passengers in Mandarin that I understood: 'this plane is overloaded in the front, please move to the back'. I was wondering how the plane was going to take-off if its front was too heavy! In a situation like this, the ability to understand Mandarin was definitely a disadvantage!

Arriving in Beijing was like stepping back into Chinese history. I was deeply moved to see, for the first time, the Forbidden City, home of the Emperors for more than 600 years. The 39 kilometers of city wall with its numerous gates that encircled the Capital, built from the Yuan Dynasty, 1000 years ago, was mindlessly torn down only 40 years ago in

1973, by a senseless decree of the leader of modern China. Tiananmen Square, large enough to accommodate a million people, is at the southern end of the Forbidden City. The People's Congress, built in nine months, and the Mausoleum of Chairman Mao flanked the two other sides of Tiananmen Square. Placed in very exact locations around the Forbidden City were the Heavenly Temple, the Earthly Temple and many other purpose-built historic imperial buildings. Most of these buildings were sacred sites for Emperors of the Ming and Qing Dynasties to make their offerings to the gods. I read of these historic sites in textbooks at school and to see them now in person was mind-boggling.

I also visited the Summer Palace, built by the Dowager Empress (*qixi taihou*) with the budget originally assigned to modernize the navy of the Qing Dynasty. In the 1980s, foreigners visiting Beijing were scarce. 'Blue-eye, red hair' foreigners always fascinated local Chinese residents. The local Chinese would often surround a foreigner, stare and call him or her *lau-wei* or 'old foreigner' in an affectionate manner. Although not blond with blue eyes, I could easily be recognised by the locals as a *lau-wei* from the way I dressed. When I was photographing some pretty flowers at the Summer Palace, a small local crowd surrounded me. Trying to be friendly, I turned to them and greeted them in my best Mandarin: '*Ni hou, zhen piao liang, shi ma?*' ('Hello, beautiful [flowers] isn't it?'). My utterance in Mandarin produced a most unexpected response from one of them: 'This lau-wei speaks Pu-tong-hua!' or 'ordinary dialect', the local Beijing term for Mandarin. I was hurt by his exclamation. Here I was, a patriotic overseas Chinese returning to my *ju guo* or motherland for the first time being called a *lau-wei* or foreigner! Sadly, not only am I identified as Chinese in Australia, Aussie in Singapore but, now, a foreigner in China! This identity crisis would follow me in these three countries that I have lived and worked in alternately all my life. Nevertheless, this was a small price to pay in return for the privilege of having made contributions in one way or another to these three countries. In anthropological terms, there are three traditional groups of Chinese in the world: firstly, *Hua ren* are Chinese who are born and live in China; secondly, *Hua chiao* are Chinese who are born in China but have migrated overseas; thirdly, *Hua yi* are those Chinese outside of China who are of Chinese descent. I belong to the last group, but a foreigner in China I am not and I was sad to be called a foreigner when I returned to China. This incident was the cause of some soul-searching on my part. I would tell my son, when he was old enough to comprehend, this story to remind him of his ancestry and how westerners would consider him as Chinese even though he was born in Australia.

The Story of 'A Foolish Old Man Moving the Mountain'

When I was a junior resident doctor in 1978, the Health Minister of China, Mr Chien, visited the Alfred Hospital. I was assigned by the hospital to be his Chinese translator. Accompanying the Minister then was Professor Tao Shou-qi, the doyen of cardiology in China and Chief of Cardiology at the Fu Wai Cardiovascular Institute in Beijing. The Fu Wai Cardiovascular Institute was and still is the national centre for heart diseases in China. Professor Tao gave me his simple name card with only one line of words: *Professor Tao Shou-qi, Physician to the late Chairman Mao*. Years later, I met Professor Tao Shou-qi again, this time in Beijing when I was invited to teach on a ward round with Professor Fang Qi and his staff at the Peking Union Medical College (Fig. 27).

One day in 1985, the President of the Fu Wai Cardiovascular Institute, Professor Guo Jia-qiang, an eminent cardiac surgeon, also visited the Alfred Hospital. Again I had the privilege of being his interpreter. My meeting with Professor Guo Jia-qiang was to have a profound impact on my medical career. Through contact with him, my work in China, spanning a period of almost 30 years now, began. Professor Guo was a visionary leader and a very dynamic and influential cardiac surgeon in China in the 1980s. He had started a cardiac surgical training programme based at the Fu Wai Hospital in Beijing for cardiac surgeons from all over China. The goal of the programme

Fig. 27. With Professor Tao Shou-qi (third left) and Professor Fang Qi (third right), the Lim family (center), Beijing, 1986.

was to increase the number of good, qualified cardiothoracic surgical units throughout China, especially in the remote areas. The Chinese Technical Cooperation and Training Center of Cardiovascular Disease (CTCTCCD) programme was thus formed in 1981. Professor Guo would personally lead a surgical team from the Fu Wai Hospital in Beijing to operate in various cities all over China, from Hainan to Inner Mongolia, to perform open-heart operations. Many new cardiothoracic programmes in China now are the fruits of his labour in the eighties. At the commencement of the CTCTCCD programme in 1981, there were only 11 qualified cardiac surgical centers in China. This number has increased to more than 200 today (Fig. 28).

During his visit to the Alfred Hospital, Professor Guo shared his surgical experience of 1300 cases of left atrial myxomas, a rare tumour of the heart, at the Fu Wai Cardiovascular Institute. The total experience of the Alfred Hospital was six at the time. After the official hospital visit, I invited him to dinner at my home that evening. During dinner conversation, in his usual serious manner, Professor Guo told me that the waiting list for congenital heart disease surgery alone in

Fig. 28. The 3rd Chinese Technical Cooperation and Training Centre of Cardiovascular Disease (CTCTCD), Fu Wai Hospital, Beijing.

China will not decrease for the next 100 years if the number of cardiac surgical units is not increased. I was astounded by this statistic and realised the enormous task ahead to improve cardiac care in China with its vast population. Qualified and competent Chinese cardiac surgeons at that time were few, and they were performing mainly congenital and valvular surgeries. Coronary artery bypass graft (CABG) surgery, the most common cardiac surgical procedure performed in the West was non-existent in China at that time. Coronary angiography had just begun in China at the Fu Wai Hospital in the early 1980s and only a handful of teaching hospitals in large cities of China were capable of performing this diagnostic procedure.

Professor Guo then asked me to help him train Chinese cardiac surgeons at the Alfred Hospital in Melbourne. My immediate response to his request was that, as a cardiologist, I could only pass on his request to my surgical colleagues at the Alfred and Epworth Hospitals where I work. After his departure from Melbourne, I approached Dr Bruce Davis, then Head of the Alfred Hospital C J Officer-Brown Cardiothoracic Unit, and Professor Brian Buxton, Head of Cardiac Surgery at the Austin and Epworth Hospitals, as promised, to ask if they would train selected cardiac surgeons from China at their respective hospitals. My two surgical colleagues agreed without hesitation. I was greatly impressed by their typically Australian egalitarian attitude to the request. Later Professor Donald Esmore, who succeeded Bruce Davis at the Alfred Hospital, also joined in this noble Sino-Australian cardiac surgical training programme. Soon the first Chinese surgeon from Fu Wai Hospital in Beijing arrived at the Alfred Hospital. Another from Hangzhou began his training at the Epworth Hospital shortly thereafter.

After CABG surgery came Percutaneous Trans-luminal Coronary Angioplasty (PTCA) in 1977. It was much less invasive than coronary artery bypass graft surgery for coronary revascularization. PTCA had been shown to be an acceptable alternative therapy to CABG surgery for patients with suitable coronary artery lesions. Dr E Manolas had initiated PTCA services at the Epworth Hospital in Melbourne in 1981 and I joined him a year later. While my surgical colleagues were training Chinese cardiac surgeons to perform coronary artery bypass graft surgery, I decided to train Chinese cardiologists to perform PTCA, the alternative to CABG for coronary revascularization, at the Epworth Hospital in 1986.

The old Chinese tale of *A foolish old man trying to remove a mountain* had inspired me as to how to plan the PTCA training programme at the Epworth Hospital for cardiologists from such a vast country as China. The story tells of an old farmer who decided to shovel away a mountain that was in his way to get to the market to sell his produce. When people ridiculed him for this silly and impossible task, he replied, 'if I am unable do it myself, my children and their children will eventually accomplish the task'. The moral of the story is that what one man cannot achieve, many will. Similarly, it is better to teach someone how to fish than to give him fish.

I therefore decided that I must train as many interventional cardiologists in China as possible instead of just performing as many procedures as possible for them in China. In principle, this was the same as what Professor Guo was trying to accomplish for cardiac surgery in

China. I carefully planned to target key hospitals in the northern, central and southern regions of China, to develop coronary intervention in a systematic way. Beijing was the target city for the north, Hangzhou in the center and Quangzhou in the south, thus covering a large portion of China for this training programme. Able young men from these cities who are potential leaders in the field will be invited to train with me overseas, in Melbourne initially and later in Singapore. Starting at the Epworth Hospital in Melbourne, the first overseas fellows to arrive were either hospital Presidents or Party Secretaries, followed by young and capable doctors. This was how my 'one man' PTCA training programme for China started in 1986.

Australia China Indonesia Singapore (ACIS) Heart Foundation

One day when I was consulting at my Epworth private outpatient clinic, I saw an elderly Singaporean Chinese female patient accompanied by her son, Mr Lee PS. In the course of conversation, I found out Mr Lee's parents and mine had migrated to Singapore from the same county of Tong-An in Fujian province, China. This *lau tong-xiang* or hometown commonality is a very powerful and positive force in establishing *kuan-xi* in traditional Chinese culture. Once connected in this manner, strangers can quickly become brothers and a close bond was immediately established. Mr Lee, or PS as I now call him, has very traditional Chinese values even though he has lived in Melbourne for many years. I asked him whether he would like to financially support my fledgling PTCA training programme for Chinese doctors at the Epworth Hospital. Without the slightest hesitation, he pledged the full amount of one hundred thousand dollars to the Epworth Medical Foundation, which I had targeted for the training programme. This donation would enable two doctors from China to be trained at the Epworth Hospital each year. Before the generous donation of PS, I had written to numerous medical companies and managed only to raise five thousand dollars from one company. My fund-raising campaign abruptly and happily ended with the single donation from PS. This Epworth-China connection started in 1987 and continued until my departure to Singapore in 1997. It was resumed when I returned to Melbourne to work at the Western and Epworth Hospitals. The training programme for Chinese interventionists continued unabated in Singapore at the National Heart Centre under the auspices of the Singapore Government. The Epworth-China connection is still alive and well at the present time.

The training programme expanded to include visits by Australian cardiac surgical teams to visit various key hospitals in China. From Melbourne, surgical teams from the Austin Hospital and the Alfred Hospital were led by Professors Brian Buxton and Donald Esmore respectively. The cardiac surgical team of the National Heart Centre in Singapore also joined in when I was in Singapore. Together we visited hospitals in Beijing, Shenyang, Dalian, Hangzhou, Shanghai and Guangzhou on numerous occasions. This foreigner-led cardiac surgical training in China complemented the local efforts of Professor Guo Jiaqiang in developing new cardiac surgical units throughout China, especially in coronary artery bypass graft surgery. While my Australian colleagues were teaching coronary artery bypass surgery, I performed and taught PTCA simultaneously at the same hospital to develop a comprehensive modern coronary revascularization programme for the hospitals that we visited.

As the frequency and cost of China visits increased, the limited Epworth Heart Foundation fund donated by PS Lee became inadequate to sustain the programme. Dr Victor Chang, who was also working independently in China around the same time, told me how he had started the first cardiac transplantation programme in Australia at St. Vincent's Hospital in Sydney with a donation from a wealthy Singaporean patient. The idea of setting up a larger foundation to assist the modernization programme for the treatment of coronary disease in China then dawned on me. With the help of four wealthy Indonesian Chinese businessmen, the Australia China Indonesia Singapore Heart Foundation

(ACIS), sounding like 'Assist', was established in 1995. ACIS is the acronym for **A**ustralia, **C**hina, **I**ndonesia and **S**ingapore.

The four donors of ACIS were Lie Siong Tay, Liem Sioe Leong, Moktar Riady and Ng Eik Chong. Lie had been a primary school classmate of my mother and was now a wealthy timber merchant in Indonesia. He was a well-known philanthropist in his hometown, Xiamen in Fujian. Education and transportation were the main targets of his philanthropy in Xiamen at that time. Through his connections, Liem Sioe Leong, the richest Chinese in the world at that time, businessmen Ng Eik Chong and Moktar Riady, were asked to donate to establish the ACIS Heart Foundation to financially support the training of interventional cardiologists from China (Fig. 29). From 1995, the ACIS Heart Foundation has helped to train numerous cardiac surgeons and cardiologists from China in Australia and Singapore. It became an integral part of the health collaborative programme of the Memorandum

Fig. 29. Benefactors of the Australia China Indonesia Singapore (ACIS) Heart Foundation (from left: YL, Liem Sioe Leong, Mayor Zhu, Ng Eik Cheong, Lie Siong Tay).

of Understanding between the Health Ministries of China and Singapore when I was based in Singapore between 1997 and 2002. In addition to the doctors' training programme, part of the ACIS Heart Foundation fund was also donated to the Medical Services International (MSI) to establish a primary care clinic and a Youth Training facility in Zhaojie, a remote village in Sichuan province, to improve the health, education and rehabilitation of drug addicts among the Yi indigenous people there.

Hangzhou Fellows

Dr Xu Wei, a Hangzhou thoracic surgeon connected me to cardiologists in Hangzhou. Hangzhou, the ancient capital of the Southern Song Dynasty, is famous for its iconic Westlake. The following Chinese verse is often quoted:

> *Above is Heaven (Tien-tang),*
> *Below is Su-Hang (Suzhou and Hangzhou).*

Of all the cities in China that I have visited, Hangzhou is my favourite because of its beauty and strong cultural heritage. Zhejiang Hospital is located in an idyllic setting, next to the Hangzhou Botanical Garden. The hospital was predominantly a hospital for retired cadres or *Gao-gans*. I arranged a short introductory course for the President of Zhejiang Hospital to visit the Epworth Hospital in Melbourne. After a short visit from the Party Secretary of the Second Affiliated Hospital in Hangzhou, the Director of Cardiology, Jin Fan, from the same hospital was then allowed to come to Melbourne to actually learn the new PTCA technique for a year. Many years my senior, Dr Jin Fan was a humble, cultivated man and very eager to learn. He was well-respected in Hangzhou and his wife Dr Ding Wen-chien, was the Director of the Coronary Care Unit at Zhejiang Hospital as well. The Jins moved in a circle of scholars and artists in Hangzhou, including the great calligrapher Sha Meng-hai and artists Lu Yan-shao and Zu Chuan-xi.

First PTCAs in Hangzhou

Percutaneous coronary angioplasty, or PTCA, for coronary artery disease was first performed in China at the Xijing Hospital in Xian in 1981 by Dr Zheng Siew Lian with the assistance of an American Chinese cardiologist Dr Liu Shijiang. Dr M. Nobuyoshi of Japan was the first Asian to perform PTCA. After Dr Jin Fan's return to Hangzhou, he became the Director of Cardiology at the Zhejiang People's Provincial Hospital. I was asked to help him start the coronary revascularization programme at his hospital. The Australian surgical teams and I visited this hospital on numerous occasions. Dr Fan and I performed the first few PTCA procedures in Hangzhou in the early 1990s (Fig. 30). At the same time, Professors Buxton and Esmore and their surgical teams worked with the President of the hospital, Professor Yan Tze-kun who was a cardiac surgeon trained at St. Vincent's Hospital in Melbourne to establish CABG surgery at the Zhejiang Provincial Hospital.

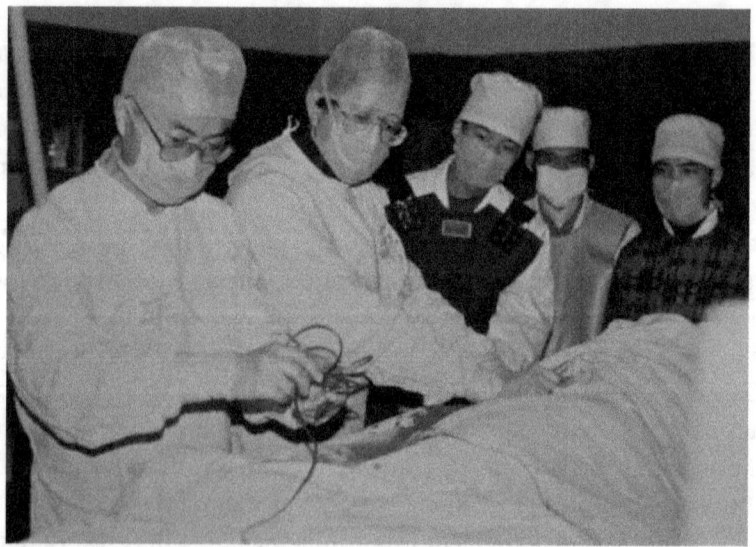

Fig. 30. Early PTCAs at the Zhejiang Provincial People's Hospital, Hangzhou 1992 (from left: Prof. Jin Fan, YL).

At the No. 1 Affiliated Hospital in Hangzhou, Chen Jun-zu was the first cardiologist to perform PTCA in Hangzhou. I was privileged to work with him in a successful but amusing case that threw light on how PTCA was accomplished in those days in China. The Zhejiang First Affiliated Hospital was the largest teaching hospital in Hangzhou then and remains so today. In the 1980s, there were no overhead monitors to visualize the fluoroscopic X-ray images during PTCA procedures. A small 14-inch ordinary television monitor placed on top of a steel trolley adjacent to the X-ray image intensifier was used as the monitor screen. No recording device was available, either, to capture cine-angiographic images. It was near impossible to visualize the guide wire used to steer across coronary lesions. When tracking the balloon along the guide wire to the target lesion, one relied more on ECG changes and the patient's experience of chest discomfort to know that the balloon had crossed the lesion. This remarkable way of performing PTCA was most anxiety-provoking not only for the patient but for the operator as well. To make matters worse, when I asked to change the angulation of the X-ray image intensifier, the radiographer in the control room told me that it was not possible. To my astonishment, the patient on the table then told the radiographer in the control room what to do to change the angle of the image intensifier! It worked and the image intensifier was moved to the desired position that I wanted. It was the one and only time where a patient had helped me to actually complete his own operation in my entire interventional career. The patient turned out to be the chief radiographer in charge of the catheter laboratory at the hospital.

'British Girl Chinese Wife'

Professor Jian Bao-dun was an unforgettable Hangzhou patient. He was an engineer by profession and one of the first Chinese citizens to be educated abroad in the dying days of the Qing Dynasty. There was a push for reformation and modernization in China, under the leadership of Qing court officials such as Zheng Guo-fan and Li Hong-zhang, to emulate the successful *min zhi wei xin* that had occurred in Japan. Many reformers were martyred but many young Chinese students were also sent to the west eventually to train in various professional fields after the overthrow of the Qing Dynasty. Jian Bao-dun was one of this handfuls of students selected to study engineering in England. While in England, he met and married a British lady, Esther Holland. By the time I met Professor Jian, he was nearly eighty years old. His wife had died of a stroke many years earlier. However, Jian gave me a copy of his wife's autobiography, entitled *British Girl Chinese Wife*. Jian had severe but stable angina and Dr Jin had arranged for me to perform coronary angioplasty for his advanced coronary artery disease at the Zhejiang People's Provincial Hospital. When we met in the cardiac ward for the first time, he said to me in perfect Imperial British: '*Hello Dr Lim, I know God has sent you to help me!*' I was startled by his reference of God in an atheist Communist country. '*Are you a Christian?*', I asked, to which he replied: '*Of course and so was my wife, she was British*'. I later read the incredible story of Jian and his wife from her little autobiography. Jian was one of the most influential engineers in China during his heyday. Because of his British wife and because he was an intellectual, he and his wife suffered harsh persecution during the Cultural Revolution. When their ordeal was over, his wife was able to publish her personal account of what it was like to live as a foreigner wife of a Chinese intellectual in Communist China and how she survived the Cultural Revolution. Before the commencement of his angioplasty procedure, we prayed together at his request, much to the consternation of my Chinese colleagues in the operating room. He went on to outlive his cardiologist Jin Fan.

'Duncan Main of Hangchow'

In a secondhand bookshop in Melbourne in 1994, I came across a book entitled *Duncan Main of Hangchow*. The name Duncan Main was not familiar to me; the name Hangchow, now Hangzhou, aroused my interest in the book immediately. I bought and read the book, written by Alexander Gammie, from cover to cover and was greatly inspired by the sacrifice of Duncan Main, a Scottish missionary doctor who dedicated 45 years of his life to China. Dr Main and his wife settled in Hangchow in 1881 soon after their wedding in Scotland. Starting his work from an opium den, he later built hospitals for tuberculosis, leprosy, women and children in and around Hangzhou and finally founded the Zhejiang Medical College that became the Zhejiang Medical University, now the Medical Faculty of Zhejiang University. The façade of the Medical College still exists today on the campus of the First Affiliated Hospital of Zhejiang University. Dr Jin Fan was able to track down an elderly nurse, in her nineties who had actually worked with Duncan Main. She recalled that the staff at the hospital affectionately called him *Mei Dai-fu* ('Doctor Blossom') in Mandarin. Mei Dai-fu always wore a red rose in his lapel. He was very humorous and punctual on his hospital rounds. If he arrived at the hospital and the junior staff and nurses were late, he would cry out: '*too late, too late, the old man has arrived!*' Main's biography would later inspire me to build a new medical school for Xiamen University. I presented my first edition copy of Duncan Main's biography to the current Second Affiliated Hospital of Zhejiang University during their 115th anniversary celebration.

Hangzhou and Beyond

The name Run Run Shaw is equated with philanthropy in Asia, in particular, China. Today all over China, a whole host of institutions, buildings and schools are named after Run Run Shaw. Sir Run-Run Shaw was born in Ningbo, Zhejiang. In the early 1990s, he wished to build a state-of-the-art hospital for Zhejiang Medical University in Hangzhou. As part of the agreement of a joint venture in China, staff from the Loma Linda University in California, USA, will manage the new hospital for the first five years. Sir Run Run Shaw had promised to underwrite the total estimated cost to build such a hospital and the hospital would be named after him. A Chinese general surgeon from Loma Linda University, Dr David Fang, was appointed as the Foundation President of the proposed new Run Run Shaw Hospital. At the invitation of Dr Fang, I was engaged to plan a new, modern cardiac unit for the new hospital (Fig. 31).

However, when the physical building was completed, many of the technical specifications had not been met. The completed hospital was obviously not the ultra-modern hospital that Sir Run Run Shaw had hoped for. The exterior looked like a five-star hotel. Sadly, despite extensive study tours of the best hospitals overseas prior to its construction, the interior design and fittings were no different to existing large public hospitals in China when it was completed in the mid 1990s. The budget also exceeded the original donation of Sir Run Run Shaw. Zhejiang government had to fill the gap the fund needed to complete the hospital.

Fig. 31. Planning the new Cardiac Unit at Run Run Shaw Hospital, Hangzhou, 1990 (from left: Fang JP, YL, Zheng Xu and two staff members).

The Loma Linda partnership came to an end after the agreed five years and now the hospital is totally owned and run by the local Chinese government. A young cardiologist Wang Jian-An, who was locally trained at the Run Run Shaw Hospital from its beginning, was appointed the inaugural Director of the Cardiac Department at Run Run Shaw Hospital. Wang was inspired by the western management style of Loma Linda and did a splendid job with the new cardiac unit at the Run Run Shaw Hospital. He remained the backbone of cardiology at the Run Run Shaw Hospital until he was appointed to his current position as the President of the Zhejiang No. 2 Affiliated Hospital of Zhejiang University (Fig. 32).

I have worked at the Zhejiang People's Provincial Hospital in Hangzhou with Jin Fan for many years since the late eighties and helped Dr Jin to develop the coronary intervention services at that

Fig. 32. Professor Wang Jian-an (first from right) and his team at the No. 2 Affiliated Hospital of Zhejiang University.

hospital. The President of Zhejiang Provincial Hospital was a cardiac surgeon who was trained in Melbourne at St. Vincent's Hospital. On his return to Hangzhou, he was appointed President of the Zhejiang People's Provincial Hospital. With an Australian-trained chief, I had high hopes that he would modernize the hospital. A memorandum of understanding was signed between the Epworth and Alfred Hospitals and the Zhejiang People's Provincial Hospital to establish bilateral technical exchanges. Regular visits by the cardiac surgical and coronary intervention teams from Melbourne were conducted successfully under this agreement. With my surgical colleagues, we helped to plan and purchase the necessary equipment and suggested appointments of personnel needed for developing coronary revascularization services for Zhejiang People's Provincial Hospital. The Australian team including myself visited the hospital at least twice a year. This project lasted many years and a great friendship and relationship was forged between the surgical teams of the Austin Hospital led by Professor Brian Buxton, the Alfred Hospital led by Professor Donald Esmore and the Zhejiang People's Provincial Hospital (Fig. 33).

The same Australian teams also operated in hospitals in other Chinese cities, helping each of them to develop both coronary bypass graft surgery and percutaneous coronary intervention services. The cities visited besides Hangzhou were Beijing, Shanghai, Guangzhou, Dalian, Shenyang and Kunming. More often, without the surgical teams, I went alone to teach coronary intervention all over China, from north to south and east to west. Over the past 28 years, the cities and counties that I have visited and worked in include Changchun, Harbin, Daqing, Dalian, Tianjin, Shenyang, Xian, Beijing, Yantai, Jinan, Qingdao, Taiyuan, Zhengzhou, Luoyang, Yinchuan, Dunhuang, Lanzhou, Chengdu, Chongqing, Leshan, Zhoujie, Fengdu, Xichang, Mianyang, Suining, Wuhan, Shaxi, Changsha, Nanjing, Yangzhou, Wuxi, Suzhou, Wenzhou, Ningbo, Hefei, Dunqi, Zhangjiajie, Kweilin, Kunming, Urumqi, Macau, Shenzen, Zhuhai, Dongguan, Guangzhou, Shaoguan, Haikou, Fouzhou and Xiamen.

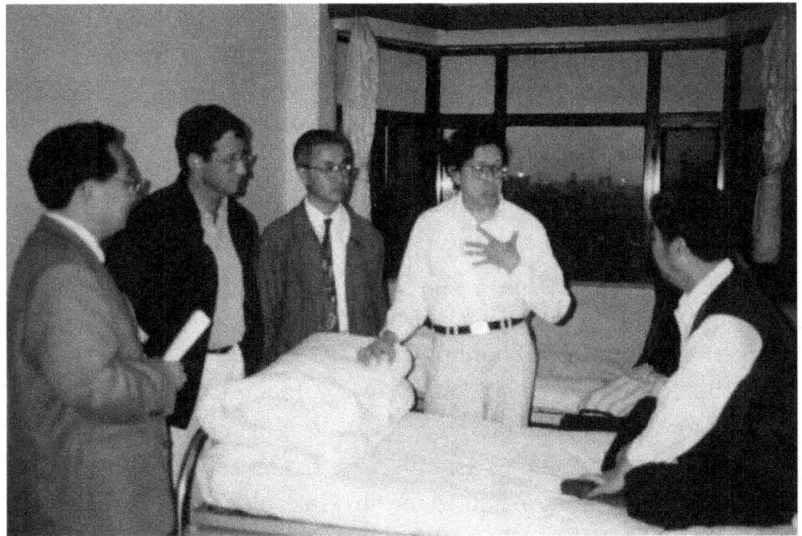

Fig. 33. The Australian surgical team evaluating a patient before CABG surgery, Hangzhou 1992 (from left: Yan ZK, D Esmore, F Jin , YL, patient).

A 'Small' Hospital

In the late 1980s, I accepted an unexpected invitation to visit Shaxi and I went to this inland city on the banks of the Yangtze River. It was not easy to get to Shaxi in those days. One had to fly to Hong Kong from Australia, then from Hong Kong to Wuhan and from there, by car for five hours before reaching Shaxi, a major city of Hubei province. On route from Wuhan, our car broke down three times. There were no road services in China in the eighties. To obtain a driver's license in China in those days, the driver had to also qualify as a motor mechanic. I was not unhappy with the breakdowns on the way to Shaxi because they provided opportunities for me to photograph the very peaceful and beautiful countryside of Hubei. It was spring and a sea of yellow 'oily vegetable flowers' carpeted the fields. The silhouettes of Jiang-nan ('south of Yangtze River') farmhouses with their classic *ma-tou qiang* (farmhouses with 'horse-head roofs'), the sea of yellow flowers and the setting sun combined to produce a most poetic and romantic image. I was busy with my camera while the driver was frantically trying to get us back on the road. We arrived very late for the welcome dinner planned by the hospital. After dinner, I was driven to the largest local hotel and given the biggest room. When I wanted to have a bath, I realised there was no hot water. In cities south of the Yangztze River, it was standard government regulation that after 7 pm in winter heating and hot water services be turned off. However, to my amazement, after informing the hotel reception of the lack of hot water, the hotel room service brought me 30 thermo-flasks of hot water on a wooden trolley to fill up the bathtub for me to have a hot bath. As for heating, I was given more hot water bottles to keep me warm in bed for the rest of the night.

The next day, I headed off to the Shaxi People's Provincial Hospital. I was politely told that the hospital we were visiting was only a small hospital. When I asked how small, they replied '*about 1000 beds*'! I realised that the concept of large or small in China was obviously quite different to that in Australia. The experience in the catheter laboratory that day at the Shaxi People's Provincial Hospital was equally unforgettable. I was to perform the first coronary angiography at this hospital. After gaining arterial access, I noticed that the pressure waveform on the monitor was a flat line. When I followed the pressure line from the patient to what should be a pressure transducer, I saw a device that looked like a hand grenade. When I asked my assistant what the 'hand grenade' was, he simply said, the pressure transducer. It was in fact a relic left behind by the Russians! What happened next was even more hair-raising. After acquiring the first angiographic image, when I lifted my foot off the X-ray foot paddle, to my horror, the X-ray image did not switch off on the screen and the X-ray could not be turned off, no matter what I did with the foot paddle. When I tried to ask the radiographer in the control room to turn off the main X-ray switch, I realised that everyone had left the control room. I had already found out earlier that all medical and nursing staff in China have a morbid fear of radiation.

With no one around to help me, I had to find a trolley nearby myself, disconnect the pressure line from the patient and move the patient onto the trolley and out of the catheter laboratory. The first coronary angiography at Shaxi People's Provincial Hospital was a flop. Happily, the X-ray equipment was fixed the next day and the case was successfully completed. I spent the next two days teaching the team of doctors, nurses, radiographers and technicians the basics of coronary angiography. The time spent in this 'small' hospital was nevertheless enjoyable if not profitable. The young female cardiologist at that hospital, Dr Li Jiali, eventually arrived in Melbourne to learn coronary angiography and angioplasty for a year before returning to Shenzen (Fig. 34).

Australian Steak Against Radiation Harm

The Fok Yin Dong Guangdong Cardiovascular Institute is co-located with the Guangzhou Provincial Hospital. The institute was named after

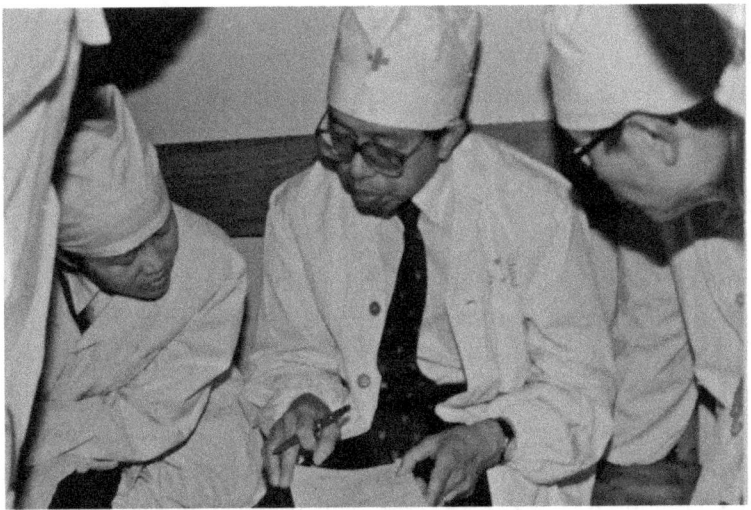

Fig. 34. Teaching coronary angiography at the First Affiliated Hospital, Shaxi, 1990 (from left: JL Li and YL).

its benefactor, Fok Yin Dong, a Hong Kong shipping magnate and philanthropist. It is by far the largest and most advanced cardiovascular center in southern China. The President of the Institute, Professor Lin Zuguang, was a pharmacologist who did postgraduate studies for a year at the University of Melbourne where we first met. I was invited to the institute to start up coronary angioplasty by the then Director of the Cardiac Department, Professor Chen Chuan-rong. Professor Chen was one of China's first cardiac interventionists. He pioneered the percutaneous mitral commissurotomy to treat mitral stenosis and was one of five Fellows of the American College of Cardiology in China in the 1980s. I taught him percutaneous coronary angioplasty and he, in turn, instructed me how to perform percutaneous mitral valvuloplasty, using his own modification of the Inoue balloon. Subsequently, his student Chen Jiyan arrived at the Epworth Hospital to train in coronary intervention. Upon his return to the Guangzhou Provincial Hospital, Chen Jiyan, now the Head of Cardiology, became instrumental in training a whole generation of new coronary interventionists in southern China.

At the Guangzhou Provincial Hospital, I was amused to see a photo of a young Chairman Mao in the control room of the catheter laboratory (Fig. 35). Beneath Mao's portrait was a bunch of bananas, presumably an offering made, in traditional Chinese custom only to gods, to the late Chairman. Just before commencement of the angioplasty procedure, the charge-nurse known to all as Madam Wong, rushed in to place another offering, this time a jar of Hunan chilly paste, a favourite of the late Chairman who originated from Hunan. She told me that the case would more likely succeed if such an offering were made! The case did go smoothly but how much of the success was due to the chilly paste remains a mystery to me to this day!

As in Shaxi, staff in the Guangzhou catheter laboratory were also acutely anxious about radiation exposure. Medical staff working in the catheter laboratory would wear specially designed headgear and heavy lead aprons to protect against irradiation (Fig. 36). More amazingly for westerners, in China laboratory staff who are getting married or are

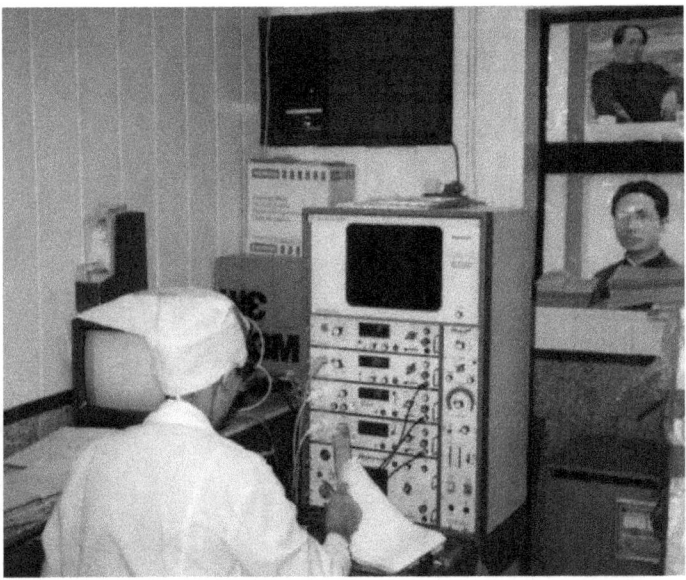

Fig. 35. Portrait of Chairman Mao in the catheter laboratory of the Guangzhou People's Provincial Hospital.

recently married are all given 'newlyweds' catheter laboratory leave for six months at a time.

Left ventriculography was not routinely performed in China. All the laboratory staff would clear out of the room whenever I performed left ventriculography. My Australian sense of humor got the better of me when I tried to explain to the Chinese staff that Australian cardiologists are not afraid of the harmful effects of radiation because they eat lots of Aussie steak! On the last day in Guangzhou I was planning to take the entire team of catheter laboratory staff out for an Australian steak lunch before my departure. I thought I could bribe them into staying with me in the laboratory during the performance of left ventriculography. After a sumptuous steak lunch, we returned to finish the afternoon's list. When the next ventriculogram was performed, they disappeared faster than they did before they had the

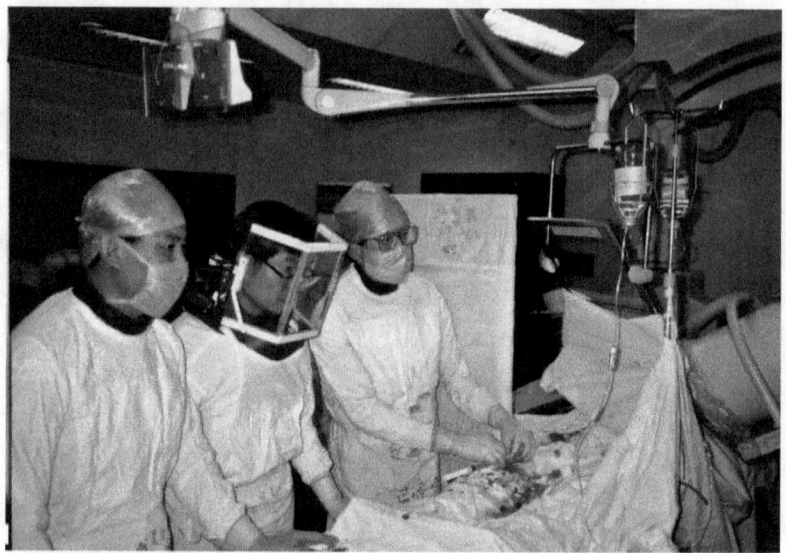

Fig. 36. Radiation protection headgear worn in the catheter laboratory of Guangzhou Provincial Hospital (from left: cardiac fellow, Chen Chuan-rong, YL).

steak lunch! Obviously my suggestion to them that Australian steak could protect against radiation harm did not wash with the Chinese doctors and nurses! It was all good fun, mixed with a lot of good will and good work.

Coronary Stenting without X-ray

I also took part in the early phase of coronary stenting at the Puxi Renji Hospital in Shanghai. The Pudong Renji Hospital in Pudong was non-existent then. Working closely with Professor Wang Bing-yau, then Director of Cardiology, and some of his younger colleagues, I performed a few cases of coronary stenting there. Coronary stenting had just begun in China at that time. One of the cases was that of a young patient who had waited many months for this procedure. The X-ray equipment at Renji Hospital was very old, but I went ahead with the coronary stenting procedure as planned. Everything went smoothly until I was just about to deploy the stent at the lesion. Without any warning, the X-ray machine died and the monitor screen went blank. No imaging could be done no matter how hard I tried. When I asked for urgent technical support, I was told that the nearest service engineer was in Guangzhou and could not arrive until the next day! With no other option, I had to retract the undeployed stent back into the guiding catheter blind without X-ray visualization. Luckily, the patient came to no harm: as the Chinese say: '*you jing wu xian*' (*lots of fear but no danger)!* However, the doctors at Renji Hospital had a tough time explaining to the patient and his family why the operation could not be completed until the next day. The machine was duly fixed and the second attempt went successfully without a hitch. Both hardware and software were less than ideal in the early days of coronary stenting in China. Ironically, twenty years later, the same experience recurred for me, this time at my own hospital in Melbourne, because the hospital could not afford to replace its decrepit X-ray equipment. In contrast, now almost all hospitals in China are equipped with the latest and most advanced equipment, housed in spanking new hospitals. Compared to any of the hospitals in China, the hospital in west Melbourne that I worked in now looked like one in a developing country. It is a remarkable turn around indeed for China in a short space of two decades.

The Wei-wei Story of Guangzhou

The connection between the Guangdong Cardiovascular Institute in Guangzhou and Epworth Hospital in Melbourne was strengthened further with the arrival of Chen Jiyan, protégé of Chen Chuan Rong. Chen Jiyan has all the qualities of a good doctor with a balance of science, practice, literature and, humanism. He is now the leading interventional cardiologist in southern China and has in turn trained many interventional cardiologists in southern and southwest China. He has been a significant figure in the realisation of the story of *'the removal of mountain by the foolish old man'.*

Two female colleagues accompanied me on one of the PTCA training trips to Guangzhou: Sister Yee Choi the Malaysian catheter laboratory nurse manager and an Australian device company representative Peta Paradine. We checked into a modest hotel in Guangzhou on the bank of the beautiful Pearl River. It was routine for me to call my wife in Melbourne to let her know that I had arrived to my destination safely. Mobile phones were not widely available then and I called from the landline phone in the hotel room. Despite following carefully the overseas dialing instructions provided by the hotel reception, all my attempts to call my wife failed with a persistent engaged signal. It was not unusual for my wife to have long conversations on the telephone and I gave up trying to call her on the first day. At breakfast the next morning, our Australian lady colleague told us that she had received a call from an unknown male. When she answered the phone, the caller asked: *'Wei-wei, you want to be friend?'* Looking at the clock showing 3 am, she replied: *'Yes, but not at three o'clock in the morning!"* and hung up. The three of us then decided to take our telephones off the hook before going to bed that night. On the second day, all attempts to call my wife still failed with a constant engaged tone. At breakfast the second morning, our Australian colleague again asked the two of us: *'Did you get a knock on your door last night?'* We replied in the negative. A man had apparently knocked on her door and said something in Chinese that she could not comprehend. Hearing this, we all felt uncomfortable with this shady hotel. By now, I had been unable to contact my wife using the hotel telephone for two days.

When we arrived at the hospital that morning, our host Professor Chen Chuan Rong, was anxiously waiting for us at the front gate of the hospital. He asked me with a suspicious look on his face: *'where were you last night, your wife called me looking for you. I sent someone to your hotel to knock on your door but there was no answer!'* That explained everything and the two ladies were giggling away with great amusement. It was hard for me to answer Professor Chen in a few words. As for all my phone calls trying to reach my wife, the hotel receptionist had given me the wrong international dialing code. When I eventually got through to my wife with the correct international dialling number, she asked me angrily *'Where have you been for the last two days?'* I related to her the whole story before she was reassured. After the incident, we nicknamed our Australian colleague *Wei-Wei* in response to her amusing phone call experience in Guangzhou.

'I want to learn Interventional Cardiology from you'

On the way back from the Guangzhou Provincial Hospital one afternoon, I saw the setting sun with its golden rays peeping out of the clouds over the Pearl River. I rushed back to my hotel to get my camera to capture this glorious image. As soon as I stepped in the hotel foyer, a young man rushed up to me and asked: *'Are you Prof. Lim from Australia?'* 'Yes', I replied. *'I want to learn interventional cardiology from you'*, he announced excitedly. I was startled by his request but I was more concerned with the rapidly disappearing sunset. *'I have to rush to photograph the sunset over the Pearl River right now, come along with me and we can discuss what you want after that'*, I said to the young man. After fetching the camera from my room, we hurried to the nearby newly completed Haiyun Bridge spanning the Pearl River. We were lucky and I just managed to capture the magnificent fading sunset with its seductive colors of dusk. Feeling quite satisfied with my shots, I turned to the young man who had helped me to carry my photographic equipment, and asked: *'Where did you come from and how did you find me?'* *'A colleague in Wuhan told me that you would be in Guangzhou today and I took a train from Wuhan last night to arrive at your hotel early this morning. Unfortunately, I was not early enough and you had already left the hotel. I decided to wait in the hotel until you returned*'. His enthusiasm to learn reminded me of a similar incident when Yehudi Menuhin visited Melbourne a few years before. A young Chinese violinist whom I know also waited all day at the Hilton Hotel trying to see him to learn from the great master. I was deeply moved by his learning spirit, like that described by Osler in the 'Alabama student' essay. I realised that the young doctor must have spent a large proportion of his monthly wage to travel from Wuhan to Guangzhou to see me. I decided to accept him as a student and invited him to dinner at the hotel that evening. I gave him a sealed envelope with a letter for his boss and instructed him not to open it until he got back to Wuhan. In it, I included his return train ticket fare to Guangzhou. This young doctor is now a senior consultant at the Fu Wai Hospital, the national heart institute of China.

Another young doctor from China who came to Australia as a language student was granted amnesty after the Tiananmen Square incident in 1989. He came to my church one day and asked me to teach him interventional cardiology. He was from Tang Shan (near Beijing) scene of the catastrophic earthquake that killed more than a quarter of a million people in 1976. He and his brother evacuated from their home when the earthquake hit. His brother perished but he miraculously survived. He was a cardiologist and befriended an Australian cardiac technician when the latter visited his hospital in Tang Shan. When he arrived in Melbourne as an English language student with very little means, the 'Good Samaritan' Australian friend took care of all his basic living needs, reflecting the mateship and the egalitarian spirit of a *fair dinkum* Aussie! His Aussie mate also helped him to find a supernumerary cardiac technician job at his hospital, the Royal Children's Hospital in Parkville. For many months, this young Chinese doctor would take the first tram to work before sunrise and returned home on the last tram. He spent the whole day at the hospital because he could then live on the free milk, biscuits and bread provided at the hospital cafeteria for staff. I was so touched by his story that I decided to take him on as an interventional cardiology fellow at the Epworth

Hospital on the condition that he must return to China at the completion of his training. He completed the training successfully and is now the Vice-President of the second largest heart hospital in China. His success story has been inspirational for many young doctors in China.

Hands-on Training in Coronary Interventional Cardiology for Overseas Doctors

Doctors learning a new operative technique on live patients must clearly understand the risk-benefits involved in such hands-on training. Hands-on interventional learning for overseas doctors does have potential risk for patients. Just as in live demonstration cases, patients' welfare must always come first during the hands-on teaching. Trainee doctors must fully understand the sacrifice patients make for them to learn the necessary life-saving skills. The reason why patients consent to this is because other patients in future elsewhere may benefit from this training. For this reason, trainees with hands-on training privileges must understand that their learning is to benefit their own patients in future. The same principle applies to research and clinical trials involving new therapeutic agents. Cardiologists from China who are given this overseas training opportunity with me are selected on three criteria, namely academic and professional competence, proficiency in the English language and a guarantee from their hospital chiefs that they will be allowed to practise what they have learnt in their own hospitals when they return to China. Only by achieving these goals would the sacrifice made by the patients be justified.

Unwitting Business Partner

The average cost of a coronary angioplasty procedure in China is approximately two years' wages for an average working class person. A large part of this cost is equipment cost. In China, one could profit greatly from selling angioplasty equipment. In the early days of coronary angioplasty at the Epworth Hospital, where most of my Chinese fellows were trained, a unique sterilization technique was developed so that expensive and hard-to-get balloon catheters could be sterilized and reused. All disposable equipment, including balloon catheters, wires, inflation devices, guiding catheters and syringes were sterilized and kept for the Chinese fellows to take back to China at the completion of their training to start the interventional programmes at their own hospitals. It was, therefore, the duty of the overseas interventional fellow to re-sterilize and store all the equipment at the completion of each angioplasty procedure.

I was flabbergasted to learn that one of my trainees actually set up a thriving business selling this training equipment instead of using it on patients on his return to China. Worse still, I became his unwitting business partner when he included me in his business plan as his overseas supplier! My philanthropic reputation built over many years of sacrificial work was almost ruined overnight. It took painstaking explanation over a considerable period of time before my good name was restored.

'To Live' but with Boomerang Instead of Aeroplane

Hu Dayi, a pioneer electro-physiologist in China, organized China's first modern international live demonstration course called the Great Wall Interventional Cardiology Congress (GWICC) in 1992. The early meetings were held at the Liangma Hotel in Beijing (Fig. 37). He and I had shared the same vision of helping a new generation of young cardiologists in China. The Great Wall Congress of Cardiology is now jointly sponsored by the American College of Cardiology. It is the largest international cardiology meeting in China with an annual attendance of more than ten thousand delegates.

When I first met Hu, he was the Director of Cardiology at the Red Cross Chaoyang Hospital, a teaching hospital of the Capital University. Hu was one of the first interventional electrophysiologists in China in the 1990s. Transluminal balloon coronary angioplasty (PTCA) had already commenced at Chaoyang Hospital under his leadership when I

Fig. 37. The Great Wall International Symposium of Interventional Cardiology (GWISIC), Liangma Hotel, Beijing 1994.

arrived there in the early 1990s. Over many years, my surgical colleagues from Australia and Singapore and I would go to Chaoyang Hospital at the invitation of Hu to demonstrate PTCA and CABG surgery there.

At the closing ceremony of one of these training courses led by the cardiac transplant surgeon from the Alfred Hospital, Donald Esmore, we presented an Australian souvenir, a boomerang, to our host as a token of our friendship and appreciation. I used the occasion and the gift to deliver an important message to the young Chinese doctors at Chaoyang, using a modified version of a popular book, later adapted into a movie, called *To Live*.

To Live encapsulated the struggle and emergence of Communist China over half a century, highlighting also the period of the Cultural Revolution. The lives of three generations of an ordinary Chinese farming family, typical of this period, were depicted. The story begins with a three-year-old girl riding on her father's shoulder. Seeing some chickens frolicking on the country roadside, the girl asks her father innocently: '*What do chickens turn into when they grow up?*' '*Geese!*', her father replies. As would any young child, the little girl asks again: '*And what do geese turn into when they grow up?*' '*Sheep*', comes the answer from dad. '*And what do sheep turn into when they grow up?*' The father thinks for a while and replies in a more serious tone: '*They will turn into water buffalos, then life will be better*'. A farmer's wealth is often measured by the possession of a water buffalo. With ownership of a buffalo, the hardship of a farmer will diminish significantly. The story unfolded with the child growing up during the Cultural Revolution. The only concern during this dreadful period in China was to live at all costs. The little girl grew up under tremendous hardships. She eventually dies during a complicated childbirth and no obstetrician was available because they were all banished to be re-educated in the countryside during the Cultural Revolution. However, the baby miraculously survives. The story ends with this baby, now three years old, being carried on her grandfather's shoulder and asking the same questions as her mother did many years before. The first two questions received the same answers from her grandpa, but to the final question the grandfather replies: '*aeroplane instead of water buffalo!*' Why aeroplane? An aeroplane is the new standard of wealth for a modern Chinese family, for it represents having the economic means to send their children overseas to study. The boomerang that I had chosen for Hu Dayi has a deeper message. Boomerangs will return if the target is missed. With this symbolic Australian hunting instrument, I wanted to convey a message to the young Chinese doctors who are sent overseas to train. I hope that all will return, like the boomerang, to serve their country at the completion of their training. They must not buy one-way aeroplane tickets when they leave for overseas. This is the purpose of my modification of the ending of the story *To Live*, by substituting boomerangs for aeroplanes.

Osler and the Peking Union Medical College

William Osler's single author textbook *Principle and Practice of Medicine* was published in 1892. About the same time, the wealthy J D

Rockefeller was looking for a worthy philanthropic project. Mr F T Gates, his CEO, was asked to find this worthy project. Mr Gates's niece was ill at that time, and he was looking for a good doctor for her. Osler, the new young and brilliant professor who had just published an authoritative textbook on medicine, was recommended. Mr Gates promptly bought Osler's textbook of medicine and even though a layman, managed to read its thousand pages from cover to cover, reflecting the captivating literary skill of Osler. After reading Osler's *opus magnum*, Mr Gates found the 'worthy project' for his boss's philanthropy. He reported to Mr Rockefeller that doctors knew a lot about diseases but very little about how to cure them. He made this observation from Osler's textbook where the pathology and clinical manifestations of all types of diseases were recorded in great detail. In contrast, treatments for all the diseases described were brief and almost the same for all diseases. Indeed, treatment of all diseases in the late nineteenth century consisted essentially of bed rest, bloodletting with leeches and some herbal remedies! Mr Rockefeller agreed and the Rockefeller Medical Research Institute was thus founded.

After the invasion of China by the coalition of the eight western nations in 1898, the United States of America was the only nation that felt guilty and repayed something to China as a goodwill gesture. Part of this goodwill gesture was the purchase of one of the imperial Qing Dynasty palaces at Wangfujin. This palace was to be used for the introduction of modern western medical education to China and to unite eastern and western medicine. Hence, the new union medical college, founded in 1906, was named the Peking Union Medical College or PUMC. The medical school of Johns Hopkins University, initially, and later Harvard University were the main western partners of this famous union medical college between the East and the West. This was the Osler connection with the Peking Union Medical College. Almost a hundred years later, I am privileged to be one of the foreign visiting teaching staff of PUMC over the past two decades. When I had the opportunity to start the new medical school for Xiamen University,

I adopted the Johns Hopkins model to appoint founding academic staff of Xiamen Medical College.

Beijing Medical License for Foreign Doctors

In the early years of the economic reform of China in the late 1970s, foreign experts who were invited by local Chinese hospitals to operate and teach needed no special practice licenses or official registration. However, over the past two decades, the Chinese authorities in all scientific and technological advances are gradually adopting international practices. Among these is the compulsory licensing of foreign doctors before they are allowed to practise medicine in China. I too had to sit a prerequisite examination to obtain a medical practice license in Beijing. I was very glad to be certified because such licensing practice will help to protect Chinese patients treated by foreign doctors. My examination consisted of an oral examination of a clinical case and the performance of a live case of coronary intervention procedure. Although well-known as a teacher to my examiners, I insisted that I should be treated no differently to any other foreign doctor. It was not customary to examine one's teacher in the Chinese tradition. Both the oral case commentary and the angioplasty procedure went without a hitch and I was duly granted a full medical practitioner license from the Health Department for Beijing. With this I was able to work legitimately in all the major hospitals in Beijing, especially at the National Cardiovascular Institute of Fu Wai Hospital, the PUMC Hospital, Anzhen Hospital and Chaoyang Red Cross Hospital.

Returning to China When I Can Walk Again

A new catheter laboratory was being commissioned at the Dalian Medical University Hospital in 1999 and I was an invited guest for the grand opening ceremony for the occasion. After the event in Dalian,

I was scheduled to attend the annual Northern Cardiovascular Symposium in Shenyang and to have an honorary Visiting Professorship conferred at the Northern Military Hospital. We were being driven in a military combivan to Shenyang from Dalian on the newly completed Shen-Da Freeway linking Shenyang to Dalian. Four doctors from the Northern Military Hospital escorted my wife and me on this trip. Unfortunately, our driver dozed off at the wheel and our van crashed into an unexpected stationary vehicle in the middle of the freeway. There were no seat belts in the van and my wife, seated in the mid-section of the middle row was thrown to the front of the car, luckily not through the windscreen. I was sitting behind the driver and sustained a repeat fracture of my left leg just above the ankle at the same site as my fracture, sustained after a fall at a friend's house in Melbourne ten years earlier. An ambulance dispatched from the University Hospital in Dalian took more than three hours to arrive at the crash site. Fortunately, I was not bleeding from my injury and no one was seriously injured. The accident occurred at dusk and very soon after, without any street lamps, the freeway became pitch black. The headlights of our van were also damaged but the car interior light was fortunately still functioning. While waiting for the ambulance to arrive, huge trucks with their glaring headlights were darting around us. In darkness and in pain, the biblical verse of Psalm 23 was most reassuring:

Yea, though I walk through the shadow of the valley of death, I will fear no evil, for Thy rod and staff comfort me.

A police road patrol vehicle stopped to investigate at our crash scene. Amazingly, the two police officers flashed their torchlights on us and mumbled, '*None dead!*' and promptly left, despite my plea for them to transport the front seat passenger with suspected facial or head injury.

Everyone was relieved when our own hospital ambulance eventually arrived and we were taken back to the same hospital we had left only a few hours earlier. It was past midnight by the time the chief orthopedic surgeon arrived to attend to my injuries. The plaster cast for my leg fracture had to be set twice and I decided not to have any analgesia or anesthesia for both procedures because of fear of needle contamination! I had a vision of the scene where Hua Tuo, the deity surgeon was extracting an arrow from the wounded Kung Kong, the legendary Chinese warrior, while he was playing chess. My wife was luckier with only superficial injuries to her face and despite complaining of neck pain, she suffered no cervical spinal injury.

Two days later, my wife and I were flown back to Singapore by a chartered medical jet at the expense of our Amex travel insurance. The cost of the airlift was 120 thousand dollars or 120 Platinum AMEX annual subscriptions! Two of my ex-fellows who are now very senior consultants at their respective hospitals in Beijing and Quangzhou stayed behind in the same hotel in Dalian to look after us until we were air evacuated. They fulfilled the Chinese saying of *'a student for a day but a father for life'*. My wife and I were deeply touched by their most attentive love and care. We also found out later that the Australian High Commissioner and China's Ambassador to Singapore had gone out of their way to arrange our air evacuation from Dalian. Upon our return to the Singapore General Hospital, I received the following personal well wishing note from the then SM Lee Kuan Yew:

> *Dear Yean Leng,*
> *My wife and I were startled to hear that you had met with a motor car accident in Dalian and that both your wife and you were injured, that you had a broken leg. What a misfortune! It is always dangerous to have an accident in China. We send you our best wishes for a comfortable and early recovery. Yours sincerely, Kuan Yew*

After this ordeal, friends and my own relatives asked me whether I would be going to China again. I replied that I would be returning to China as soon as I was able to walk again. Despite six months of intensive rehabilitation, the fracture had further weakened my polio affected right leg. It would be nearly a year before I was able to return to China (Fig. 38).

'Three Wise Men of Christmas' at Dunhuang

Dunhuang is famous for the caves that contain the frescos of Buddhist art, painted over a thousand years, from the third to twelfth centuries. These cave paintings and sculptures were perfectly preserved by the dryness of desert air. The famous twentieth century Chinese artist, Zhang Da-chian, copied many of these frescos that helped to make Dunhuang the 'Mecca' for Chinese artists and Buddhist pilgrims. It is an essential stop along the Silk Road, the trade route that Marco Polo travelled to link China to the west. My dream of visiting Dunhuang to see these frescos was realised when one of the fellows, Dr Liu Chao-zhong,

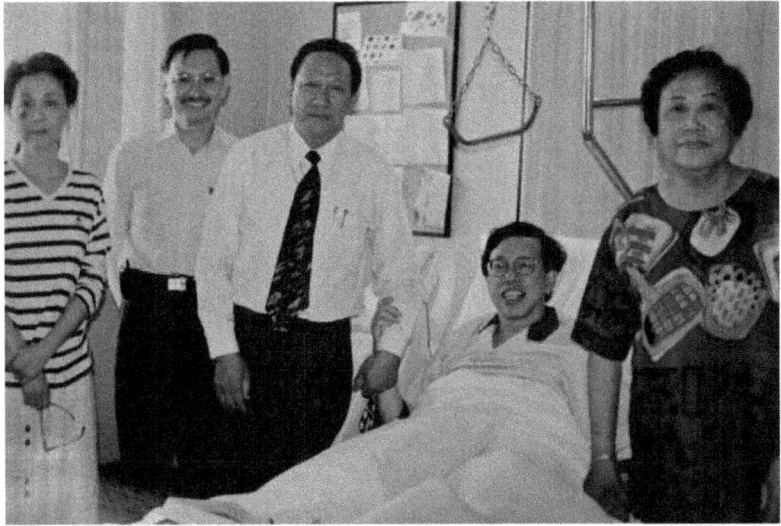

Fig. 38. Air-evacuated to Singapore General Hospital after Dalian car accident (from left: Joy, a friend, Rev. Steven Tong, YL, mother).

invited me to speak at a coronary intervention meeting in Lanzhou, not far from Dunhuang.

From Lanzhou, we made a special one-day visit to Dunhuang. We woke early the next morning to see the sunrise at *Mingshasun* or the 'Singing Desert Mountain' on camel back. I could not manage the steep sand dune to see the sunrise. When the sun eventually rose over the desert peaks it cast three elongated images that looked like pictures of the three wise men bearing gifts to the newborn King on Christmas cards. Taking photographs with one hand while clinging to the saddle was challenging. The camel's back was not broken but mine almost was (Fig. 39).

A few years later, I was invited by Professor Cia Shaobin, another ex-fellow who is now the Vice-President of Ningxia People's Provincial Hospital, to visit and work in his hospital at Yunchuan, capital of Ningxia. There, I had my second camel ride on a unique tourist site

Fig. 39. '*Three wise men*', photograph taken from a camel's back at Mingshasun, Dunhuang (from left: Liu Chao-zhong, YL, Joy).

called Sahu or Sand Lake. Sahu is a series of lakes situated in the middle of a vast desert not far from Yinchuan. This site was recently listed as a world heritage nature site. From my boat in the lake, the image of speedboats creating waves against the backdrop of a camel train in the desert was most unusual. These were the bonuses and unexpected joy of working in remote areas in China.

'Goodness not Grief'

To my knowledge, the first private hospital in China, the Beijing United Family Hospital, was opened in Beijing in 1996. It was a small obstetric and family hospital of twelve beds, owned and run by an American expatriate, Ms He Mujia. Today, the Beijing United Family Hospital has expanded into a large franchise of private hospitals, spread over many major cities in China. Healthcare in China is predominantly public, provided by two parallel systems, the military and the civilian. I have had the privilege of working in both civilian and military hospitals. Xijing Hospital in Xian is one of China's largest military hospitals in China, an affiliated hospital of the Fourth Military Medical University. The Chief of Cardiology of Xijin Hospital was Professor Cia Guo-liang, a pioneer of coronary intervention in China. His Chinese name, literally translated, means *well nation*. Hanging on the wall of his office at Xijin Hospital was a Chinese couplet, given to him by a grateful patient, with the following inscription:

> *Excellent skill and good ethics*
> *Essential to make a nation well;*
> *Sincerity and sagacity*
> *Vital to heart patient's hearts.*

The couplet is especially relevant to cardiologists who deal mainly with hearts. I quote this couplet extensively in my lecture 'How to be a good doctor' in China and elsewhere (Fig. 40).

Fig. 40. The Cia Guo-liang couplet, calligraphy by YL.

A Chinese artist, Lin Xiang-xiong, painted for me a Chinese brush painting (Fig. 41), based on my '*Bird on a branch*' coronary artery photograph reproduced on the cover of this book and inscribed on it the following poem:

Presenting to the world, the coronary painting,
At the twilight of one's brief life,
Like the benevolent Hua Tuo
Vowing to return to common folks,
Goodness not grief.

Fig. 41. Coronary painting by Lin X.X., containing the poem '*Goodness not Grief*'.

Indeed, my father's last illness and his encounter with the medical profession, gave us all in the family deep and lasting grief. Throughout my medical career, I wanted to train doctors who will give their patients and relatives goodness not grief, after the encounter with their doctors. I can say that after 40 years of medical practice, I have returned mostly goodness and not grief to most of my patients and their families.

'Tao Li Fen Fang'

In 2006, many of my previous Chinese fellows organised a surprise party in Shanghai to celebrate the twentieth anniversary of my work in

China. A traditional Lion Dance greeted my wife and I on our arrival at the party. Many ex-fellows who are all eminent cardiologists in China now made sincere and grateful speeches to celebrate the occasion. Those who could not attend also shared their thoughts on video clips. A local Shanghai artist was also engaged to write on the spot for me a four Chinese character calligraphy, '*Tao Li Fen Fang*', meaning '*fragrance of peach and plum blossoms everywhere*' (Fig. 42). Peach and plum blossoms represent the fruits of one's labor evident all over the country and fragrance annotates their success. It is a traditional Chinese phrase used to honour a teacher who has produced distinguished students in all parts of the country. My wife and I were deeply moved by the sincere friendship and respect shown in such a traditional manner by so many past students. We feel very privileged indeed to have played a part in their very successful lives.

Fig. 42. Calligraphy '*Tao Li Fen Fang*' with Fellows at my Erin Street Clinic in Richmond, Victoria 2006 (from left: Chen Ming, Zuo Luning, YL, Zhu Tie-bin).

Following Father's Footseps (*Zi Chen Fu Yue*)

Most Chinese parents hope that their sons will one day turn out to be dragons and their daughters phoenixes. Coincidentally our only child, Iefan, was born not only in the Chinese calendar year of the Dragon but also under the western zodiac sign of the Lion (Leo), both of imperial significance. The two Chinese characters of his name mean '*to surpass the common*', in other words, *superman*! Iefan has a unique way of achieving what he wants. As a child, he was asked the question, '*Are you going to be a doctor like your father when you grow up?*' The answer was invariably a firm '*No*'. He turned out to be a doctor anyway. He was faced with the next common question from our well-meaning friends after he graduated as a doctor, '*Are you going to be a cardiologist like your father?*' The answer was again, '*definitely not!*' As it turned out, he is now not only a cardiologist, but also an interventional cardiologist like his father! Iefan's classic 'NO' for an answer reminded one of a story told by the Nobel Laureate, Louis Ignarro. Ignarro was one of the three joint winners of the Nobel Prize in Medicine in 1998 for solving the mystery of Endothelium-Derived Relaxing Factor (EDRF), that turned out to be Nitric Oxide or NO in molecular term. Before this discovery, Ignarro was often asked the question by scientific reporters: '*Professor, do you know what exactly is EDRF?*' His answer was always '*No*'. After identifying EDRF as NO, he lamented that he had the correct answer all along without even knowing it!

Iefan had an all round education. He was gifted as a violinist with the gift of perfect pitch according to his violin teacher, the late Nellie Shkolnikova. He was leader of the Melbourne Grammar School orchestra. His mother and I are immensely happy and proud that he has turned out to be a good son and a practising Christian doctor, full of compassion and care for his patients. As a busy cardiologist father, I was not able to spend enough time with him when he was growing up. Watching a football match on television with me one day when he was 27 years old, he turned to me suddenly and said, '*Dad, you did not come to my Saturday school football match ever, not even once, did you?*'

The price one pays to be a busy cardiologist is steep indeed. His decision to follow in my footsteps and become an interventional cardiologist of his own volition has fulfilled the traditional Chinese quotation, '*zi cheng fu ye*', which literally translated means '*son following father's profession*'. I was very pleased when he became one of my cardiology trainees at the Western Hospital in Melbourne and I taught him just like any other young budding cardiologist (Fig. 43). In the Chinese tradition of *Kung Fu* training, he was my last pupil, the so-called '*kuan men di tze*' that is of special significance in the Chinese tradition.

On 5th December 2010, Iefan married his long-term sweetheart, Krystal Bergin, an Australian of Italian-Irish descent. Krystal's grandmother-in-law in Taiwan gave her a Chinese name *Jin-Jin*, or crystal in

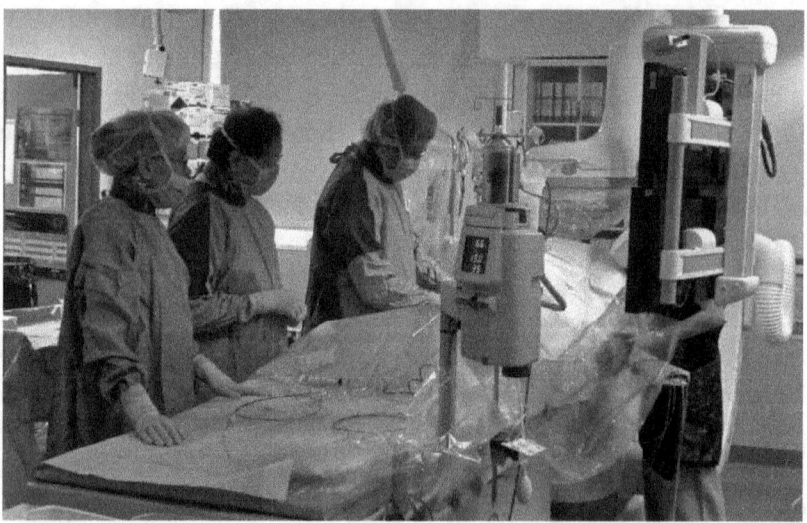

Fig. 43. Working with Iefan in the cardiac catheter laboratory at the Western Hospital, 2007.

the Chinese translation (Fig. 44). Krystal, elegant and intelligent, is training to become a hematologist. With Iefan as a vascular interventionist, the union of blood vessel with blood is most natural.

Fig. 44. Wedding photograph, Iefan and Krystal Lim, 5 December 2010.

5

Xiamen University Medical College

The Tallest House in Chen-chang

My father was born in the village of Chen-chang, Tong-An County and my mother in the neighboring island city of Xiamen or Amoy, both belonging to the province of Fujian, in the southern part of China. I am therefore a Hokkien speaking southerner. Mr Lie Siong Tay, a Xiamen born Chinese merchant, was my mother's primary school classmate. He had been trying for a few years to get me to return to Xiamen to help improve the healthcare standard of Xiamen city. Mr Lie was a philanthrophist and had done many good things for his hometown, building roads, schools and many other public facilities but had not been involved in the healthcare area. Mr Lie eventually persuaded me to get involved with Xiamen healthcare and I arrived there with my wife and son for the first time in 1995.

On a trip to Xiamen with my youngest brother Yean Teng in 2000, we wanted to visit our roots in Chen-chang. Xiamen University staff swiftly arranged a van to take us there. Chen-chang was a village outside a small town called Maxiang. We had to abandon the van soon after crossing the township of Maxiang and walked the remaining distance to Chen-chang that could not be reached by car. I was very emotional because it was the first time I had returned to the village that my father had come from. My mother had told me to look for the tallest building in the village, a three-storey house that she had built for father's relatives. Sure enough before reaching the village I saw a tall building sticking out like a sore thumb. I could not wait any longer and excitedly asked the first person we met on the way: '*Where is the Lim's residence?*' To my astonishment, he replied '*We are all Lims in this village, who are you looking for?*' I then realised that *Chen-chang* is a village of the Lim clan! When we arrived at the tallest house, a plaque on the wall with the Chinese inscription *Lim Koon Yaw Residence* was clearly visible. Tears welled spontaneously in my eyes. A large crowd had gathered to greet us in front of the house. They were all related to my father, one way or another. Dad had three older brothers and one older sister. He was the youngest in a family of five children. Two of his older brothers, the second and third, had migrated to Indonesia. The oldest woman of the Lim clan who came out to greet us was the daughter of my eldest paternal uncle. In other words, she was my first cousin. She and her children and grandchildren had been waiting anxiously for our arrival that day (Fig. 45).

To my dismay, when I asked all my relatives present to write their names on a piece of paper so that I could identify and give each one of them an '*ang-pow*', the traditional greeting present of a red package with cash, none of them could because they were illiterate. An elderly man who was the village letter writer volunteered to complete the task for me. I could not help thinking that if my father had not immigrated to Singapore, I would be just like one of them, illiterate and running around the village bare-footed!

Tan Kah Kee's 75 Year-old Dream Realised

A Singaporean Chinese philanthropist, Tan Kah Kee, founded Xiamen University in 1921. Tan was a successful rubber merchant who dedicated his life and fortune to improving education for the masses, both in Singapore where he had lived and in Xiamen where he was born.

Fig. 45.   A visit to the Lim clan at the village Chen-chang in Tong-an, Fujian 2000.

Apart from Xiamen University, he also built many primary and secondary schools in Singapore, Malaysia and Zimei, his hometown in the outer suburb of Xiamen. The Communist Party in China regards him as a national hero even today. My connection with Tan Kah Kee started at Tao-nan Primary School that he founded in Singapore. Tao-nan was the first school that I attended, at the age of five. In 1921, when Xiamen University was founded, Tan Kah Kee recruited Dr Lim Boon Keng, another Singaporean doctor who was trained in England, to be its Foundation President. With this appointment, Tan was hoping to establish a medical school as the first school for the new university. This wish might have been motivated by the fact that the University of Hong Kong, founded earlier in 1905, had the Medical Faculty as its first school. More significantly, among its first intake of medical students was Dr Sun Yat-sen, father of modern China. For various reasons, the medical school that Tan had wished for did not eventuate for 75 years.

After the establishment of the People's Republic of China in 1949, two further attempts by the Chinese government to fulfil Tan's wish also failed.

China's economic reform in the late 1970s set things in motion and Xiamen was declared the second autonomous Special Economic Zone in the 1980s, after Shenzen. The time was then ripe for a medical school at Xiamen University in the 1990s. There is a Chinese saying, '*Tien si di li ren he*', meaning that the timing and necessary ingredients must be all in place before a plan can eventuate. This was certainly true for Xiamen University to be able to have its medical school established eventually in 1995. I was merely the catalyst to make it happen, more by good fortune than any careful planning. During the meeting with the Mayor of Xiamen City to discuss the building of Xiamen Heart Centre, I suggested to the Mayor, a brilliant and progressive man, that a heart centre of excellence could not be accomplished without being affiliated to a university with a good medical school. With this suggestion, the 75 year wish of Tan Kah Kee would eventually materialize (Fig. 46).

Birth of a New Medical School

Xiamen University is one of about forty national universities in a total of just over one thousand universities in China. Universities in China are graded in three categories, national, state and local universities. Accordingly, the intakes of undergraduates at the national, state and local universities are derived respectively from the entire nation; from within a state or province; or locally, within a city or county. National universities are funded and governed by the central Education Ministry in Beijing while the provincial and local universities are under the auspices of the provincial and local governments. Xiamen University was a national university with a full range of faculties but not medical before 1995.

Mr Lie Siong Tay, an important benefactor of Xiamen, took me to the city as agreed after he helped me to establish the ACIS Heart

Fig. 46. First batch of medical undergraduates of the new Xiamen University Medical College, 1996.

Foundation to train interventional cardiologists in China. As soon as I arrived at Xiamen in April 1995, I requested to be taken to visit the famous Xiamen University, built by my fellow Singaporean, Tan Kah Kee. I was deeply impressed by the beautiful campus and the vitality of the young students that I met. The President of the university then was a chemical engineer by the name of Lin Ju-geng. When I asked him to show me the medical faculty, he lamented: '*We do not have a medical school, even though we have all the pre-clinical disciplines for a medical school at the Science Faculty*'. He then added a crucial comment '*we were waiting for the right person to help us plan the clinical departments to start a medical school for the university!*' Hearing his comment, I replied instantly, '*Clinical teaching is my forte, I will help you plan the necessary clinical departments to start the medical school*'. He was greatly excited with my off-the-cuff offer and asked me to suggest it to the Mayor of Xiamen city, Mr Hong Yong-shi, with whom I had an appointment for a breakfast meeting the next morning to discuss the building of a Heart Centre for Xiamen.

Mayor Hong was a very capable and progressive leader. He had transformed Xiamen from a backwater town into the fourth fastest growing economy in China during his first term as the city's Mayor. When the Mayor found out that my parents were from Xiamen and I could speak the native Xiamen or *Mingnan* (southern Fujian) dialect, an immediate and magical bond developed between us. Prior to my arrival in Xiamen, the Mayor had already approved funding for the building of the Xiamen Eye Centre, the Xiamen Heart Centre and the Xiamen City Emergency Centre. With the help of another Singaporean, an ophthalmologist, Dr Arthur Lim, the Xiamen Eye Centre had already been established. Arthur was the Director of the Singapore Eye Centre when I was appointed the Director of the National Heart Centre in Singapore. Arthur is also a writer, artist and a famous art collector. After the Xiamen Eye Centre, Mayor Hong was eager to quickly follow with the building of the Xiamen Heart Centre and the Xiamen City Emergency Centre.

Understanding the close relationship between emergency medicine and cardiology, I suggested to the Mayor that the two centres should be combined. My experience working with politicians in Singapore had taught me that if one wants a politician to agree to one's proposal, the best way was not to ask for more money. With a pre-existing model of the Alfred Hospital Clinical School in Melbourne in mind, I was quite confident that I could use the budget of the two planned centers that Mayor Hong wanted and add the clinical departments of a medical school without significantly increasing the budget. The model was my own clinical school at the Alfred Hospital, one of the three Clinical Schools of Monash University Medical Faculty, located at Prahran, Melbourne. Not only one of the teaching hospitals of Monash University, the Alfred Hospital is also the Trauma Centre for the State of Victoria. I also highlighted to the Mayor that without the university academic influence, clinical excellence will not be achieved for the planned new heart centre.

The Mayor was visibly excited with my proposal and asked the Deputy Mayor, Mr Wang Rong, to organise a meeting with all the relevant departments involved for the planning of a new medical school for Xiamen University before my departure from Xiamen in the afternoon. An ad hoc committee for the establishment of the Xiamen University Medical College and the Xiamen Heart and Emergency Centres was formed instantly. The historic meeting took place at 10.30 am on the same day, chaired by Deputy Mayor Wang Rong, and was attended by the Presidents of Xiamen University, Zhongshan Hospital, the directors of the relevant departments of the Ministries of Education, Health, and Town Planning and Development, Mr Lie Siong Tay and myself (Fig. 47).

Fig. 47. Meeting where the discussion of the new Xiamen University Medical College took place, Xiamen 1995 (from left: Lie Siong Tay, Wang Rong, Lim Zugeng, three government officals, Chou AT, YL, Wang LM).

Elitism with high standards was the vision Mayor Hong and I shared for the new medical school of Xiamen University. The elitism refers to the selection and recruitment of high calibre students and academic staff, inspired by Osler and the founders of Johns Hopkins Medical School when it was started. Mayor Hong also had a revolutionary idea for the governance of the new medical school by a western Board structure, with himself in the Chair. Thus, a board-governed new medical school, the first of its kind in China, was born. The first intake of 25 medical undergraduates, who came from all parts of China and Taiwan, commenced study in the following year, in 1996 (Fig. 46).

Traditionally, only Chinese nationals are allowed to be full-time Deans of national universities. However, Mayor Hong was insistent that I should become the inaugural full-time Dean of the new medical college at Xiamen University. Xiamen was one of three Special Economic Zone cities in China in 1995, the other two being Shenzen in Guangdong and Qingdao in Shandong. The quick thinking Mayor made a personal appeal to Beijing to allow a foreigner to be the Dean of the new medical school in Xiamen, citing 'Special treatment for a Special Economic Zone!' This special request was eventually approved by the then Minister for Education, Mr Li Lan-qing, after seven months. I was thus officially appointed the Inaugural Dean of the new Xiamen University Medical College on 11th October 1996 at the official opening ceremony of the new medical school (Fig. 48). Although appointed as full-time Dean, I performed all my duties on a part-time and without stipend basis, from Melbourne and Singapore. This was only possible because of a very capable deputy, Zhang Bei-mong, who was appointed as the inaugural Professor of Surgery and Deputy Dean. He was effectively the real full-time Dean and Professor of the new medical school as well as the Head of surgical services at the Zhongshan Hospital, the first teaching hospital of the new Xiamen University Medical College.

Fig. 48. Inaugural Dean appointment at the Opening Ceremony of the Xiamen University Medical College, 11 October 1996 (YL , Mayor Hong YS).

Doctors with Knowledge and Humanity

Xiamen University Medical College was officially opened on 11th October 1996. The opening ceremony of the Xiamen University Medical College was a grand occasion with the appointment of the governing Board of Directors of the college and the inaugural Dean. Representing the Central Government was Professor Wu Jie-Ping, a retired urologist and Chairman of the *Jiu San Xue She* (93 Scholars Committee). Wu was also appointed as the Honorary Dean of the new College at the Opening Ceremony. The appointment of Wu, a high-ranking Communist Party official, indicated the importance of the founding of the new medical school that fulfilled the wish of Tan Kah Kee, a highly regarded educationist and national hero of the Communist Party in China.

My inaugural Dean's speech at the official opening ceremony was entitled 'Doctors with Knowledge and Humanity'. Humanism is vital for a good doctor. Without this, the healer is a mere technocrat. A good doctor must possess not only the knowledge and clinical skills required to diagnose and treat diseases, but more importantly the qualities of kindness and compassion. The importance of research, the search for truth and the use of English in the curriculum of the new medical course were also emphasized in the Dean's opening speech. My wish was that future graduates of the new Xiamen University Medical College would become part of the global medical community and contribute to new knowledge and discoveries in the same way as their western counterparts.

The medical education system in China then, and now, is quite unlike that in the West. The medical courses at a university are designed for either a five-year undergraduate bachelor degree, a graduate seven-year master's degree or an eight-year doctorate degree. Mayor Hong's initial wish for an elite high standard school with only doctorate level students proved to be impractical and impossible according to strict national education department requirements. The lack of adequate teaching academic staff was the main reason for the new medical school not to start at this level. The new medical college therefore was only able to offer the most basic five-year undergraduate bachelor degree course initially. The first student intake was only 25, in line with the '*few but excellent*' recruitment policy expounded by the Mayor. The first enrolled students were mainly from the Fujian province, and only a handful from other provinces in China, including one from Taiwan. The use of English was encouraged and emphasized for learning and teaching alike. Both students and teachers were urged to attend English classes provided by the Arts Faculty of the university. In the early days of the new medical school, as the Dean and one of only a handful of teaching staff, I had to personally lecture and teach clinical medicine at the bedside to the first batch of undergraduates (Fig. 49).

Despite my best efforts to design a new curriculum and to modernize the medical course, the curriculum was not acceptable to the central Ministry of Education in Beijing. I wanted to introduce the Problem Based Learning (PBL) method of clinical teaching used in the western

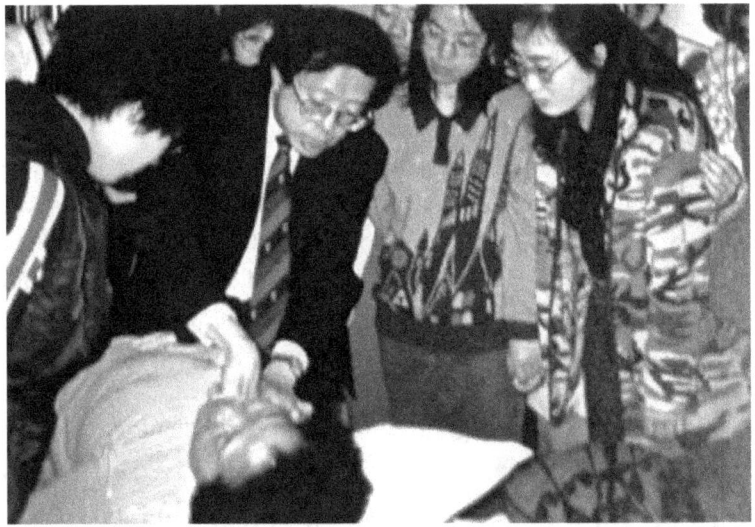

Fig. 49. Teaching bedside clinical medicine at the Xiamen University Medical College, 1996.

medical curriculum rather than the traditional eastern factual retention style of learning. The effort was thwarted by regulatory curriculum constraints dictated by the Education Ministry. Nevertheless, I tried to encourage students to engage in broad and lateral thinking as much as possible and not to waste time on poor lectures and narrow and dogmatic teaching. Students were encouraged to balance learning and leisure, with a healthy dose of extra-curricular activities, especially in sports and the arts. The 25 youthful Chinese medical students who went through high school education in a strict and authoritative manner, found the liberal approach to learning emphasized by the new Dean most refreshing! However, the conservative party secretary of the medical school was flabbergasted with my revolutionary ideas. He took copious notes when I was sharing my learning methods with the new students, and I was certain all these were reported at the regular Party self appraisal sessions. Nevertheless, the new learning technique adopted by the first batch of medical students was justified when they distinguished themselves by achieving the highest scores in the annual internal university examination performance.

With the graduation of the first batch of medical students in 2001, three were offered residency positions in Xiamen's top teaching hospitals, a definite stamp of approval for the new medical school. Today, there are 1500 undergraduates and 200 postgraduate students each year at the Xiamen University Medical College. The school offers courses in all disciplines of health sciences, including pharmacy, dentistry, paramedical sciences and traditional Chinese medicine. The reseach activities of the fifteen-year-old medical school also attracted one of the largest research grants and awards in China today.

Professors for Xiamen University Medical College

Johns Hopkins Medical School was the model I wanted to emulate in the staffing of the new medical school at Xiamen University. The painting that hangs in the library of the Johns Hopkins Hospital in Baltimore by the American impressionist, John Singer Sargent, entitled '*The Four Professors*' immortalized the four founding professors of Johns Hopkins Medical School. The four professors, namely Osler, Halstead, Kelly and Welch, were appointed to head the departments of medicine, surgery, obstetrics and gynecology, and pathology in the new school respectively. For the initial teaching faculty of the Xiamen University Medical College, existing staff from the Science Faculty of Xiamen University were conjointly appointed to teach the pre-clinical subjects such as physiology, biochemistry, histology, embryology and biostatistics. Proficiency in the English language would be an advantage for the joint appointments. Three essential appointment criteria were stipulated for Foundation Chairs, namely the age of forty years or less; the possession of an overseas PhD degree and the appointee must be a Chinese national. A flexible and negotiable appointment term was approved by the Board to attract the best appointees for the new medical school.

Two separate funds were set up by the Board at my instigation, one for capital expenditure (hardware) and the other for operational expenditure (software), for staffing and educational advancement purposes.

A vigorous fund raising campaign was started. Since its inception, Xiamen University has received generous financial support from the Lee Foundation in Singapore. The philanthropist Lee Kong Chien, son-in-law of Tan Kah Kee, founder of Xiamen University, established the Lee Foundation. Lee Kong Chien had been a Chancellor of the University of Singapore. In addition to Xiamen University, the Lee Foundation has regular endowments established to promote the arts and education in Singapore, China and many other South-East Asian countries. Mr Lee Seng Gee, eldest son of Lee Kong Chien and grandson Tan Kah Kee, agreed to donate 200,000 yuan per annum towards the education fund of the new Xiamen University Medical College. This generous donation enabled the school to appoint its first few key academic staff members from overseas for the various clinical departments of the new medical school.

An electronic library was one of the priorities in the early planning stages of the new medical college. Electronic learning would be a feature of the new Xiamen University Medical College. Computers and learning software were made available to all the students and teachers of the new school. Funds necessary to acquire the electronic library were donated by a one-off donation made by Mr Moktar Riady (Li Wen Jen), Chairman of the Lippo Group. Mr Moktar Riady also donated ten million yuan to build the first administration building of the Xiamen University Medical College. This first building, the *Wen Jen Building* named after its benefactor, was officially opened in 2001, during the 80th anniversary celebration of Xiamen University (Fig. 50).

Affiliated or Teaching Hospital

In China, hospitals owned and operated by the universities are known as *Affiliated Hospitals*. They are funded and administered entirely by

Fig. 50. The first Xiamen University Medical College Building, named after Li Wen Jen (Moktar Riardy), Chairman, Lippo Group.

the universities under the auspices of the State or Central Departments of Education. On the other hand, hospitals that are owned and administered by the local Ministry for Health but used as teaching hospitals of the various universities are known as *Teaching Hospitals* of those universities. Zhongshan Hospital in Xiamen is a Teaching Hospital of Xiamen University. The Xiamen Heart Centre, housing the various clinical departments of the new Xiamen Medical College, is co-located at the Zhongshan Hospital. The ownership and the control of the proposed Heart Centre building at Zhongshan Hospital became a sticky issue. For maintaining high academic standards, I was keen for Zhongshan Hospital, together with the new Heart Centre, to be an Affiliated Hospital and Specialized Centre of Xiamen University. This would allow the university to have autonomy and full control of the clinical departments at Zhongshan Hospital as well as the Heart

Centre. However, this would require the transfer of ownership of the hospital from the Health Ministry to the Ministry of Education. I was very naïve to think that this transfer would be possible. Despite many appeals to the relevant authorities and Mayor Hong himself, the attempt to make Zhongshan Hospital an Affiliated Hospital of the Xiamen University failed. This decision would set back the reform, planning and progress of the new medical school significantly.

Xiamen Heart Centre

The Melbourne architecture firm, Eggleston & McDonald, was engaged to design the 'three-in-one building', combining the Xiamen City Emergency Centre, the Xiamen Heart Centre and the Clinical Departments of the Xiamen University Medical College. The building would be co-located within the campus of the Zhongshan Hospital, at Hubin Road, adjacent to the lake in Xiamen city. On my recommendation, the Melbourne architect Mr Collin Stevens was engaged to design the building with local architects. We traveled to Xiamen together and worked with a local architect firm for a week to draw the initial plans. In the mid-1990s and even now, it was popular for hospitals in China to be 'tall and slim', much like modern five-star hotels. When I tried to propose a more functional 'short and fat' design model for the new Xiamen Heart Centre, my concept met with significant resistance from the conservative local architects. The basic concept of the building was finally agreed with the 'tall and slim' model gaining victory. The agreed building would be a twelve-storey building, with a helipad on its roof. The state-of-the-art headquarter of the Xiamen Emergency Centre would be located on the twelfth floor below the helipad and the Emergency Department itself would occupy the ground floor with adjacent ambulance parking bays. The diagnostic imaging services, operating theatres and the intensive care unit would occupy the second floor. The Heart Center with inpatient wards would occupy six floors, from the third to the eighth floor. The university clinical departments would occupy floors nine to eleven, with an auditorium and library on the eleventh floor (Fig. 51).

The building would be the latest in hospital design for China at the time of its completion, with emphasis on efficiency, functionality and traffic flow, separating patients, staff and visitors and isolating potential infections among patients. Most hospitals in China have inadequate and poor elevator services. Separate lifts for visitors, staff food deliveries, and laundry and maintenance services were planned for the new

Fig. 51. The 'Three-in-one *Zhen-he building*' housing the Xiamen Heart Centre, Xiamen Emergency Centre and the XUMC Clinical Departments (Left: Zhang Beimong, YL).

Xiamen Heart and Emergency Centres. The three-in-one building was completed in 2000 and named the *Zhen He Building* after its main benefactor, Li Zhen-he, who donated 15 million yuan towards its construction. The Australian architect firm whose architect had accompanied me to Xiamen generously waived the consultancy fees at my request. Such was the goodwill and friendship between Australia and China in those days. I was deeply touched.

Top Surgeon or Pioneer Dean

Being the focus of the cross-strait tension between China and Taiwan, Xiamen city was held back in development until the economic reform program of China that started in the late seventies. Xiamen lagged behind many major cities in China in terms of modernization, especially in health and technology. The government in Xiamen tends to be ultra-conservative in their policies, favouring Party lines instead of Government initiatives. It was Chairman Deng Xiao-Peng who gave the go-ahead for Xiamen to catch-up with the rest of China when he visited the city in the late 1980s. Within a few years and under the able leadership of Mayor Hong Yong-shi, the city was transformed. High-rise buildings mushroomed all over the island. A remarkable esplanade motorway became a major tourist attraction of Xiamen city. Today the locals call this beautiful esplanade the *namecard* of Xiamen. Chinese who lived overseas returned to Xiamen in droves to invest in the new buzzing city.

By the mid-nineties, the local government had begun to invest in science and technology. The new medical school came about in this milieu of growth and expansion. However, changes in healthcare policies did not follow at the same pace. Many health reform policies, already in force in other major Chinese cities such as Guangzhou, Shanghai and Beijing, could not be implemented in Xiamen. The battle to try to build for Xiamen University a modern western medical faculty was uphill all the way. Xiamen was not ready for radical reform in the mid-nineties and I was therefore reluctant to make my Deanship appointment full-time and kept my position in Melbourne and Singapore while attending to the growth of the new medical school in Xiamen. In order to progress the new medical school, one of the most urgent tasks was to find a capable local Chinese Deputy Dean who would share my vision for the new school. I found such a person at our local church in Melbourne, an act of God I believed.

His name is Zhang Bei-mong, a young and energetic liver-transplant surgeon from Guangdong. Zhang graduated from the famous Zhongshan Medical University in Guangzhou. He obtained his PhD from Uppsala University in Sweden and had completed a post-doctoral research-training course in Paris prior to coming to Melbourne where I met him. He was doing further research at St. Vincent's Hospital, a teaching hospital of the University of Melbourne and had planned to return to Zhongshan University in Guangzhou at the completion of his training in Melbourne to take up an appointment as one of its youngest Professors of Surgery. To me, Zhang was an ideal candidate for the inaugural Chair of Surgery at the new Xiamen University Medical College and in my assessment, the potential to follow me as Dean. We shared a common vision of producing a new breed of doctors for China. I challenged him with a choice of being remembered as a renowned Professor of Surgery in the well-established Zhongshan University in Guangzhou or as a pioneer and visionary Dean of a new medical school in Xiamen. After much soul-searching and consultation with his wife, he chose the latter and was appointed the Foundation Chair of Surgery to the new Xiamen University Medical College and Head of the Department of Surgery at Zhongshan Hospital in Xiamen and Deputy Dean of the new Xiamen University Medical College. The Vice-President of Xiamen University Professor Pan Shi-mao had to go personally to the Human Resources Department of the Zhongshan Medical University in Guangzhou to negotiate his job transfer to Xiamen University and residency relocation to Xiamen from Guangzhou. I had succeeded in attracting the first high calibre full-time senior academic staff member for the new medical school.

Professor Zhang Bei-mong was, in reality, the full-time Dean on site. He worked tirelessly to design the curriculum, recruit junior teaching academic staff, attend to all administrative work, as well as fulfilling a very hectic clinical workload at the Zhongshan Hospital. Shortly after his arrival in Xiamen, he was named one of the ten outstanding young achievers of Xiamen city. He was responsible for the day-to-day running of the medical school in my absence. Whenever I arrived in Xiamen, I would attend to the important policy and governance decisions, fund raising, new senior academic appointments and some lecturing and bedside teaching for students. Unfortunately, the hard work of Zhang Bei-mong was not appreciated fully when a new Party Secretary and President of Xiamen University was appointed in the new millennium. My hope for his succession as Dean did not eventuate.

Big Party Secretary and Little Party Secretary

Before my arrival in Xiamen, it was already decided that the proposed heart centre would be located at Zhongshan Hospital because of Mr Lie Siong Tay's connection with that hospital. In fact, the No. 1 Hospital in Xiamen, the largest and most established public hospital at that time, would have been a better teaching hospital for the new medical school if I were given a choice. Nevertheless, connection or 'kuan-xi' is all-important in China and Zhongshan Hospital became the teaching hospital of the new Xiamen University Medical College by default. My proposed three-in-one building to incorporate the Heart and Emergency Centres as well as the clinical school gave Zhongshan Hospital the opportunity to become the first teaching hospital of the new medical school.

The clinical standard of Zhongshan Hospital was suboptimal for a tertiary teaching institution and the governance was weak. The leadership style of the hospital was more in line with the values of the Cultural Revolution era. Many senior hospital management personnel had no formal medical training. The majority of the doctors, nurses and technologists were also poorly trained. To transform such a hospital into a tertiary teaching hospital is an arduous task indeed.

With the appointment of Professor Zhang Bei-mong, the heavy clinical burden of transforming Zhongshan Hospital into a teaching hospital fell squarely on his shoulders. He was immediately appointed Deputy President of the hospital with executive power to improve the clinical standard of Zhongshan Hospital. His reform met with significant resistance from the existing leadership, in particular, the hospital's Party Secretary. It was obvious that unless someone sympathetic to the reform replaced the 'small' hospital Party Secretary, the chances of transforming the hospital into a teaching institution would be slim. I conveyed this message to the Mayor of Xiamen who was simultaneously the 'big' Party Secretary of Xiamen city. The 'big' Party Secretary promised to effect this change within six months. Unfortunately, after the passage of two 'six months', Xiamen city was rocked by the notorious '*Yuan Hua*' corruption case. Although innocent, the one-in-all Mayor and 'big' Party Secretary was held responsible for the scandal that had occurred in Xiamen during his watch. Ironically, as one often experiences in this world of ours, the bad 'small' Party Secretary survived and the good 'big' Party Secretary was replaced.

One Pen

The new medical school had limited operational autonomy after it was founded because of its small size and the fact that I was not always around. A deputy president of the university Professor Pan Shi-mao was appointed to oversee daily operational needs of the medical school, including all financial and academic matters. The President of the University was in charge of the budget for the medical school. The traditional 'one pen' policy was exercised in the new medical school by the President himself. This 'one pen' policy is widely used in China to make sure that only one person is authorized to sign off any financial expenditure, large or small. The pen in the case of the new medical faculty was firmly in the hand of the University President and not the Dean for the entire time that I was in office. Despite having raised a substantial amount of both the capital and education funds, mainly through the Lee Foundation in Singapore, I had no direct control of the finances of the medical school. Requests for mobile phones and a vehicle for the use of the medical school were never approved. To complicate matters, without consultation, the President of the university appointed the retired president of a Harbin Medical University who was well-connected to the central Ministry of Education as Honorary Dean to ensure alignment of the new medical school to the requirements of the Ministry of Education in Beijing. The Honorary Dean was not a reformer and the modern curriculum that I had planned did not conform to his conservative views. He started to dismantle the new curriculum that my deputy and I had put in place. The authority of my on-site deputy was eroded and he was insidiously marginalized.

Search for a Local Successor

Against all odds, the vision of a modern western-style medical school with the flagship heart centre was firmly adhered to during my tenure as the inaugural Dean and Director of the Xiamen Heart Centre. However, right from the beginning, I was constantly looking for a local Chinese leader to take over. I would pass the baton on as soon as such a person could be found. The first local Chinese I thought of was Hu Dayi, then the Director of Cardiology at the Chaoyang Hospital in Beijing. He and I initially shared the same vision of creating for China a new generation of young cardiologists when we first met in the 1990s. He confided to me while attending the CSANZ meeting in Brisbane that he longed for his *Camelot*, a place where he could build his dream of training good doctors for China, a dream very close to my heart. When the Xiamen Heart Centre was being built, I thought of him and his Camelot immediately and invited him to Xiamen to inspect a potential Camelot at the Zhongshan Hospital. He duly arrived and met with the relevant authorities in Xiamen. Unfortunately, the Xiamen Heart Centre was not his ideal Camelot.

The next candidate I turned to was a most respected cardiac interventionist, Zhu Guo-ying. She was a pioneer interventional cardiologist and teacher of most of the early batches of interventional cardiologists in China. Zhu was born in Guangzhou and trained in France. When I approached her she was Professor and Head of Cardiology at the No. 1 Affiliated Hospital of the Peking Medical University, now the School of Health Sciences of Peking University. She visited the newly established Xiamen Heart Centre at my invitation to assess the centre first hand. After nine months of negotiation with the local Xiamen city health authority, she found the local health system too rigid and not amenable to positive changes. Before she could make a decision for Xiamen, she was offered the position of President of the first private cardiac hospital for China in Wuhan. She then abandoned the Xiamen position and went to Wuhan. It was a great loss for Xiamen and the Xiamen Heart Centre.

The last local candidate that I tried to attract to Xiamen was Cia Guo-liang of Xijing Hospital, an affiliated hospital of the Fourth Military University in Xian. Cia, like Zhu, was a pioneer interventional cardiologist in China. He was trained in Japan and, like Zhu Guo-ying, had trained an entire generation of interventional cardiologists in China. Cia also came to Xiamen to see the new heart centre for himself. After a careful consultation with local authorities, he also found Xiamen authorities to be too conservative for new reforms. The gap in healthcare policies between Xiamen and the other major cities of China at that time was wide indeed. The local Health Ministry officials obviously did not share Mayor Hong's wish of attracting the best talents for Xiamen.

With the search for a local candidate coming to a dead end, my attention turned to outstanding overseas Chinese nationals. One candidate, He Guo-wei, a distinguished researcher in mammary graft physiology, clearly stood out. Professor He was educated in Anhui and trained as a cardiac surgeon at the National Cardiovascular Institute at Fu Wai Hospital, Beijing. I met him when he was completing his PhD at the University of Melbourne under the supervision of my surgical colleague Brian Buxton. After his doctorate in Australia, he did post-doctoral research in Canada and then Dallas. He was appointed Director of Research in Portland, Oregon, working with Albert Starr, of the Starr-Edwards prosthetic valve fame. From Portland he was invited to the Chair of Cardiac Surgery at the University of Hong Kong, a rare distinction for a Chinese national. He had published more than 300 papers that influenced the routine clinical use of internal mammary artery conduit in coronary bypass graft surgery. To attract such a person back to China would require some extraordinary incentives. I had earlier tried to attract him to the National Heart Centre in Singapore but failed because of resistance from local cardiac surgeons. Xiamen Heart Centre would be attractive to him because of his Chinese national origin. He was enthusiastic about the position and the prospect of a research institute of his own. I managed to persuade the Xiamen Government and the entrepreneur businessman Mr Lie Siong Tay to come up with a suitable employment package that would make his relocation to Xiamen possible. He would initially be appointed with the combined roles of Director of Xiamen Heart Centre, Professor of Cardio-thoracic Surgery and Director of Cardiovascular Research at Xiamen University Medical College. Professor He agreed to the offer and the carefully worded contract was signed with a three-component salary package from the university, the Ministry of Health and a final top-up guaranteed by Mr Lie.

Loss of a Local Successor

Mr Lie Siong Tay, a timber tycoon, however, had a different idea about He Guo-wei's appointment. He was always unhappy with my peripatetic style of Deanship at the Xiamen Medical College. He was impressed with Guo-wei, and had decided that he would make a better full-time Dean than myself. Known to be a kingmaker in Xiamen, Lie was able to convince Mayor Hong that Guo-wei should replace me as full-time Dean. Without prior warning, I was asked to attend a special Board meeting in Xiamen in May 2000 planned by Mr Lie. Mayor Hong announced at that meeting that I would be stepping down from my full-time Deanship and assume the role of Honorary Dean. The proposal of appointing He Guo-wei as my successor was also announced at the Board meeting. However, He Guo-wei being a personal friend was placed in a difficult situation. Although very keen, he was not prepared to accept the post offered without my agreement. If Mayor Hong or Mr Lie had consulted and discussed this proposal with me prior to the shocking announcement, I would have seriously considered it. I would have suggested to them to appoint Zhang Bei-mong instead as he was almost ready to assume the Deanship by then. Unlike He, Zhang had after all done most of the hard work in shaping the budding medical school. Professor He eventually did the right thing and declined the offer of full-time Deanship and all the agreed appointments by the Board. After this debacle, I distanced myself from Xiamen. At the same time, even though innocent, Mayor Hong had to relinquish his official posts as Mayor and Party Secretary of Xiamen because of the Yuen Hua scandal in Xiamen but remained on the Board of the Xiamen University Medical College until recently.

A young hematologist by the name of Wang Sin Ru was appointed to succeed me as the new Director of the Xiamen Heart Centre. This same person would later become the Director General of the Health Department of Xiamen city. Another liver surgeon succeeded Wang Li-min and became President of the Zhongshan Hospital. A retired cardiac surgeon, Dr Liow from Fuzhou, became the Head of the Cardiac Surgical Services at the Xiamen Heart Centre. An interventional cardiologist from Hong Kong, Dr David Ho, subsequently took over as Director of the Xiamen Heart Centre on a part-time basis. A research cardiologist and member of the Science and Engineering

Academy of China from Shandong University, Professor Zhang Yun succeeded me as the second Dean of the Xiamen University Medical College. He too was part-time and held a simultaneous Deanship of the Qilu Medical University in Shandong. After a short period, an ophthalmologist, Professor Liu Zu-guo was appointed as the third and current truly full-time Dean of Xiamen University Medical College.

Four years after the commencement of the new medical school, President Lin Zu-Geng retired and the University Party Secretary, Chen Chuan Hong, became both President and Party Secretary of Xiamen University. He showed little interest in the new medical school and did not get along with my Deputy Dean, Zhang Bei-mong. Zhang regularly failed to attend university administrative meetings because of his heavy clinical responsibilities at the Zhongshan Hospital. Zhang Bei-mong lost his role as Deputy Dean of the medical school and as a result, my carefully planned local successor for the Deanship was ruined. I was saddened by the thoughtless act of the new university President. With hindsight, the decision made by Zhang to trade his bright future as a young professor of surgery at the well-established Zhongshan University in Guangzhou for the embryonic Xiamen medical school appeared to have been a mistake for Zhang but not for the medical school in Xiamen. I owe Bei-mong much for his personal sacrifice and regretted asking him to go to Xiamen. During his tenure as Deputy President of Zhongshan Hospital, he had transformed Zhongshan Hospital from a mediocre public hospital into a worthy tertiary institution. He brought liver transplantation and many other innovative education programmes to Zhongshan Hospital. Through his sacrificial hard work, the young Xiamen University Medical College was put on a solid foundation for it to become what it is today. The 15-year-old medical school today has more than 1500 undergraduates and 200 postgraduate students annually. He will be fondly remembered indeed as a pioneer of Xiamen University Medical College in years to come.

Dragon or Worm

As dean and director of the Xiamen medical school and heart centre, I was also full-time Director of the National Heart Centre in Singapore. In addition, I had to attend many cardiovascular symposia and hospital teaching commitments throughout China. The unforeseen car accident on the Dalian-Shenyang highway in northern China halted my travel to China from Singapore for six months. My duties as full-time Dean at Xiamen University were neglected during this period. Lie Siong Tay, the kingmaker in Xiamen, was unhappy that I had not physically spent enough time attending to my duties as full-time Dean in Xiamen. He wanted me to relinquish all my other work, including my many important roles in Singapore and relocate to Xiamen. Contrary to his assessment, after years of work in China I have come to realise that as a foreigner, I would be more effective in achieving my goals for China if I were overseas than if I were to reside in China. Just as it is written in the Bible, local prophets are never highly valued in their own town. My good friend, Zhu Guo-ying, the teacher of many coronary interventionalists in China, often warned me against working full-time in China, saying: *'an overseas expert is like a dragon in the sky, whereas a local expert is like a worm on the ground'*. She spoke from personal experience and was absolutely correct. Coming from Australia or Singapore, I can arrange a meeting with any high government officials in China at the drop of a hat. My views would be considered immediately and carefully. Over nearly three decades, I have chosen to work freely and effectively in and out of China, like a dragon in the sky, rather than be treated like a worm on earth.

6

Health Reform and Centres of Excellence

I Left My Heart in Singapore

One night in October 1996, I was woken by a telephone call around midnight local time in Melbourne. A familiar voice at the other end said, '*Hi, Yean Leng, it's Charles here. How are you? I'm calling to ask whether you would be interested in coming to Singapore to direct the Singapore Heart Centre?*' Not fully awake, I replied that I had just accepted the full-time Deanship at Xiamen University Medical School and that it would be difficult to do both. The caller said, '*Oh, I see, perhaps we can talk again later*', and hung up. The next morning, I remembered the midnight caller was Charles Toh, an eminent Singaporean cardiologist. I had been employed by Charles as his locum at his busy practice at Mount Elizabeth Hospital in Singapore many years previously. I felt burdened by his call because as a Singaporean by birth, my country needed me then. Besides, I had not fulfilled my obligation under the Colombo Plan of returning to serve the country, even though my bond was legally absolved. The vow to train better doctors that I had made at the time when my father was gravely ill returned to haunt me as well. Deep down, I knew that it was a call I could not reject. Yet there were many hurdles I had to clear before I could respond positively to this challenging call, coming from my country of birth. In Melbourne, I had one of the busiest private cardiology practices and I had just started a brand new Department of Cardiology at Box Hill Hospital. In China, I had been given the important task of building the new medical school of Xiamen University. I could not possibly do all these jobs and take on the Heart Centre job in Singapore. I wanted a clear signal from God that it was His will to leave Melbourne where I was also Chairman of the Board of the Chinese Theological Education Foundation then. My wife and I prayed for God's settlement of all the above issues plus the sale of our large Toorak house and the purchase of a secure apartment to house our collection before we could relocate to Singapore. I was also hoping for a two-year leave of absence from Box Hill Hospital and Monash University, a five (two plus three) year contract and a promotion to full professorship in Singapore, before I would make the move. My wife and I had decided that if it was truly God's will for us to leave Melbourne, then all these obstacles would be cleared. Fortunately at that time, our son Iefan had just left Melbourne to study medicine at the Royal College of Surgeons in Dublin, Ireland and we could travel freely. Our prayers were answered and all the seemingly impossible hurdles were promptly removed one after the other in a short space of time. The unexpected midnight call became the next major turning point in my life.

On the 1st of July 1997, my wife and I arrived in Singapore. To my amazement, the Singapore Heart Centre that I was asked to direct was located within SGH, adjacent to Boyer's Block where my father passed away 32 years ago. The first part of my vow, to return to the hospital where my father passed away, was realised. My vow to train better doctors at this hospital was left for me to materialize. An article, entitled: 'I left my heart in Singapore', was published in the local newspaper the *Straits Times* to introduce the new director of the Singapore Heart Centre (Fig. 52).

Fig. 52. *Straits Times* article 'I left my heart in Singapore', 1997.

Uniting the 'Cardiological Factions'

I was headhunted to return to Singapore mainly because I was Singaporean by birth and would have a good understanding of the local culture to help me achieve the goals of the job set for me. In my official letter of job offer of the Directorship of the Singapore Heart Centre, signed by the Permanent Secretary of the Ministry for Health, three terms of reference for the job were specified in order:

> Firstly, to build for Singapore, a state-of-the-art Heart Centre, secondly, to unite the three factions of cardiology in Singapore and finally to produce a national programme of international repute.

Singapore was and still is a nation that thrives on competition. For a long time, cardiac services in Singapore were split into three competing camps. The rivalry between the oldest and most established, SGH and its off-shoot, the National University Hospital (NUH), has been intense. The third faction is the private sector healthcare. Unlike western healthcare, Singapore Government policy does not allow simultaneous appointments of senior medical staff in the public and private sectors. Experienced and senior medical officers from the public sector have to choose to leave their jobs 'inside' the government hospitals if they wish to start more financially lucrative practices in the private sector 'outside'. They could therefore only be either 'inside' or 'outside' in local terminology. This practice is still in force today. Traditionally in Singapore, the three cardiological factions worked antagonistically rather than synergistically with each other. Therefore one of the main objectives of my job as the Director of the Singapore Heart Centre was to unite the three factions and build a united national cardiac care programme for Singapore. Being an outsider and also older with sufficient professional clout and suitable cultural insight, I had the best chance, the Singapore Government thought, to achieve this goal for them.

Aussie Humor not Appreciated

The population of Singapore is predominantly Chinese with traditional Confucian or *Ru Jia* values. In *Ru Jia* tradition, the order of a society is strictly hierarchical and obedience to superiors is taken for granted. The Australian way, in contrast, values individuality and egalitarianism. Having lived most of my adult life in Australia, my values although essentially Confucian, are in many ways Australian-orientated. Fortunately, many traditional Confucian values that I had acquired from my 'texts, teachers and tongues', to quote Osler, are still goal posts for my life, the most important being biblical values. I was not accustomed to the hierarchical way of life when I first returned to work in Singapore. Instead I was keen to promote Australian egalitarianism at work. To this end, I had arranged various 'meet-the-staff' sessions at the Singapore Heart Centre. To each group I tried to emphasize that everyone in the Heart Centre is equal, from the CEO to the most junior staff member. I encouraged all staff, irrespective of their station, to approach me directly if they had any grievances, no matter how small. For six months, not a single junior staff member took up my offer because it was not customary for Singaporeans to approach the boss directly.

Soon after my arrival on the scene, I had arranged a meeting with the entire nursing staff hoping to praise and encourage them. I told the assembled group that nurses and teachers are the two professionals I admire most, because they both share the common admirable goal of wanting to 'help people who cannot help themselves'. The sick do not know what they need to get better and the students do not know what they need to learn to improve themselves. I exalted the nurses for their unenviable tasks of feeding, clothing and washing their helpless patients day in and day out. I then went on to say that if they do not have this self-sacrificing attitude, they would be happier as florists, working in an environment surrounded by nice fragrance and beautiful flowers; or they could become cinema attendants, enjoying free movies in air-conditioned workplaces. My characteristic negative-style Aussie humor, however, did not go down well with the straight-forward literal-minded Singaporeans. Instead of being positively encouraged, they were very deflated by being told by their boss to choose other professions. When my 'offence' was pointed out to me the next morning by the matron, I realised that Singaporeans take everything said to them literally and they are unaccustomed to the typical Australian '*Ocker the knocker*' sense of humor. I had to reschedule another meeting with the nurses to praise all of them in the most direct and positive terms. I learnt from this incident that I had to change my 'Aussie' way of speaking in Singapore to be productive.

Professionalism for Nursing and Medical Technologist

The nursing profession in Singapore, and Asia in general, does not receive the high professional esteem that it deserves. The first Health Minister of Singapore that I had the privilege to serve was a particularly young and enlightened individual and quite approachable. Three months into my job, the Minister invited me to lunch at his office to ask my early impressions of healthcare in Singapore. I replied to his question by asking him another question that took him by surprise. '*Do you have a daughter, Minister?*', I asked. He looked perplexed and amused because I was an unlikely candidate to be his son-in-law! I quickly followed with the next question: '*If you do, Sir, would you want her to become a nurse?*' I then went on to say, '*Sir, pardon me for saying this, if you were ill and admitted to the Heart Centre, as your doctor I would visit you for about half an hour each day, the remaining 23 and a half hours, you would be looked after by nurses. Are nurses important, Sir?*' He then understood my series of questions to him in reply to his question of healthcare in Singapore. I told him more directly that nurses in Australia are highly esteemed and treated as healthcare professionals and not workers. They should be treated as professionals, with skills no different to the doctors or technologists in the hospitals, public or private. Nurses in Singapore and Asia are less well-trained professionally, I said. They should be highly regarded like the doctors which is the situation in western developed nations.

I spent the next five years trying to instill professionalism and self-esteem into the nurses at the Singapore Heart Centre. I worked closely with the Director of Nursing to evolve a career path for nurses at the National Heart Centre and urged all medical staff to treat both nurses and medical technologists as equal professionals. I propagated the concept of the three equally robust pillars essential to sustain any good healthcare institution; they are the medical, nursing and technical pillars. This is standard in western hospitals but not those in Asia. Weakness in any one of these three pillars will cause the institution to collapse. With nursing leadership, we designed comprehensive in-house nursing training programmes. I personally taught nurses to perform many routine medical procedures such as venous cannulation, venipuncture and basic bedside clinical physical examination techniques that were previously done only by medical staff. This comprehensive career path and the nursing training programmes at the Singapore Heart Centre were very popular and highly sought after by nurses throughout Singapore. While other public hospitals were chronically short of nursing staff, the Singapore Heart Centre enjoyed a surplus of nursing applicants each year. The Director of Nursing was subsequently awarded the prestigious President's Nurse Award as a result of this nursing reform at the National Heart Centre.

First Asian Medical Technology Diploma Course

Medical technologists make up the third pillar of modern healthcare teams, together with doctors and nurses. However, like the nurses, medical technologists are not appropriately trained or esteemed in Asia. There were no formal tertiary education courses nor practical training facilities for medical technologists, especially cardiac technicians who are the key to good diagnostic and therapeutic services in cardiology. In the West, cardiac technicians have to qualify with a tertiary education diploma in order to be employed. Most countries in Asia do not have a formal training programme for medical technologists. They are trained on the job like motor mechanic apprentices.

A pilot training programme for cardiac technologists was introduced at the Cardiac Unit of the National University Hospital a few years before my arrival in Singapore, but it did not mature into a formal tertiary educational programme. Recognizing this deficiency, I designed and developed a partnership with one of the three local universities, aiming to create a medical technology diploma course. I was fortunate that the Senior Minister of State for Health at that time, Dr Aline Wong, was simultaneously the Senior Minister of State for Education. She was a very progressive politician and a great intellect. She listened intently to my case for developing the first diploma course for medical technologists for Singapore and South-East Asia. She quickly approved funding for the creation of such a diploma course. The National University of Singapore and the Nanyang Technology University both declined my invitation to set up such a course, while the Singapore Polytechnic enthusiastically agreed to develop such a diploma course in partnership with the National Heart Centre. With the blessing of the Senior Minister of State for both Education and Health, all necessary prerequisites for the establishment of the tertiary diploma course were quickly fulfilled. Within a year of its inception, the first batch of undergraduate medical technology students was enrolled at the Polytechnic in the year 2000. The course curriculum was decided and the theoretical and practical components of the course were to be taught at the Singapore Polytechnic and the Heart Centre respectively. The course proved to be very popular, with participation by medical technologists from hospitals within Singapore and from neighboring South East Asian countries. This diploma course for medical technologists at the Singapore Polytechnic course was the first of its kind in Asia. The graduates are now working in many heart centres throughout South-East Asia. The standard of cardiac care in Asia has significantly improved as a result of programmes such as this. This is a fine example of what can be achieved when a clear vision is supported by wise government decisions.

Role Model Leadership

One of the main reasons that prompted my return to Singapore was to fulfill the vow of training better doctors, a promise made at my father's bedside in Ward 23, then the surgical ward in the Boyer's Block of the Singapore General Hospital. I constantly reminded all my medical staff to be compassionate to patients and their relatives and treat them as if they were their own family members. During routine ward rounds, I would often ask young doctors how they would treat the patient under their care if the patients were their own parents. I showed them personally how to talk to their patients and their relatives and how to explain the exact nature of the patients' illnesses and the treatment choices in a language that any layman could understand. I also insisted that they should always convey hope to their patients and relatives even when prognoses were grim.

A patient-centered work principle was demanded of all medical and nursing staff at the National Heart Centre. I introduced a *5-minute response* to paging rule for all medical and nursing staff. If no response from resident medical staff were received by the nursing staff within 5 minutes of the resident being paged, the nursing staff would page the next level medical staff after every five minutes until the director, myself was paged. This was both refreshing and threatening for the nursing staff in Singapore, who would never dream of calling the director or professor directly.

In order to gain first-hand knowledge of both patients and medical staff at the Heart Centre, I rostered myself in equal rotation with all my senior medical colleagues for both public inpatient and outpatient clinic responsibilities. In addition, I conducted professorial teaching ward rounds for advanced cardiology trainees and senior nurses once a week, except when I was overseas. The teaching session also served as a quality assurance round to indirectly supervise the practice standards of my consultant medical staff on ward service. I consider inpatient ward services the important clinical privilege for any consultant medical staff.

On one occasion, I received a call from a house medical officer at 3 am in the morning appealing for my intervention in the management his young patient who had a heart attack. The brave young doctor had a different management plan for his patient to that of the medical consultant on ward service. He thought that the optimal treatment for his patient was early reperfusion by immediate coronary angioplasty instead of the thrombolytic therapy orderd by the on-call consultant.

After listening to his case carefully, I agreed with the junior doctor's suggested therapy. I then got out of bed and went to the hospital to perform the primary angioplasty procedure. The procedure was successfully completed in a timely manner. When the consultant concerned realised the next morning that the Director had overruled the management plan of his patient, he never again offered second best treatment to his patients because of personal reasons. This role model leadership has resulted in improvement in the clinical standard of care for patients at all the institutions that I have had the privilege to serve, including the National Heart Centre in Singapore and the two cardiac services in eastern and western Victoria in Melbourne. I had the satisfaction of knowing that the vow of training better doctors that I made at the age of 17 at the time of my father's death had been fulfilled.

Outpatient Clinic Bullying

One day the outpatient nurse unit manager brought a sobbing Malay junior nursing aid to my office. The manager complained to me that the behaviour of one of my Chinese senior consultants was most unacceptable. He was extremely rude to the Malay staff who could not speak Chinese. This particular consultant was well-known for his abrupt behaviour and I had already received numerous complaints about him prior to this incident. This was the straw that broke the camel's back and I had already decided to teach him a lesson. Together with both the Malay nursing aid and her manager, we headed to speak to the consultant in question at the outpatient clinic. When I arrived at the outpatient clinic, the waiting room looked like a fish-market, packed with impatient patients to the rafters waiting to be seen by the consultant. I understood immediately that the consultant's irrational behavior that day was precipitated by an excessive workload. I too, had lost my cool on such occasions. So instead of going to the consultant's cubicle to chastise him, I asked the nurse unit manager to open one of the empty clinic rooms for me to see some of the waiting patients. I told her and the junior nurse that I would deal with the consultant later. She was puzzled by my actions and change of heart. When the consultant came out later to find that the number of clinic patients had dwindled and realised that the director was seeing his patients, he was confused and alarmed. When he asked the nurse unit manager why I was there, he was embarrassed. Without uttering a single word, I had achieved a better outcome by role model leadership. From that day on, the consultant changed his attitude towards the nursing staff for the better. The same consultant became a valued colleague and a close friend to this day. When he found out that I was leaving Singapore, he led the vast majority of the medical staff in writing a letter of confidence to try and persuade the Ministry of Health to retain my position at the National Heart Centre.

Quantifying Academic Excellence

Academic excellence is basic to all good healthcare. Whilst reforming the nursing and medical technology pillars of the Singapore Heart Centre, I emphasized the importance of every doctor's need to strive for academic excellence. In the public sector in Singapore, a doctor's total salary package consists of three different components. The first is the basic salary; the second is the income derived from treating private patients; and the third and last component is an annual performance bonus. The CEO of the institution at the recommendation of its departmental heads traditionally decided the amount of the last variable component, the bonus. As the Director of the National Heart Centre, I combine the roles of both the administrative CEO and medical director of the centre. I therefore have to finally approve the amount of annual bonuses of all of my medical staff based on their performances. Such a performance-based bonus is non-existent in the western industrial system. Once I understood this remuneration system in Singapore, I realised the great potential of using this performance-based bonus to drive excellence. For performance to be objectively assessed, a quantifiable system of excellence, especially academic excellence, must be developed. The amount of annual bonus for each individual staff can then be objectively meted out in accordance to a derived score that would reflect excellence of performance based on acceptable international academic standards.

In healthcare, academic excellence is traditionally measured by the three key components of research, clinical service and training. The weight and importance of these three components can be adjusted in accordance with the desired goal or vision of a particular hospital or healthcare institution. To achieve academic excellence, the emphasis needs to be in the order of research, followed by clinical service and finally training excellence. Tertiary teaching hospitals of research universities, such as Harvard or Cambridge, would accord high weight to research compared to service and training excellence. Service-oriented hospitals, especially for-profit private hospitals would distribute large portion of their goals to service excellence. The governing body of a particular healthcare institution would eventually decide the type of hospital they want and quantify the size of the three different areas of excellence they want and utilizes their resources to achieve their goals accordingly.

In all the leadership positions in hospitals in Asia or Australia that I was entrusted with, attaining a high level of academic excellence, in accordance to international criteria, has been my leadership goal. There must be a common vision between the institution and its appointed leader. The weight of the three pillars, viz, research, service and training, can then be adjusted accordingly to this common goal and vision. Research must precede service excellence but the two should not be very far apart. For the National Heart Centre, a major teaching hospital affiliated with the National University of Singapore, out of a score of 100, I would recommend a weighting of roughly 45, 40 and 15 to research, clinical service and training respectively. The governing Board must share this decision of course. For each of the three components of research, service and training excellence different grading methods can be developed. For research, I used a scale of 5, 3 and 1 points to recognise contributions made at international, national and local levels respectively. This applied to all peer reviewed journals articles with their variable impact factors and oral and poster presentations at scientific meetings at the three levels. Clinical excellence can be graded by performance reports from supervisors, heads of department and the director of the institution. Finally, training excellence can be graded by feedbacks from trainees and the amount of time spent in teaching and training junior staff. Last but not least, a small component amounting to 15-percentage points or so can be accorded to professionalism, including attitude and behavior. This objective system of quantifying academic and professional excellence could then be objectively applied to determine the size of the performance-based bonus as well as the objective grade of each medical staff to determine whether he or she is a Category I (clinician-scientist), II (clinician-teacher) or III (service clinician) staff that each healthcare institution needs in varying proportions. This quantification of academic excellence was particularly useful for Asian countries such as Singapore and China where a performance bonus is a significant part of a medical worker's pay package. Not only was the quantification of academic excellence useful for objective payment of bonuses, more importantly it allows accurate placement of each medical staff into three academic categories using internationally accepted criteria. Category I staff are doctors of international reputation with frequent international speaking demands and scientific publications in international peer review journals. Category II staff are those with national standing and finally Category III are staff who are locally prominent. Using this quantifiable criteria, there were no Category I staff when I first arrived at the National Heart Centre and only a handful of Category II staff. The majority were robust and hardworking Category III staff. Before I left NHC, few had moved from Category III to II but none had made the Category I grade.

I have shared this concept of quantification of excellence with the various hospital chiefs and management groups in Singapore and China and presented this at the annual national hospital presidents' conference in Wuxi. I was also privileged to have a private meeting with the Deputy Minister for Health, Professor Huang Jie-fu in Beijing, to put forward to him my paper on healthcare reform for China that included this important hospital management concept (Fig. 53).

Fig. 53. Meeting with vice-minister Huang Jiefu, Ministry for Health, Beijing 2009.

Pyramid of Excellence

Excellence in any important medical therapy should follow a pyramidal approach that I called the 'Pyramid of Excellence'. The base or bottom of the pyramid is *knowledge transfer*. At this level, basic clinical knowledge and technical skill are acquired through teaching and training. The middle level of the pyramid is *new knowledge*. Here, new knowledge is generated through research. The top of the pyramid is *knowledge exchange*. At this level, the new knowledge obtained in the previous level is communicated and compared at local national or international scientific meetings or published in peer review journals. Percutaneous Coronary Intervention (PCI) is an important medical therapy. To achieve excellence in PCI development in any country, this pyramidal approach must be followed (Fig. 54). In most Asian developing nations, PCI prgrammes are still in the knowledge transfer zone at the bottom of the pyramid. Little new knowledge in PCI has come

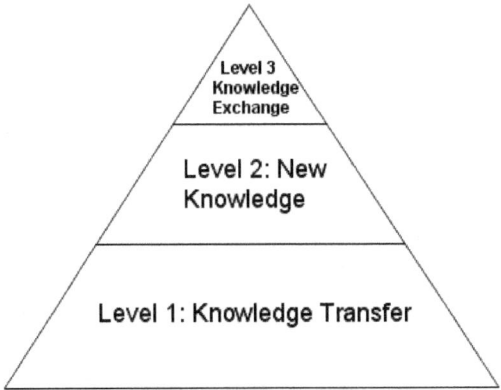

Fig. 54. Pyramid of excellence in percutaneous coronary intervention.

from the Asia Pacific region, despite the large number of patients being treated by PCI in this region. Singapore and China are entering the second level of the pyramid of PCI excellence now.

Staff Appointment and the Electoral College System

The Electoral College system is a robust and transparent system that is used to appoint senior academic and hospital staff in Victoria, Australia. The Electoral College is essentially a fixed term selection committee, activated whenever needed to appoint senior tenured healthcare and academic staff in a public government-funded tertiary institution. Professors, directors and heads of clinical services at public hospitals fall into this category of appointments. The job of this selection committee is to ensure that the best-qualified person, based purely on academic merits, is appointed to the important vacant job position. The Electoral College must also ensure that a minimum standard for the position is met. It will not make an appointment recommendation if no suitable candidate among the applicants meets this minimum standard. If more than one suitable candidate is found, the committee will rank the candidates for appointment and offer the job in the order of the ranking. The composition of the Electoral College typically consists of members from the institution offering the job, senior members of the medical profession, the university, representatives from specialist medical societies and lay persons from the community. The president of the institution offering the job chairs the committee and the institution cannot have more than half of the Electoral College votes. However, the institution has the final right to accept or reject the Electoral College's recommendation. This system not only provides expertise and transparency but safeguards also the public's interests and ensures that ordinary lives in the community are in the best of hands. The heads of clinical services in a public hospital make decisions that often affect people's lives. In contrast, politicians make decisions that only affect people's way of life. Much more care should therefore be given to these appointments and the Electoral College is very suited to this important task.

Singapore thrives on meritocracy and the Electoral College system should be readily acceptable for appointing senior public servants, especially heads of healthcare institutions. I recommended the introduction of the Electoral College system to the Minister of Health for appointing very senior and key medical staff to the National Heart Centre. After months of procrastination and debate, I managed to convince the Ministry for Health to agree and adopt the use of a modified Electoral College to appoint very senior medical staff at the National Heart Centre as a pilot project.

'Kiasu-ism' — A Unique Singaporean Trait

Singapore has virtually no natural resources and its long-term survival depends heavily on good governance. Governance generally is that of a meritocracy and hierarchical or top-down Confucian order. Competition to get to the top is usually intense. Singaporeans tend to be more self-centered, perhaps for survival reasons, in a world with limited resources.

This self-centered attitude could have its origin from traditional Confucian teachings. Thus the famous Tang verse, exalting one to '*sweep only the snow on one's own door-step but not to clear the frost on the roof of one's neighbor*' is well-known to all Chinese. This prevailing Chinese ethos has evolved into a uniquely Singaporean phenomenon, known locally as *Kiasu-ism*. *Kiasu* is a local Hokkien idiom that, literally translated, means 'afraid of losing'. *Kiasu-ism* is a common trait, especially among Singaporeans of Chinese descent. I noticed that *Kiasu-ism* was also widespread at the National Heart Centre and insisted a paradigm shift of this *kiasu* culture there. I urged all my staff to shift their goals from a 'self' to a 'team', a doctor-centered to a patient-centered culture; a parochial to a global perspective. In fact I listed 14 paradigm shifts that were necessary to improve the culture at the National Heart Centre (NHC) (Table 2):

Table 2. Paradigm shift in culture needed to improve NHC.

Old culture	New culture
Service Excellence	Academic Excellence
Doctor-centered	Patient-centered
Self-interest	Team-interest
Experience-based	Evidence-based
Hierarchy	Equality
Division	Integration
Destructive criticism	Constructive criticism
Narrow-minded	Broad-minded
Selfishness	Generosity
Old glories	New achievements
Accepting dogmas	Challenging status quo
Isolation	Communication
Incumbency	Insurgency
Parochial	Global

At the annual Singapore Monash University Alumni dinner held at the Raffles Hotel in 1998, I was invited to be the respondent to the speech of the guest speaker, Sir James Gobbo AC, then the Governor of Victoria. His speech was about the importance of egalitarianism in society, in contrast to the *kiasu-ism* that prevails in Singapore. My response in part was as follows:

> *His Excellency spoke of early contact with Singapore through Singaporean students attending Melbourne University under the Colombo Plan in the sixties. I was one such student attending Monash University. Many more Singaporeans, sponsored or otherwise, have received an excellent education in Australia. The majority of them have returned to help shape Singapore into what it is today. What a totally different country it is compared to the one I left in the sixties. This reflects the determination, hard work and vision of the founding fathers and the people of this nation. Many prominent Singaporeans, including some Government Ministers, have been educated in Australia. Australia therefore can claim to have played a role in the success story of Singapore.*
>
> *His Excellency was one of the seven Founding Members of the Immigration Reform Group in the early sixties. The Group's pioneering effort led to the reformation of the White Australia Policy. This immigration reform has forever transformed Australia into a unique and successful multicultural society. It is indeed a unique achievement for Australia because no other Western nation in the world today, in my knowledge, can claim to possess the spirit of 'genuine respect for the culture of others and a recognition of the value of the culture of others', referred to by His Excellency...his Excellency quoted the Singaporean Minister for Arts and Information B G George Yeo's ideal vision of Singapore, 'a nation characterized by good governance, civic responsibility, honesty, strong families, hard work and spirit of voluntarism'. His Excellency has chosen to focus on the spirit of voluntarism tonight.*
>
> *In the Straits Time Review yesterday, the headline 'Civil society will anchor community in the long run' was most apt. The American*

pre-eminent management guru Peter Drucker argues that voluntary community work must play a major part in any successful stable economy. He pointed out that 50 percent of Americans work at least four hours a week in a voluntary association, either in a church or the community. When one thinks of notable voluntary work, names such as Albert Schweitzer in Africa, Mother Theresa in India, and our own eye surgeon Fred Hollows in different parts of Asia rapidly come to mind. Some of us here tonight, I am sure, who have been engaged in charitable work may feel self-content. But we are reminded by His Excellency not to be hasty in congratulating ourselves when social issues are involved, 'for civic responsibility, co-operation and enlightenment are subject to setbacks and disenchantments'. 'Charity and voluntary work, strictly benevolent or not, is recently being promoted by the Government of Singapore. This is to counteract the quaint social phenomenon of 'Kiasuism' (a term which in the local Hokkien dialect means 'afraid of losing'). This local characteristic has spurred intense competition and self-interest among Singaporeans. While it has produced the desired effect of a hardworking, productive and much better educated society, it has at the same time produced the undesirable effect of suppressing community spirit and benevolent voluntary work', he concluded... Humanitarian goals, charitable and voluntary work in the community might heighten one's self-esteem and lower one's stress. This may very well be the right prescription for reducing the stress level of Singaporeans...We thank His Excellency for his timely reminder of the importance of civic engagement in a healthy democratic society.

'You Are On the Wrong Side'

Soon after arriving in Singapore, I was assigned by the Ministry for Health to be a member of the taskforce to implement the Australian Diagnostic Related Group (DRG) system of healthcare funding in the public, or 'restructured' hospitals as they were called in Singapore. At the Box Hill Hospital in Melbourne, I had first–hand experience working with the Victorian casemix funding system at Box Hill Hospital for five years prior to coming to Singapore. Before rolling out the DRG funding scheme, a Singapore delegation, headed by the then Minister for Health, had to obtain the official agreement of the Australian Health Department to use the Victorian casemix in Singapore. I was one of the members of this delegation to visit Canberra for the signing of this agreement (Fig. 55).

The Ministerial delegation duly arrived in Canberra and was given a warm reception at the Australian Parliament at Capital Hill. At the reception, the team from Singapore was lined up on one side and their counterparts from Australia on the opposite. I was standing with the Singapore team. The Australian Health Minister, Hon. Dr Michael Woolridge, a colleague of mine when he was a resident at the Alfred Hospital, headed the host team. The official protocol called for the introduction of the members of both teams by their respective

Fig. 55. Meeting of health ministers of Australia and Singapore to sign the DRG MOU (from left: Moses Lee, YL, Willie Tan, CT Yeoh, M. Woolridge).

Ministers. When it came to my turn to be introduced by the Health Minister from Singapore, Dr Woolridge took one look at me and said '*I know this man, he used to be my tutor and he is on the wrong side!*' Suitably impressed, the Singapore Health Minister quickly replied, '*Oh, we have temporarily seconded him*'. As for myself, I was really unsure on which side I should be standing!

The team returned to Singapore after successfully obtaining the agreement to implement the DRG Victorian casemix funding system in Singapore. I was promptly recruited into the casemix committee of the Ministry of Health. My main task was to explain the medical aspects of casemix funding to the clinicians at all the restructured hospitals and to win over their confidence for DRG funding. For DRG hospital funding to be successful, the role of the clinicians is crucial. Learning from past experiences in Victoria, a Casemix Clinical Committee was set up from the outset to modulate and formulate the Singapore casemix. The National Heart Centre and the Changi General Hospital were chosen to be the two pilot sites to implement Victorian casemix funding in Singapore for the first year. With the successful implementation at these two hospitals, the DRG casemix funding was rolled out to all the Singapore restructured hospitals in 18 months. In contrast, it took five years to implement DRG funding for all the public hospitals in Victoria.

'All-or-none'

Public and private healthcare sectors in most western countries are not mutually exclusive but complementary. Medical manpower in western countries is efficiently deployed in both private and public hospitals to the benefit of patients in both sectors. The best and most successful clinicians are given privileges in both public and private hospitals to treat their patients. In Australia, medical consultants in public hospitals are given private practice privileges of varying degrees and even the so-called full-time staff is accorded private practice rights for a quarter of their time.

However, in most Asian countries, the 'all or none' rule applies to all senior medical staff of public or governmental hospitals. This rule dictates that medical consultants cannot have private practice privileges outside of their public hospitals. In Singapore, the difference in income for medical practitioners in the public sector, known commonly as 'inside', and the private sector, or 'outside', is very steep, in favour of doctors 'outside'. Therefore, whenever senior doctors 'inside' are sufficiently confident of a successful practice in the private sector 'outside', they will invariably opt out of the public system to set up their own private practices in the greener pastures 'outside'. Public hospitals by default become a perpetual training ground for younger and less experienced doctors. This chronic and persistent loss of experienced clinicians is a serious weakness of public hospitals in Singapore. To compensate for this wasteful loss, some Asian countries, notably Malaysia and Indonesia, have made it compulsory by law for doctors in the private sector to spend a proportion of their time in public hospitals.

Therefore as expected, four of my senior consultant staff decided to resign from 'inside' and move 'outside' to start their private practice on the third year of my watch at the National Heart Centre. After lengthy discussion with each one of them, I found out that all four would rather stay inside if only dual appointments of 'inside' and 'outside' were allowed. I then made a formal appeal to the Ministry of Health to allow dual appointments in order to retain these experienced and precious staff, on part-time contracts, citing my personal experience in Australia. This is a brave new frontier for the Ministry for Health in Singapore. The Minister was sympathetic and eventually allowed such dual appointments to be tried at the National Heart Centre as a pilot project. I was tasked by the Ministry of Health to draft guidelines to supervise the implementation of this dual 'inside and outside' appointment system to ensure that the standard of care of patients 'inside' is not compromised. I duly drafted the operational guidelines and implemented them successfully at the National Heart Centre. I demonstrated that it was possible in Asia to retain senior and highly trained medical staff in the public sector while allowing them some private practice. Unfortunately, this successful pilot project at the National Heart Centre terminated with my return to Australia. The dual appointment scheme that was vital for senior staff retention has not been rolled out to the other restructured hospitals in Singapore to this day. In contrast, the scheme of multi-site appointments for senior doctors is being implemented in many major cities in China today.

Review of Medical Education in Singapore

During my time at the National Heart Centre, there was a strong move among senior doctors at SGH to have a second medical school for Singapore. This was partly motivated by a significant shortage of medical manpower in the country, especially junior medical officers in public hospitals. This shortage was a direct consequence of a government policy implemented a decade ago to restrict the influx of foreign medical graduates. Singapore, with a population of 3.5 million, could easily accommodate two medical schools. I was asked to chair the Ministry for Health's Committee for the Review of Medical Education to restructure medical education for Singapore in the new millennium. After a year of deliberation, the committee submitted a report recommending an increase in the intake of medical undergraduates to 250 students per year, with ten percent of them targeted for the emerging life sciences industry. Furthermore, the report recommended a new graduate medical school be built to enhance healthcare and promote life science research in Singapore.

It is customary for the Singaporean Government to seek independent endorsement from an external expert committee on all recommendations by its own local committees. To this end, a heavyweight international panel led by Lord Oxburgh, with four other medical education experts from the United Kingdom, Sweden, Australia and USA, was asked to write their independent report to review and overhaul medical education in Singapore. After many site visits and a year of intense study, Lord Oxburgh's panel made their independent recommendations to the

Singaporean Government. In their final report, many of the recommendations were in fact similar to those made by the local Medical Education Review Committee. In essence, the external report concluded that Singapore should not continue to rely on importing doctors that were trained abroad. It observed that clinical research relating to the treatment of patients is not well-developed in Singapore, and the bio-industry is severely hampered by a lack of doctors who are well-trained in research. The Oxburgh Committee advised that if Singapore were to grasp the commercial opportunities of biomedicine, new initiatives and a profound cultural change must follow. The role of the physician-scientist must be established and people in this role must be well-remunerated and able to dedicate most of their time to research. Academic appointments must be held conjointly between research institutions, hospitals and the university and close collaboration between these bodies must be fostered. For these reasons, planning should begin for a new medical school. The second clinical school or stream should be based at SGH with its own teaching, research and clinical academic staff. This second clinical stream should have an exclusively graduate entry and should compete in teaching with the existing undergraduate school based at the National University Hospital to harness the research capabilities of SGH. It must be recognised that along with constructive internal competition, close internal collaboration in many areas is essential if Singapore is to be internationally competitive.

Today ten years later, such a graduate school in partnership with Duke University of the United States of America is now up and running in Singapore, located within the SGH campus as recommended 10 years previously.

NMRC, BRMC and A*STAR

In addition to my role as Director of the National Heart Centre, I was invited to assume the role of Chairman of the National Medical and Research Council (NMRC) of Singapore in 2000. Once on board,

I realised that the operation of NMRC was suboptimal. I sought advice from the then Chairman of the NHMRC of Australia, Professor Richard Larkins, later, the Vice-Chancellor of Monash University to revamp the NMRC of Singapore. Prior to this, I had nominated Professor Larkins to be one of the members of the Oxburgh Panel to review medical education for Singapore, and he was well-acquainted with the medical research scene in Singapore at that time.

Quite fortuitously, the Peter Wills Report on the NHMRC of Australia entitled *Virtuous Circle* had just been published. The report described the circular relationship between the three key components of biomedical research, namely science, industry and government. These three components complement and coerce each other. Singapore was strong in two of the three components in the circle, namely government support and industrial venture capitals, but was relatively weak in science. Australia, on the other hand, was strong in science but weak in industrial and governmental support. I presented my views for the revamp of the NMRC, adopting most of the arguments listed in the Peter Will's Report to enhance biomedical research in Singapore, at the first meeting of the Inter-Ministerial Executive Committee for Life Sciences, chaired by Dr Tony Tan, then the Deputy Prime Minister and now the President of Singapore. Until 2000, the Board of the NMRC of Singapore had focused only on the selection and funding of research projects but not the outcome of the funded projects. The funding process often lacked rigorous scientific scrutiny and the Research and Ethics Committees of the re-structured hospitals conducting clinical research were not robust. A new NMRC Board was appointed, consisting of scientists, clinicians, academics and industry representatives. Technical officers were sent to Canberra to study the operations of the Australian NHMRC. New computerized tracking of applications, selection, funding status and outcomes of all medical research grants was developed. The annual budget of the NMRC was increased from 40 to 45 million dollars. Greater accountability and outcome assessments of the awarded grants were achieved.

Soon after the restructuring of the NMRC, a meeting of the Chairmen of the National Science and Technology Board (NSTB), the Economic Development Board (EDB) and myself was organised. At this meeting I suggested the pooling of all the biomedical research funds of the three relevant ministries, namely Health, Education and Trade and Industry, into one to optimize biomedical research in Singapore. The discussion took place during a breakfast meeting at the Raffles Hotel and agreement for combining the resources of the three biomedical research organizations was obtained. The name Biomedical Research Council (BMRC) was coined at this meeting. BMRC would remain under the auspices of the Ministry of Trade and Industry that has the lion share of biomedical research funding. Soon after its formation, BMRC was renamed the Agency for Science Technology and Research (A*STAR), and this remains its name to this day. An international expert panel comprising some of the top scientists in the western world was also established to advise the Inter-Ministerial Executive Committee for Life Sciences that funds and oversees all biomedical and life sciences research in Singapore (Fig. 56).

'Mamas Always Come to Us'

Since 2000, biomedical research has grown from strength to strength and Singapore has become a major global life science research and investment hub for international players within a relatively short time. The Chairman of A*Star, was a very energetic and zealous leader. Prior to this role, he was Chairman of the Economic Development Board (EDB), the economic engine of Singapore. He was also the architect for the first three successful economic waves of Singapore, namely commerce, electronics and information technology. Realising the economic potential of the biosciences, the government had targeted bioscience as the fourth economic wave for Singapore and chose the same person to drive this latest venture under the auspices of the Ministry of Trade and Industry. Anyone who has worked with this dynamic Chairman will be

Fig. 56. Inter-ministerial executive advisory committee for life sciences, Singapore 2001.

familiar with his *allegro* working tempos and his *presto* decisions and actions. Under his leadership, the training of bright young Singaporean scientists was turbo-charged and boosted. The concept of a Biopolis, the geographic center for Singapore's bioscience industry, was conceived and it would be located in the precint of the existing National University of Singapore. This Biopolis is now fully functional and is one of the finest bioscience parks in Asia, attracting a large number of multi-national pharmaceutical and biomedical companies to base their Asian headquarters and research facilities there.

Cardiovascular research in Singapore was virtually non-existent when I arrived at the National Heart Centre of Singapore. With my Melbourne connection, a collaborative Memorandum of Understanding (MOU) with the Melbourne Baker Medical Research Institute, now renamed the Baker International Diabetic Institute (Baker IDI), was signed. A NMRC funded Baker IDI laboratory was soon established at the National Heart Centre and one of the Baker IDI senior scientists was appointed to supervise the local NMRC funded research projects there. A year later, a delegation from Baker IDI, led by the Institute's Chairman, was invited to visit Singapore. One of the highlights of the visit was to meet the legendary Chairman of A*Star at his office in the Raffles City Tower. He managed to keep the visitors waiting for more than half an hour. When he eventually turned up, the Chairman literally waltzed in and without greeting his guests, proceeded to draw on the white board in the meeting room, the 'life cycle of Bioscience', as he called it. Referring to multi-national pharmaceutical companies as big *Mamas*, he proudly proclaimed that big '*Mamas always come to us*'. I noticed the absence of doctors or clinicians in his 'Bioscience life-cycle' and interjected: '*With all due respect Sir, all Mamas eventually must come to, the doctors, to have their products tested clinically*'. Without clinical trials involving real patients, no products of biomedical research will ever come to the market. I was trying to highlight the fact that doctors are often forgotten in the medical research equation in Singapore. This is reflected in the relatively small research budget for NMRC from the Ministry of Health, compared to the disproportionally large research budget for A*Star from the Ministry of Trade and Industry. To be competitive in the global biomedical research sphere, Singapore needs to support the clinical component of bioscience research in a much more substantial way.

'S' Stands for Singapore

Many pharmaceutical and medical device companies came to the National Heart Centre for evaluation of their products. One day the President of Biosensor, a partly Singapore-owned device company, met with me and asked me to do a local clinical trial of a new balloon and stent that his new company had manufactured in California. The company was also hoping to gain financial assistance from the National

Science and Technology Board of Singapore (NSTB) in the form of a research grant. With part Singapore ownership, I was keen to help the company. However, after evaluating one of the company's newer products, an 'over-the-wire' balloon and the stent, I was unimpressed and told the president to modify his balloon catheter and manufacture a 'rapid exchange' system instead. Within six months, he returned with the new rapid exchange balloon and stent. This time his product gained my approval and I agreed to test the new stent at the National Heart Centre and also recommended the company for the research grant assistance from the NSTB. I suggested to the President of Biosensor Company that he should name the new stent, the 'S-stent'. I told him that 'S' stands for Singapore, and not the 'snake-like steerability of the new stent that he was trying to impress me with. I then went on to complete the Phase 2 clinical trial for the 'S-stent' at the National Heart Centre. The company later took off with the advent of a new drug-eluting stent and became one of the mainstream medical device companies in the world. This was one of the first success stories of Singapore's bioscience push, one that the National Heart Centre helped to launch, in the 'fourth wave' of Singapore's economic development.

Demise of the New National Heart Hospital

When I arrived in Singapore in 1997, the Singapore Heart Centre (SHC) was located at the Mistri Wing, a building located on the campus of SGH. The Mistri Wing used to house the pediatric services of the SGH. The SHC building has no inpatient beds and caters only for ambulatory patients. The 186 beds (140 cardiology and 46 cardiothoracic) of SHC were located in two wards in Block 7 of SGH. The third term of reference for my appointment as the Director of the Singapore Heart Centre was, to '*build for us (Singapore) a state-of-the-art new Heart Centre building*'. With initial full support of the first two Ministers for Health that I had worked with, the planning of a new world-class state-of-the-art heart hospital was in full swing. After repeated hard bargaining with the Ministry of Finance, a budget in excess of 180 million dollars was eventually approved for the planned new heart hospital.

The first site chosen for the new heart hospital was adjacent to the Emergency Department of the SGH, abutting Outram Road. A new heart hospital Building Committee was formed. An overseas study tour of some of the leading heart centres in Europe and the United States was undertaken. Various members of the planning committee for the 'state-of-the-art' heart hospital visited world-renowned heart hospitals in Leipzig, Munich, and Paris to see the latest developments in cardiac facilities in Europe. I also visited American centres in Washington and Boston on my own to try to incorporate American perspectives into the new heart hospital. The name of Singapore Heart Centre was changed to the National Heart Centre of Singapore to reflect its national character, with official government sanction. A new Board of the National Heart Centre was also created, initially chaired by the Director of Medical Services, Dr Chen Ai-jou.

However, two years into the planning of the new National Heart Centre, a new Minister for Health arrived on the scene. He was the third Minister for Health that I had to work with in my short five years at the National Heart Centre. The new Minister decided to split healthcare into two geographic clusters, one in the east with the SGH as the hub and one in the west with the National University Hospital or NUH as its hub. The national heart programme that I was asked to direct for Singapore was no longer relevant. A new Board for each cluster was appointed, each with its new CEO. The new Health Minister called six senior public hospital administrators, including myself, to nominate for the three top jobs, namely the Director of Medical Services and the two clusters' CEO positions. I declined to be one of the three nominees, and wanted instead to dedicate my total time and energy to the building of the new heart hospital and the reorganization of the NMRC. Overnight, all my superiors were changed and the carefully planned new heart hospital was being '*reviewed by the new health administration in light of the two health clusters*'! This review would lead to the abortion of the new heart hospital despite numerous public announcements confirming its construction and funding secured from the State Treasury and approved by the Cabinet.

The demise of the new heart hospital occurred in stages. The new CEO of SGH was previously the Director of the National Eye Centre, adjacent to the Heart Centre. He was a close colleague and good friend. Apart from his CEO role, he was also the Co-Chairman of the National Land and Development Board. Wearing the latter hat, he had plans to redevelop the Outram Road SGH campus site. With this redevelopment plan in mind, he initially asked me to move the planned new heart hospital to a new site adjacent to the Boyer block. Reluctantly I had to agree, because it was within his privilege to do so in his new role. I was, after all, only an imported 'foreign talent', trying to do a technical job for Singapore. Within a few months after the first suggested relocation of the planned new heart centre, he again asked me to consider moving it to yet another site, opposite the Cancer Centre. Again I had to agree.

With each proposed move of the new heart hospital site, I had to write to the Minister to seek his concurrence, without quoting the new CEO's requests. The Minister was understandably not impressed with all the changes in a short space of time. He called for an urgent meeting to announce his final decision with regards to the proposed new heart hospital site. At the meeting, he was obviously annoyed and opened the meeting with these words: '*My confidence with you lot is zero*', looking straight at me and making the zero sign with his thumb and index finger. '*Before I could even finish reading your first proposal, you came up with another. I want the new heart centre completed as soon as possible according to your original plan*'. At this point, the Permanent Secretary of Health, who knew well the background to these changes, winked and grinned at me. The Minister's decision was not what I expected but certainly what I wanted. I was quite pleased, in fact, with the 'zero confidence' the Minister had in me.

Not long after this meeting with the Minister, I was summoned out of the blue to the office of the CEO of SingHealth. The CEO, a person whom I had supported to get him to where he was, delivered to me the devastating news that there will be no new Heart Hospital. No reason was offered and I left his office dumb-founded. All the hard work and expenses, in excess of a million dollars, had gone down the drain. The widely publicised and cabinet approved world-class project that I came to implement for Singapore was abandoned with no clear reason. The 180 million dollars approved by the Finance Department for the project was eventually returned to State Treasury. Officers in the Finance Ministry later told me that this was unprecedented.

The Fateful Letter

I was bewildered at the sudden change of heart by the Ministry for Health in terms of national programs of health and the building of a world-class heart hospital for Singapore. I sought advice from Dr Charles Toh, the person who brought me to Singapore to direct the heart centre and the cardiac care programme for Singapore. He too was shocked by what happened and advised me to write a letter to SM Lee Kuan Yew, to seek his intervention. Dr Toh had a close professional relationship with then Chief Justice of Singapore, C J Yong Pang How. He suggested that I send a draft of the letter to the SM to CJ first for his approval before delivering the final version to the Senior Minister. I did exactly what Dr Toh suggested and the letter was delivered to the SM's office at the Istana, at the insistence of the Chief Justice. The letter listed the following four reasons why the planned new heart hospital should not be abandoned:

1. The standard of tertiary cardiac care will be compromised for current and future generations of Singaporeans.
2. The opportunity for Singapore to have a world-class stand-alone heart centre will be lost.

3. The morale of the NHC staff will be severely affected.
4. The reversal of this widely publicised project that might affect the welfare of the entire population is politically unwise.

Within two days, the SM replied, through his Principal Private Secretary, as follows:

Dear Prof. Lim,
Thank you for your letter… to Senior Minister Lee Kuan Yew. PS (Health) has informed me that the Ministry of Health has not changed its mind about building the new National Heart Centre. Rather, it cannot be built on its original site. It will have to be co-located with the redeveloped SGH, to improve accessibility and to optimize land use, freeing up land with a market value of $3 billion compared to the $1 billion required to redevelop the SGH. I understand that you will be meeting with the Minister of Health next week to discuss this matter. If you agree, I will send him the letter that you have sent to Senior Minister Lee, so that he can deal with the specific issues you have raised. I hope you will continue to contribute to the development of the new National Heart Centre. …
with best wishes.

My initial gut feeling was not to have my letter forwarded to the Minister of Health, knowing intuitively that he would not react kindly to the fact that I had written to the SM. The decision to write to the Senior Minister was not mine but that of my two advisors, both very senior and respected members of the Singaporean Government. I had telephoned the Chief Justice, firstly to inform him of the SM's reply and secondly to ask for his advice as to whether my letter should be forwarded to the Minister for Health. After hearing me out, the Chief Justice laughed light-heartedly and said: '*Don't worry, have the letter sent to the Health Minister, he will find out sooner or later*'. Deep inside I knew that this would be a mistake and I would not have done it myself. On the other hand, the advice of the Chief Justice is not something one should ignore. I then phoned the SM's Principal Secretary and agreed to have the letter forwarded to the Minister of Health. My fear for the worst was subsequently proven. The advice that I had received from the highest legal authority of the land did not help to resurrect the new heart hospital; instead my contract at the National Heart Centre was not renewed when it expired. With that all my other roles and potential contributions to Singapore also came to an end. I was however, offered any other role that I wished except that of the Director of the National Heart Centre. I politely declined this secondary offer citing that I was initially headhunted to Singapore to do just this specific job. When the SM found out that I was leaving Singapore to return to Australia, he sent me a personal email as follows:

> *I hope…you will find a more permanent perch which will keep you with one foot in Singapore, if not both feet. Your contributions to Melbourne and to the Australians can easily be made up. Your contribution to Singapore will be far greater and not just in cardiology. China will also be much closer for you to help … I hope you will find a way to keep a base in Singapore. I wish there was an institution that could give you a perch in Singapore.*

The SM's wish was realised to a small extent when I started the new Department of Cardiology at the new Raffles Hospital. This position allowed me to have what the SM later described as a 'toe-hold' in Singapore. Ten years after I left the National Heart Centre, a new National Heart Centre building was completed. It was not the world-class state-of-the-art heart hospital that I had been asked to build for Singapore 15 years before, but a revamped model of the existing ambulatory heart centre of SGH.

Without Brain or Heart

Simon Shorvon is a world-class neurologist, renowned for his research work in epilepsy. He was the Professor of Neurology at Queens Square,

University of London, when he was headhunted to direct the newly completed Neuroscience Institute in Singapore. With his Singaporean wife, he moved his world-class research to Singapore. As Chairman of the National Medical Research Council, I was one of the members of the selection committee responsible for his appointment and I was keen to make sure that his research needs at the Neuroscience Institute were met. In conjunction with the newly created Biomedical Research Council, he was awarded a large research grant to relocate some of his key London research team members to the new Neuroscience Institute. With this, he took up his appointment as the inaugural Director of the Neuroscience Institute. His arrival in the year 2000 was widely reported in the local media as a major coup for the fledgling bioscience industry in Singapore.

Being expatriates, Simon and I had much in common and we had plenty of work experiences in the new environment to share. He was promptly recruited to be a new member of the Advisory Committee for the National Medical Research Council. The Advisory Committee gained much from his extensive experience in research, especially in the assessment and award of research grants with our relatively small research budget.

During one of our regular lunch meetings, he appeared very agitated and told me about some new administrative changes that were occurring at the Neuroscience Institute. He was no longer the chief administrator even though he was the Director. Things got worse quickly and he was accused of conducting 'unethical research', which was hard to believe. A pre-requisite for the National Medical Research Council to award research grants was the approval of all research projects by the Research and Ethics Committee of the hospital where the research would be conducted. The combined Research and Ethics Committee of the Neuroscience Institute and Tan Tock Seng Hospital had earlier approved his clinical research project prior to commencing any human research. However, an internal hospital inquiry eventually found him guilty as charged and he was removed from his position as Director of the Neuroscience Institute. He had to accept the inquiry's findings before the report was released and left Singapore hurriedly after signing his acceptance of the report.

On his return to London, an independent inquiry conducted by the University of London found no basis of unethical research and he was exonerated and reinstated to his original post as Professor of Neurology at Queen Square, University of London. The General Medical Council (GMC) of the United Kingdom also conducted an inquiry of its own and again found Shorvon not guilty of the charges. The Singapore Medical Council however, made an appeal to the High Court of the United Kingdom. The Judge presiding over the case eventually dismissed the case and the matter was put to rest. Simon made an indirect reference to this unfortunate incident in an article published in the *Lancet* entitled 'The prosecution of research-experience from Singapore'. The aim of this article was to warn against the GMC's new ruling to abolish its own independent inquiries and to accept the rulings of malpractice established by foreign medical boards against British doctors, citing his own personal experience in Singapore. The SMC's rebuttal to this article was not published by the journal.

In our last luncheon together before his sudden departure from Singapore, when Simon found out that my departure from Singapore was also imminent, he lamented: *'Without brain or heart, what's left?'*

'Idealists Must Suffer'

The Lee Foundation is famous for its philanthropy. The Chairman of the Lee Foundation is Lee Seng Gee, son-in-law of the late Lee Kong Chian, a businessman who made his fortune as a rubber merchant. Lee Kong Chian was the Chancellor of the University of Singapore in his time. The Lee Foundation was well-known for its support of education, arts, music, sciences, and many other worthy social and charitable causes in Singapore, Malaysia, China and Indonesia. Lee Kong Chian's father-in-law, Tan Kah Kee, was the founder of Xiamen University, China. The Lee Foundation is still regularly financing and maintaining the Xiamen University today. The Chairman of the Lee Foundation in fact contributed to finance and created a Research and Education fund at the newly established Xiamen University Medical College to employ senior academic staff. The wish of Tan Kah Kee in 1921 to have a medical school at Xiamen University was not fulfilled until 1996, hence the generous support of the new medical school by the Lee Foundation.

When things were not working out the way they should for me at the National Heart Centre, I sought counselling from Mr Lee Seng Gee. In his wisdom, he told me that *'idealists must suffer'.* He told me that bad decisions could not be easily undone; there are many other interrelated factors. Instability would result if any of these factors were disturbed. I understood what he was trying to tell me and thanked him for his continuing support of the medical school in Xiamen. I left his office, high up on the 38th floor overlooking Singapore River and Boat Quay with a heavy heart. A poem entitled 'What the world needs' written by an unknown author came to mind:

>*The world needs men and women*
>*who cannot be bought*
>*whose word is their bond*
>*who put character above wealth;*
>*who possess opinions and a strong will*
>*who are larger than their vocations*
>*who do not hesitate to take risks*
>*who will not lose their individuality in a crowd;*
>*who will be as honest in small affairs as in greater*
>*who will make no compromise with wrong*
>*whose ambitions are not confined to their own selfish desires*
>*who will not say they do it 'because everybody else does it'*
>*who are true to their friends through good and bad,*
>*in adversity as well as in prosperity;*
>*who do not believe that shrewdness, cunning, and hard headedness are*
>   *the best qualities for winning success*
>*who are not ashamed or afraid to stand for the truth when it is unpopular*
>*who can say 'no' with emphasis, even though the rest of the world says 'yes'.*

'How is He?'

Without prior arrangement, the surgeon who operated on my late father during his last illness came to see me as an outpatient at the National Heart Centre. He was 78 years of age by then and had developed coronary artery disease. The table had been turned and he needed my medical expertise. When he walked into my consulting room, I greeted him in the usual way and said: '*We have met before.*' '*Oh, when?*' He was surprised. '*You operated on my father many years ago*', I replied. '*How is he?*', he asked casually. '*Unfortunately, he passed away many years ago*', I said sadly. '*I'm sorry to hear that*', he replied in his usual manner. The image of my father lying in a bed in ward 23 of SGH flashed vividly in my mind. The scene at that moment could have been taken straight out of a classic Chinese *kung-fu* book or movie. After a short hesitation, I asked the surgeon calmly, '*What can I do for you?*' and continued the consultation in my routine professional manner. At long last, I had the satisfaction of treating the doctor who operated on my father during his terminal illness. I was certain that my father would have been proud of me if he could have been in the outpatient clinic at that time.

In Singapore, it was customary for families to place memorial notices in the local newspaper to remember their loved ones. So on the 40th anniversary of my father's passing on the 25th of November 2005, my mother and all of us posted a notice in the Straits Times newspaper, with the heading: '*In memory of my husband, our father, grandfather, father-in-law and great-grandfather*'. Forty years ago the vow that I had made in Ward 23 of Boyer's Block was finally fulfilled. I had returned to SGH and I had trained better doctors at the National Heart Centre and elsewhere. My father had not died in vain.

'Where Exactly are We in Health?'

Soon after starting work at the SHC in 1997, I realized that B2 and C classes of subsidized public patients in Singapore have only a very limited range of drugs in the 'standard formulary' made available to them for chronic illnesses, such as hyperlipidemia, hypertension and diabetes mellitus. Unlike Australia where the Government through the Pharmaceutical Benefits Scheme (PBS) subsidizes all drugs, newer and more expensive drugs were not among the standard formulary in Singapore public hospitals. To me coming from Australia, it was also apparent that SM Lee's autobiography entitled '*From Third World to First*' is yet to be realised in healthcare in Singapore. After some hard negotiations, I managed to have at least one of each of the classes of the latest anti-hypertensive and lipid-lowering drugs added in the standard formulary list. I was impressed by the resolve and speed of the Ministry of Health leadership towards improving healthcare for its grassroots citizens, once sound evidence was presented. In both developed and developing countries, politicians are accused of not providing the right resources to health and education often because of the lack of communication between experts and responsible government officials. If dialogue between funder and funded can take place frequently and effectively, positive outcomes from these dialogues can be expected in most instances if the government has the interest of its citizens at heart.

I received a lunch invitation from the then Prime Minister (PM) Goh Chok Tong at the Istana just before leaving Singapore. Instead of a farewell luncheon, it turned out to be a private two-person luncheon. I guessed reports of my leaving the country must have filtered up to him and he wanted to find out first hand why when I have contributed so much and positively. He started with a question that I had anticipated. '*Professor, where exactly are we in health?*' Knowing that the occasion would be a once-in-a-life-time opportunity to speak to a nation's leader, I had rehearsed the answer many times before coming to the Istana. Prior to answering his important question, I requested permission to convey a sentiment of many grassroots Singaporean patients. He agreed and I remarked, '*Sir, patients in the restructured hospitals hold the view that "A xai xi, boay xai pi"!* Translated, this sentiment in the local Hokkien dialect means '*one can afford to die but cannot afford to be sick' (in Singapore)!* It highlighted the unaffordability and accessibility issues of healthcare in Singapore, even in the restructured public hospitals at that time. The PM acknowledged with a nod. I then went on to answer his question by pointing out the gaps in healthcare delivery standards between Singapore and Australia in five main areas:

1. Lack of a comprehensive pharmaceutical benefits scheme to ensure the availability of all therapeutic drugs to needy patients. This is further compounded by the common practice in most eastern countries where the prescribers are also the dispensers of the drugs in Singapore, and Asia in general. Such conflict of interest is not allowed in the West in general.
2. The lack of a comprehensive private health insurance system.
3. Service excellence takes precedence over academic and research excellence in most eastern countries, including Singapore.
4. Nursing, technological and paramedical training is not at a tertiary or equivalent professional level compared to that in the West.
5. Healthcare operations are more centrally controlled and less autonomous compared to the West.

The discussion was refreshing to the PM and the issue of my imminent departure from Singapore was never raised. The PM thanked me for my candid opinion and walked me to the car. I too thanked him for his kind gesture and the unique private session before leaving the Istana with a sense of mission accomplished (Fig. 57).

A New NAFA

Nanyang Academy of Fine Art, known locally as NAFA, was the first tertiary fine art academy in Singapore. Lim Hak Tai, an eminent Chinese artist who had immigrated to Singapore from Xiamen, China, founded it in 1938. He was a close friend of my maternal grandfather Lau Teck Jin, one of a handful of English speaking youth in Xiamen in

Fig. 57. Luncheon meeting with PM Goh Cheok Tong at the Istana 2002.

1930. My mother's family migrated from Xiamen to Singapore around the same time as Lim Hak Tai. My connection with NAFA started in 1959 when the school was located at St. Thomas' Walk, off River Valley Road in Singapore. As mentioned previously, my mother managed to persuade Lim Hak Tai, the principal of NAFA, to enrol me as a regular student of NAFA when I was 11 years old and I graduated in 1961 at the age of 13.

On my return to Singapore in 1998, I received an invitation to the 60th anniversary celebration dinner of NAFA, not as an alumnus but in my capacity as Director of the National Heart Centre. When I arrived at the dinner party and told the Principal that I was an alumnus, he was astonished. Soon after the 60th anniversary celebration, when he confirmed that my name was indeed present in the graduate class of 1961, he invited me to become a member of the Board of NAFA. I subsequently became the Chairman of the Board and the Building Committee that oversaw the building of the new NAFA campus in Bencoolen Street (Fig. 58).

Fig. 58. NAFA Graduation Ceremony 2002 (from left: Minister Ng Eng Hean, Principal Ho KL, Fu CA, clerk, YL).

NAFA in 1998 was a different school to the one I knew when I graduated in 1961. Over the years and successive administrative changes, NAFA had transformed from its original school of fine art into a tertiary centre for learning for all forms of arts, including fashion and graphic design and multi-media art as well as a music school for young talented musicians. As one of Asia's four economic 'dragons' in the late 1990s, the Singapore Government wanted also to transform the island state into a commercial, technological and cultural hub. To this end the government had decided to invest in and promote the arts. The Ministry of Education had earlier approved a budget of 70 million to the relocation and reconstruction of NAFA at a new site in Bencoolen Street, close to the Museum of Fine Art. The new school would consist of three separate buildings, one each for the Schools of Fine Art, Music and Fashion. The celebrated Singaporean architect Liu Tai-ge was commissioned to design the three buildings and a Japanese firm won the tender to be the construction company for the major project. I chaired the Building Committee to oversee the construction of the three buildings. Regrettably, I was not invited to the official opening of the new NAFA campus when it was completed in 2004, a year after I left Singapore.

Together with the construction of the new physical building for NAFA, and Chairmanship of the Board of Directors, I was also given the unenviable task by the Ministry of Education to overhaul its academic and administrative structure. Two appointed officers of the Ministry of Education worked closely with me to give NAFA not only new premises but also a new leadership team. Before this monumental task could be finished, I had to return to Australia. A new Principal and Board Chairman were duly appointed to complete the intended changes. Despite my premature departure that prevented the completion of the task assigned, I had the satisfaction of serving my alma mater and had played a significant role in its modernization. At the valedictory dinner specifically requested by the then Minister for Education, he publicly acknowledged the major contributions that I had made to the making of a new NAFA.

Professor and the Beauty

I would like to finish this chapter of my time in Singapore with a light-hearted and amusing incident. With my wife back in Melbourne, a cardiac surgical colleague had invited me to dinner one Sunday evening. Shortly after arriving at the restaurant, a Chinese lady and her European companion arrived. With total confidence and vitality, the young lady greeted me with an outreached hand and said, '*I am Michelle Yeoh*'. I shook her hand and replied politely: '*I am Lim Yean Leng*'. She appeared startled and quickly followed: '*My uncle is Yeoh Ghim Seng*'. The name was unfamiliar to me and I responded with slight embarrassment: '*I am very sorry, I have just arrived in Singapore from Melbourne and don't know too many people here*'. She looked disappointed and asked no more questions. The other guests then arrived and we were ushered to our table. By sheer chance, she was seated next to me. No sooner had we sat down, a waitress came up to the table with a large guest book and asked for her autograph. I was intrigued and said to the waitress with my usual Aussie sense of humor, '*Do you ask all of your guests to sign autographs?*' My cardiologist colleague and friend Professor Chia Boon Lok interjected before the waitress could reply, '*Only pretty ones, Yean Leng*'. The waitress secured the young lady's autograph and left highly excited. Out of courtesy, I decided to start a conversation with my neighbor: '*Where do you live?*', I asked Michelle. '*Sometimes Hong Kong, sometimes Los Angeles, sometimes Ipoh,*' she replied. I surmised that she might be a wealthy executive-type globetrotter. '*What do you do, Michelle?*', I continued with our small talk. '*I make films*', she replied without hesitation. Being a photographer, I automatically interpreted her 'films' to be photographic films or negatives and quickly summed her up as a CEO of a film company such as Kodak or Fuji. By this time, Professor Chia who had been eavesdropping could stand it no longer and yelled at me: '*Yean Leng, don't be silly, Michelle is the Bond girl!*' With the not-so-subtle prompt, I was jolted to remember the latest James Bond movie filmed at the twin towers in Kuala Lumpur in which an Asian girl instead of a blond partnered the hero. With great excitement I exclaimed, '*that's right, Michelle, I saw your movie but only half of it! I saw the part from when you were chained to James Bond on the motorbike*'. Indeed I saw the movie on an older model SIA inflight entertainment programme when one could not manually watch any movie from the beginning. Michelle did not appear amused and did not bother to answer. '*When you karate chopped the villains, was it real or stunt?*', I tried desperately to carry on the conversation. '*I am a black belt karate*', she replied impatiently. With that answer, I shifted my seat a fraction away from her. To my surprise, she then volunteered, '*I am making my next movie with Jackie Chan*'. '*Who's she?*', I asked. '*Jackie Chan is a he not a she!*', she replied in exasperation. '*A male with the name Jackie?*' I continued in my ignorance. With that remark, she gave me her first smile for the whole evening.

I gathered she no longer felt insulted when she realised I did not know who Jackie Chan was either! At the end of the dinner, Michelle was so entertained by my ignorance of her that she autographed the menu on the table for me alone, to the envy and annoyance of all the other male guests around the table. On it she wrote. *'To Professor Lim, with love'*, and signed Michelle Yeoh, in both Chinese and English! With the unexpected honour, she said to me: *'All night I have been trying to figure out whether you were pretending or genuine and concluded that you haven't the foggiest idea who I am!'* I guessed it was rare and refreshing for her to find someone who genuinely did not know who she was. Most people queue for hours to catch a glimpse of her and there I was, sitting next to her and asking her what she does for living!

My wife would call me daily if we were not together to find out whether I was alright. This night was no exception and she called as usual, after dinner. Before she could say anything, I started the conversation, *'Guess who I had dinner with tonight?'* She could not guess. *'Michelle Yeoh'*, I said. There was a short pause and I heard her yelling excitedly to my 21-year-old son who must have been sitting across the room: *'Dad had dinner with Michelle Yeoh tonight!'* *'Did he get an autograph?'*, I heard my son asked loudly. *'Tell him not to worry, I've got one'*, I said to the boy's mother with some satisfaction. Looks like I was the only one in the family who had not heard of Michelle Yeoh. The following Chinese New Year, I was pleasantly surprised to receive a personal greeting card from Michelle Yeoh. I was impressed that she still remembered me. Since then, I have made a special effort to see all of Michelle Yeoh's movies, including her Oscar winning film, *Crouching Tiger, hidden Dragon*. I was moved to tears with her performance of Aung San Suu Kyi in *The Lady*.

When I narrated this story to my old school classmate, who at that time was the chief editor of the local Chinese newspaper *Lianhe Zhaobao*, he published this amusing story with the title 'Professor and the Beauty' in his daily column. In the article he said: *'It is understable that Michelle Yeoh knows not of Lim Yean Leng. It's equally understable that Lim Yean Leng knows not of Michelle Yeoh'*.

7

Asia Pacific — The Third Block

Live Demonstration Courses in Interventional Cardiology

Andreas Gruentzig, who performed the first percutaneous transluminal coronary angioplasty (PTCA) in man, was an enthusiastic teacher. He was keen to disseminate the technique involved in this very important life-saving operation to others. He initiated live demonstration courses, known as 'live demos' in the trade, to teach and disseminate PTCA technique. The first such course was conducted at the auditorium of the University Hospital in Zurich in 1978. During these live demos, Dr Gruentzig would perform the procedure in the catheter laboratory of the University Hospital and the entire procedure would be transmitted live to an audience in the remote auditorium. PTCA is a minimally invasive procedure to clear a blocked coronary artery in the heart of a patient using a very small balloon catheter introduced from the patient's femoral artery in the leg under local anesthesia. During the live demo, Dr Gruentzig would first outline the patient's clinical problem; then explain the strategy of his treatment and the technical details of the procedure. The operation would then be broadcasted live in real-time. Being a delicate heart operation, unexpected complications could occur and the operator-teacher would then demonstrate to the audience how the unexpected complications were actually handled. As one would expect, in a heart operation the atmosphere was usually highly charged for the operator and the audience, not to mention the risk involved for the patient. At the end of such a live demonstration course, the attendees, who are often very senior and experienced cardiologists themselves, would learn the technique and return to their individual hospitals and perform the PTCA procedure themselves on their patients. The learning curve is steep for the first 50 or so procedures for any new operators. Once proficient and experienced, the senior operators would then conduct their own live demo courses and the technique would thus be disseminated.

Percutaneous Coronary Intervention, or PCI as it is commonly referred to today, is a much less traumatic operation than an open-heart bypass graft operation. PCI has helped millions of patients and is an alternative to open-heart surgery when revascularization therapy for their coronary artery disease is required. Because of the prevalence of atherosclerotic coronary heart disease, PCI has become the most common medical procedure performed in the world today. These live demos in PCI remain a unique method of procedural training in cardiology as no other medical disciplines have adopted this mode of real-time live demonstration to teach new and complex operations. Today, a multitude of interventional cardiologists criss-cross the world at regular intervals to attend live demo courses and to learn the latest technology. Over a period of three decades, a whole new industry of live demo courses has developed with significant implications to healthcare costs worldwide.

Andreas Gruentzig Society 30th Anniversary Celebration

I was privileged to participate in the 30th anniversary celebration meeting of the International Andreas Gruentzig Society in Zurich, 2007, commemorating the performance of the first percutaneous balloon coronary angioplasty (PTCA) in man in 1977. The meeting was held in the same auditorium at the University in Zurich where the first live demonstration course was conducted with Andreas Gruentzig as the Course Director. Many of those who were present at the first course also attended the 30th anniversary meeting. Some of the attendees at the first meeting had passed on, including Gruentzig himself. There was much nostalgia and I was glad to be present on that historic occasion (Fig. 59).

During that meeting, I had the privilege to meet Gruentzig's wife Michaela and daughter Sonja as well as the first man who received PTCA therapy, Mr Dolf Bachmann and his wife (Fig. 60). Dolf Bachmann had a simple obstruction at the beginning portion of his left anterior descending artery, commonly referred to as the 'widow-making' artery. He was determined not to have the open-heart bypass graft surgery. At that time, Andreas Gruentzig had only performed the PTCA procedure successfully in five dogs. Somehow, in his unique flamboyant

Fig. 59. 30th anniversary of first PTCA in man performed by A. Gruentzig on 16 September 1977. University Hospital lecture theatre, Zurich 2007.

Fig. 60. With Dolf Bachmann, the first man to receive PTCA treatment (left: YL, Dolf & Mrs Bachmann).

style, Gruentzig managed to convince the courageous patient to have the PTCA procedure on the 16th of September 1977, using a balloon catheter that he had manufactured in his kitchen. History was created when the procedure was successfully completed after three hours. The patient is alive and well today but sadly the doctor died in a plane crash in 1985.

The history of modern cardiology leading up to the performance of the first coronary angioplasty was detailed in a book entitled *Journey into the Heart* by David Monagan. Andreas Gruentzig's eventual coronary angioplasty would not be possible without the pioneering efforts of Werner Forssmann, Mason Sones and Charles Dotter. I was privileged to have met Gruentzig personally on two separate occasions when he visited Melbourne and Perth before his untimely death in 1985 at the age of 46.

Gruentzig's pioneering balloon angioplasty treatment of coronary atherosclerosis has saved many lives. Today, with refinement, patients whose lives are being threatened by sudden heart attacks are the real beneficiaries of this technique. The technique has also revolutionized cardiology and changed the lives of many patients as well as doctors. PTCA has defined my medical career and I am a beneficiary of this technology both as a patient and a doctor. I had the privilege to teach this technique to other doctors in Australia, Singapore and China. In China, my initial training programme was focused on the transfer of technical skills of angioplasty to the local practitioners. Today, thirty years later, the Chinese doctors are more skillful than the western doctors in the technical aspects of coronary angioplasty because of the necessity to treat large numbers of patients there. Due to the lack of alternative bypass graft surgery in many hospitals in China, more patients with complex diseases normally requiring surgical revascularization are being treated successfully by PCI.

Although technically competent, many doctors in China are lacking in clinical training to appropriately select their patients for myocardial revascularization therapy. Everywhere I go to teach in China today, I emphasize the clinical reasons of why and when PCI is necessary rather than the technical aspects of how the procedure is to be performed. I have said right from the start that there are two questions a doctor must answer before performing coronary angioplasty on a patient. Firstly, he must be able to tell the patient why the percutaneous coronary intervention is necessary and the current evidence that the procedure will improve his or her survival and or quality of life. Secondly, whether the doctor must be able to assess accurately the technical risk and probability of success of the angioplasty procedure. If the doctor cannot adequately answer the first question, he *must not* perform the treatment on the patient. If he is unable to answer the second question, he *cannot perform the* angioplasty successfully. In short, coronary angioplasty must be performed to *treat patients, not just lesions* and the principle of *first, do no harm* must always prevail.

Singapore Live Course in Endovascular Therapy (SingLIVE)

Soon after the first PTCA was successfully performed in man in Europe in 1977, Dr M. Nobuyoshi of Japan performed the first PTCA in Asia, in 1981. He also started the first live demo PTCA Course in Asia, known as the 'Kokoura Live Course' in Fukuoka, Japan. The Singapore Heart Centre Live Demonstration Course followed in 1991, directed by Dr Arthur Tan, the first Director of the Singapore Heart Centre. It had been running for six consecutive years when I took over from Dr Tan in 1997. It was a very popular course for cardiologists in South-East Asia. In 1998, the Singapore live demonstration course was given a new name, 'SingLive', an eponym derived from '**S**ingapore **L**ive Demonstration of **V**ascular Endo-therapy' (SingLIVE), coined by Dr Mak Koon Hou at the Singapore Heart Centre. The logo of SingLive was the English word *LIVE* written in traditional Chinese calligraphy by myself (Fig. 61).

Singapore is the geographic center of South East Asia as well as the entire Asia Pacific region. SingLive could therefore be a forum to launch interventional cardiology in this vast region. In trade and commerce,

Fig. 61. Calligraphic logo of the 'Singapore Live Intervention in Vascular Endotherapy', now part of EuroPCR-SingLIVE.

Singapore has traditionally been the gateway between Asia, Europe and America. In the same way SingLive could one day become the key meeting for transfer and exchange of knowledge and skill in percutaneous vascular intervention between the East and the West. This was my vision for SingLive. The meeting could be a platform to launch promising Asian interventional cardiologists onto the world stage. Singapore will then become the focus of the third or Asia-Pacific block of endovascular therapy in the world. This 'Third Block', as I called it in an editorial article in 2000, will follow the other two already well-established blocks of endovascular intervention therapy in North America and Europe. To achieve this goal, the National Heart Centre of Singapore offered to be the headquarters of the Asia Pacific Society of Cardiology (APSIC) and I was elected its Permanent Secretary.

The building of the Third Block in the global interventional community started inconspicuously at the international forum, the SingLive of National Heart Centre. Indeed within a short space of five years, a network was established between budding interventional cardiologists in the developing nations in the Asia Pacific regions and the more mature professional colleagues of the western developed nations. Key contributors from the prestigious Trans-Catheter-Therapeutics (TCT) in Washington, USA and the Europe Paris Course in Revascularization (EuroPCR) in Europe were invited to attend SingLIVE regularly to lecture and demonstrate the latest technologies and disseminate their knowledge. Australia, Japan and South Korea were more advanced than other countries in the Asia Pacific region in vascular intervention in the late nineties. After the success of SingLive, many other live demo courses were started in Asia, notably in China, Malaysia, India, Taiwan, Thailand, Hong Kong, and Vietnam. With much larger patient pools, the technical skills of the Asia Pacific operators, especially in the performance of complex angioplasties, developed quickly and were soon recognised and acknowledged by their western counterparts. Bilateral exchange of skills and knowledge quickly followed.

Each year six interventional live demo courses in the region were officially sponsored by APSIC. They included the Angioplasty Summit, now called TCT-Asia Pacific, in Seoul, the Complex Catheterization Therapeutics (CCT) course in Kobe, the China Interventional Therapeutics (CIT), now called CIT-TCT, course in Beijing and the SingLive course (now PCR-SingLive) in Singapore.

Twenty years after its inception, the role played by APSIC in global percutaneous vascular intervention has matured significantly. To have reached this point, the support it has received and is still receiving from many western nations must be fully acknowledged and sincere gratitude be expressed. The contributions by APSIC's member nations towards global vascular intervention is growing rapidly and the vision of the Asia Pacific 'Third Block' of global intervention has been realised.

Asia Pacific Society of Interventional Cardiology (APSIC)

The Asia Pacific countries together have more than half the world's population, yet the volume of PCI procedures in this entire region is less than half that of the USA alone. With the rapid economic growth and improvement in healthcare seen in many of the developing Asia Pacific nations, PCI and other vascular intervention treatment procedures are growing rapidly and will soon catch up with the western developed nations. This is especially true for China, India, Thailand, Malaysia, Indonesia, Pakistan, Myanmar, Bangladesh, Sri Lanka and Nepal. In other Asia Pacific countries such as South Korea, Japan, Australia, New Zealand, Taiwan and Singapore, the growth of PCI and other vascular interventions has more or less reached a steady state.

The Asia Pacific Society of Interventional Cardiology or APSIC was conceived at a meeting in Sydney in 1992. It was formally established in Singapore in 1993 by a group of like-minded interventional cardiologists with the objective of *'promoting interventional cardiology, especially in the field of coronary intervention, in the Asia Pacific area'*.

Peripheral vascular intervention was still embryonic at that stage; hence the name of the Society was restricted to *Cardiology* when it was first formed. Peripheral and structural cardiac intervention is now an integral part of the Society but the name change of the Society is yet to be made. APSIC was first constituted with 14 member nations in 1998. This has now increased to 20. The member nations and regions include Australia, Bangladesh, Cambodia, China, Hong Kong, India, Indonesia, Japan, South Korea, Malaysia, Myanmar, Nepal, New Zealand, Pakistan, Philippines, Singapore, Sri Lanka, Taiwan, Thailand and Vietnam. Membership of the Society is targeted at physicians who are '*active practitioners of cardiac catheterization and angiography, coronary and peripheral vascular intervention who have interest in devoting themselves to the development and promotion of interventional cardiology in the Asia Pacific region*'. An Advisory Board with national and regional representatives from all the participating nations governs the Society. Every two years, one member country will be elected to represent the Society as the President Nation, from which the President and Secretary General of the Society are nominated. The President and Secretary General are supported by a Permanent Secretariat, initially based in Singapore and later moved to its current permanent office in Hong Kong. The APSIC constitution was drafted and approved by the Advisory Board during Japan's presidency in 1998.

The development of PCI and other endovascular therapy was inhomogeneous within the various countries of APSIC at this stage. To make them more even, nations that are more advanced scientifically and technically should help and support those that are just starting to develop this technology. This has been the goal of the Society. At its inception, it was decided that the leadership of the Society was to rotate through six nations, namely Singapore, India, Japan, Australia, New Zealand, Malaysia, each for a two-year period. Diplomas of Full and Associate Fellowship, Membership and Emeritus Fellowship of the Asia Pacific Society of Cardiology (FPSIC) were awarded for the first time in 2006. The inaugural Fellowship Convocation ceremony was held during the APSIC sponsored 2nd Asian Interventional Cardiovascular Therapeutics (AICT) meeting in New Delhi. Merger of the Boards of APSIC and AICT took place this year in 2013 and the 9th Asia Interventional Cardiovascular Therapeutics (AICT) in Bangkok became the first official scientific meeting of APSIC. Convocations of Fellowships have been held in Malaysia, South Korea, Japan, China and Thailand in conjunction with the scientific meeting hosted by the Presidency Nation of APSIC of that year. Another milestone of the Society occurred when the scientific journal of the American Society of Catheterization Angiography and Intervention (SCAI), *Catherization and Cardiovascular Intervention* (*CCI*) was adopted to be the official journal of APSIC. Most reputable international endovascular interventional meetings such as EuroPCR, TCT, ACC and the South American cardiac societies have APSIC partnership. The society has come a long way and the future is bright indeed.

Two Philosophies of APSIC Governance

Compared to the more advanced European and American interventional cardiology blocks, the standard and development of interventional cardiology among the membership countries of the APSIC block is more uneven. Two distinct and different philosophies of governance of APSIC could be adopted. The first is an inclusive philosophy that supports the idea of the 'strong helping the weak'. This was the hope of the founding members of the Society. With this approach, the more advanced members of the society would nurture the less advanced countries and every membership nation would have an equal chance of representing the Society at a global forum. The alternative philosophy supported the notion that only the scientifically advanced nations would represent the Society. The more scientifically advanced nations were Australia, New Zealand, Japan and South Korea in the early phase of the Society. There were pros and cons for the two philosophies. The first supports egalitarianism whilst the second would better represent the Society at global intervention forums. As Permanent Secretary of the Society in its first decade, I had always supported the first philosophy of governance for APSIC.

In the second decade of the society, the Presidency nation chose to adopt the second approach of governance to advance the scientific credibility of APSIC. This represented the second phase of the Society. With the merger of the Society and AICT, a third phase of the Society may be starting and no doubt the Society will grow from strength to strength in time.

China's Role in the Third Block

Percutaneous Transluminal Coronary Angioplasty (PTCA) was embryonic in China in the early 1980s. I have adopted the Pyramid of Excellence model in the planning of my training programme for cardiologists in China from the beginning. At the base of the knowledge and skill transfer phase, I chose hospitals that could potentially be developed into geographic training centers in China to do my training work. Potential leaders were also selected from these centers to train with me overseas. Most of my work in China was a solo effort and required significant personal sacrifice and perseverance over nearly three decades. As described earlier, the training programme that I have planned for my work in China was inspired by two Chinese fables, 'the removal of a mountain by the foolish old man' and the 'train the trainer' approach.

Professor Chen Hou-zu of Shanghai performed the first coronary angiography in China. A few years later, Dr Djeng Siew-lian in Suzhou successfully completed the first PTCA in 1984, with the assistance of a foreign doctor. Soon after that many foreign experts, including myself, were invited to perform and teach coronary angiography and angioplasty in the more advanced hospitals in major cities. These included the Fu Wai Hospital in Beijing, Xijing Hospital in Xian and the Fok Yin Dong Cardiovascular Institute in Guangzhou. I performed my first balloon coronary angioplasties in China in 1986 with Professor Chen

Jin-ju at the Zhejiang First Affiliated Hospital and then with Professor Jin Fan at the People's Provincial Hospital in Hangzhou. Coronary stenting was first performed in man by Ulrich Sigwart in the United Kingdom in 1987 and quickly became the standard method of percutaneous coronary intervention (PCI) in the late 1990s. In 1992, together with Drs Stephen Lee of Hong Kong and Professor Chen Chuan-rong of Guangzhou, coronary stenting using the self-crimping Palmar-Shatz stents was introduced at the Fok Yin Dong Cardiovascular Institute in Guangzhou. Dr Antonio Colombo of Milan, Italy was the world pioneer in coronary stenting at that time. I invited him to demonstrate coronary stenting at the Chaoyang Hospital in Beijing in 1998 (Fig. 62).

In 1995, the number of PCIs performed in China began to increase after the return of some of the young doctors who were trained overseas, mainly in Singapore, Japan, USA, Australia, Paris, Germany and India. They in turn train others and most of the interventional cardiologists in China are locally trained. There is now a formal training

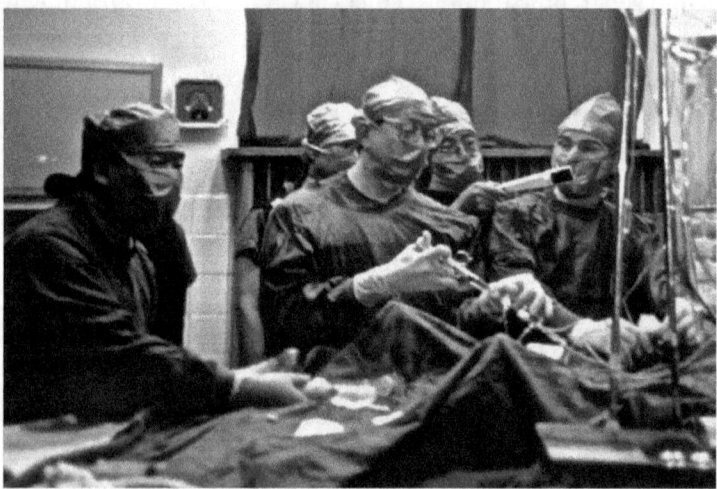

Fig. 62. Live demonstration of coronary stenting by Dr A. Colombo at the Chaoyang Hospital, Beijing 1998.

programme as well as official accreditation and credentialing processes approved by the central government for hospitals providing PCI services in China. A central web-based database at the Health Ministry in Beijing is also established to capture all PCI procedures performed throughout China. The knowledge transfer part of the pyramid of PCI excellence has already achieved much in the short space of two decades.

Coronary Intervention Salons of China (CISC)

Traditionally and culturally, Chinese doctors tend to work in isolation. Interventional cardiology meetings have become a useful and popular academic forum for cardiologists in China to learn from each other. Live demonstration courses in PCI have mushroomed all over China in the past two decades. At last count, there are more than 300 large and small PCI 'live demo' courses in China each year. Historically, the Great Wall Interventional Cardiology Conference (GWICC) was the first live demonstration course in cardiovascular intervention in China. It was started by Hu Dayi, an American trained electro-physiologist, at the Liang Ma Hotel in the Chaoyang District of Beijing in 1991. The GWICC is now a general cardiology meeting and renamed the Great Wall Congress of Cardiology (GWCC) after its partnership with the American College of Cardiology (ACC). GWCC also incorporates live demonstration of PCI and other novel cardiovascular interventions in its scientific programme. Western, Eastern and Southern branches of GWCC have also been established in major cities in the corresponding parts of China. Other large regional cardiovascular symposia and live courses include the China Interventional Cardiology Salon (CICS), the International Heart Forum (IHF) of Fu Wai Hospital, the China Cardiovascular Interventional Forum (CCIF), the Oriental Congress of Cardiology (OCC), the annual Lingnan Congress of Cardiology in Guangzhou, the Northern interventional live course in Shenyang and Harbin, the Southwest China Cardiovascular Symposium and the Qianjiang Interventional Cardiovascular Congress (QICC) in

Hangzhou. The proliferation of all these endovascular therapeutic meetings has promoted the introduction of important live-saving procedures to the multitude of heart disease patients all over China, including those in remote cities and rural areas.

By 2004, there were more than 500 well-qualified local Chinese interventional cardiologists. Under the leadership of Professor Lu Shu-jen of the Anzhen Hospital in Beijing, an all-Chinese society for interventional cardiologists named the Coronary Intervention Salon of China or CISC was formed. To become a member of this salon, the entry criteria were Chinese nationality and primary PCI operator experience of at least 50 cases per annum. The Salon held annual national scientific meetings in various cities in China. The first Salon was held in Huangshan city, gateway to the famous scenic Yellow Mountain or Huangshan. As an exception, I was granted honorary membership at the second meeting. However, I was treated as a foreigner and it took another three years before I was granted 'ordinary' local membership. The first year, my name was the only one listed in English in the membership list. The following year, my name appeared in Chinese but with Australia in brackets behind my Chinese name. It was only at the fourth Salon meeting that my name appeared no differently to all the other local Chinese members. I was invited to deliver a short speech at the opening ceremony at that meeting in which I highlighted the following:

> It's a rare honour and privilege to be allowed membership to this prestigious and exclusive Salon and to take part in its fourth annual scientific meeting. Being an overseas Chinese, my wish that one-day, I would be accepted as a 'fair dinkum' Chinese has been realised! I thank the Organizing Committee for this rare honour. The name 'Salon' chosen for this society intrigued me, for it was a name used by like-minded artists in France to form a group to advance their art. Here, the interventional cardiologists in China have decided to use 'Salon' to name their scientific organization. I take it as your desire to combine science and

the humanities in interventional cardiology, a wish very dear to my heart. Perhaps this will distinguish Chinese interventional cardiologists from others. The Chairman of the Salon, Prof. Ruilin Gao, has also highlighted the features of this scientific meeting, namely 'to demonstrate evidence-based medicine using cases that have been performed to further enhance excellence in interventional cardiology in China'. A revered pioneer, Prof. Zhu Guoying, also alluded to the huge responsibility facing Chinese interventional cardiologists today. She believes that China will lead the world in interventional cardiology in future, a vision I share wholeheartedly. Professors Cia Guoliang and Shen Weifeng, the other notable pioneers of coronary angioplasty in China, also reminded us that technical perfection must not be the goal of coronary intervention. We must be patient-oriented and the safety, comfort and cure of our patients should be the ultimate criteria of success. A really good medical therapy must be both successful and affordable to all patients and not only to the privileged few. I was greatly encouraged to read the comments of our young colleague Dr Liu Jian, who reminded us all that 'we should treat patients and not lesions ... We are doctors, not technicians, artists not artisans', quoting directly from my lecture on 'How to be a Good Doctor and Interventionist'.

China Interventional Therapeutics (CIT)

Currently in China, a total in excess of 400,000 coronary angioplasty procedures per annum are performed. The number is increasing at a rapid rate. If China were to have the same rate of PCI per population as America, then nearly 4 million PCIs procedures each year would need to be done. At present the low rate of PCI performed in China is due to the lack of adequate technical expertise and facilities in many parts of China and the high costs for the procedure. China and many other developing nations in Asia have a long way to go to catch up with the PCI standard of the western developed nations.

China is the largest nation in the Asia Pacific region and it is conceivable that it will become the leader of the Third Block of global cardiovascular intervention communities. China will need to evolve a high caliber scientific meeting for the Third Block similar to TCT and EuroPCR in the American and European blocks respectively. With SingLive as the platform, global experts from the West and budding Asian interventional cardiologists were brought together. With some political maneuvering on my part as Permanent Secretary, China not only was admitted to membership of APSIC, but the existing membership of Taiwan was also preserved. China quickly became the Presidency nation of APSIC and Ruilin Gao and Weifeng Shen were elected President and Secretary General of APSIC respectively for the two year term commencing 2001. During this period, the idea for China to evolve a large meeting to showcase endovascular intervention in the Asia Pacific Third Block was conceived. The idea received the full support of the President, Professor Ruilin Gao. I suggested the name of CIT (*China Interventional Therapeutics*) for this large meeting in the third or eastern block, to match that of TCT and PCR in the other two western blocks of endovascular intervention. The name was agreed to by Professor Ruilin Gao and supported by Mr Teddy Chien, Chairman of Neich Medical Company who had kindly donated an office in his company building in Hong Kong to be the new headquarters and provided a full-time secretariat for APSIC. Professor Gao would direct CIT and the Fu Wai Hospital would be CIT's base hospital. It was designed for CIT to replace the existing annual scientific meeting of Fu Wai Hospital but this did not eventuate. The inaugural CIT meeting was successfully held in Beijing in 2003. With the connection of FU Wai Hospital and Professor Gao, the faculty dinner of the first CIT meeting was held at *Diao Yu Tai* or The Fishing Pavilion, a state function venue reserved normally for elite Chinese governmental officials only. After dinner, an *impromptu* concert was organized with a musical item from members of each country present. I put together an international choir and sang the hymn, '*Amazing Grace*' that most western foreigner guests

Fig. 63. Gala dinner of the First CIT at *Diao Yu Tai*, Beijing 2003.

are familiar with. The choir performed superbly without rehearsal to the delight of all present. That could very well be the first time that a hymn was sung in *Diao Yu Tai* (Fig. 63).

After a decade, CIT has indeed become the largest and most important live demonstration course in cardiovascular intervention not only in China but the whole Asia Pacific region. It is now held in partnership with TCT and the meeting will be in Shanghai for the first time in 2014. Professor Ruilin Gao was awarded the Ethica Award at the 2011 EuroPCR Course in Paris; this annual award serves to recognise an individual who has made an outstanding contribution to endovascular intervention in general. Following Ruilin Gao at APSIC, Junbo Ge of Shanghai was elected President of APSIC in 2011, succeeding Dr S. Saito of Japan. It is the second time around that China has led the Third Block of global endovascular intervention. China has no doubt reached the pinnacle of the Pyramid of PCI Excellence.

The modern 'Marco Polo' of interventional cardiology has emerged, this time travelling in reverse direction, from the East to the West. The traffic of scientific communication between the East and the West has become bilateral, no longer one way from the West to the East.

East West PCI — from 'Cross-Fire' to 'Co-Evolution'

The wish for China to represent the Asia Pacific block in PCI was realised when China was invited to transmit live cases from the Fu Wai Hospital in Beijing to the APSIC session of the EuroPCR meeting in Paris in 2002. This occurred after a trial transmission from the same hospital in Beijing to the SingLive meeting in 2000, witnessed by the EuroPCR Course Director, Professor Jean Marco. After this, the transmission of live cases from China to Paris was agreed, targeted for the 2002 EuroPCR (Fig. 64).

There are significant differences in the practice of percutaneous coronary intervention (PCI) between the developing countries in Asia and the developed western nations. I was invited to deliver a keynote lecture entitled '*Cardiovascular Intervention: Intercontinental Crossfire*' in the Asia Pacific live transmission session during the 2011 EuroPCR meeting in Paris. Surgical coronary revascularization by

Fig. 64. Live transmission from Fu Wai Hospital to EuroPCR 2002 (left: Gao R, YL, M. Claude-Morice).

coronary artery bypass graft (CABG) was well-developed in the West before the advent of percutaneous coronary revascularization by angioplasty in 1977. In contrast CABG is still not readily available in most hospitals providing PCI therapy in the Asia Pacific countries. The reasons for this are complex. The lack of surgical expertise and facilities, socio-economic, philosophical and cultural preferences all play a part. The relative ease in starting PCI services compared to CABG surgery services is one of the key factors as well. The rapid economic progress in many Asian nations has also enabled PCI services to mushroom in many hospitals in Asia Pacific countries over the past decade, notably China.

The lack of CABG facilities in many Asian hospitals providing PCI leaves these hospitals no choice but to treat all patients needing coronary revascularization therapy by PCI, including those with very high risks and complex cases. This is a vicious cycle and further hampers the development of CABG surgery in many Asian hospitals. Without comparable CABG experience and expertise, the practice guidelines for the choice of coronary revascularization recommended by the ACC/AHA and ESC cannot be applied in Asian practices. Pivotal clinical trials such as SYNTAX cannot be used for patients in the Asia Pacific countries because the mortality and MACE rates of CABG quoted in trials such as SYNTAX cannot be achieved in many hospitals in the East. The recommendation of PCI or CABG to patients requiring coronary revascularization therapy in Asia therefore cannot be based on results obtained from large western clinical trials. More recently, some large Asian countries have tried to develop their own local practice guidelines and risk assessment, such as the Chinese PCI guidelines of 2009 and the SinoScore. Radial access is the default approach to perform PCI in most Asian institutions, notably those in Japan, China and South Korea. This practice with its potential clinical benefits is only gaining momentum in the West. PCI is the only coronary revascularization modality available in many Asian hospitals without CABG services. As a result all patients needing coronary revascularization, irrespective of existing guidelines, are being treated by PCI. It is important to remember that the equivalence of the long-term clinical outcome of PCI and CABG is yet to be proven scientifically.

The relatively high cost of PCI is still a very important consideration in the choice of therapeutic modality for individual patients in developing countries. Often, a second best choice has to be accepted because of cost constraints or the unavailability of CABG surgery. For cost reasons, cheaper locally developed drugs and devices are frequently used clinically in some Asian countries without trial data of their efficacy or safety.

PCI training in the Asia Pacific region deserves special attention by the West. Relatively few interventionists from Asia have the privilege to learn PCI first-hand in western centres of excellence. Most of them learnt their art and technique locally from proctorships by overseas experts at their hospitals and also during global live demonstration courses such as the EuroPCR and TCT. These western live demonstration courses in PCI have played a significant role in the development of PCI in Asia Pacific countries. A healthy collaboration between the East and the West has evolved over the last decade, resulting in hybrid East-West live courses such as TCT-Asia Pacific, SingLive-EuroPCR, CIT-TCT and many others. Trainers during these live courses will do well to emphasize the clinical reasons of *why* and not just the technical issues of *how* PCI should or could be performed to optimize patient outcome. The principle that patients who agree to participate in live demonstration courses are there, first and foremost, to be treated rather than taught, must be observed at all times. PCI operators in the East now enjoy the labour of research, educational activities and the clinical rigor of the West, with little input from the East. In turn the West can capitalize on the unique skills accumulated through the sheer necessity of performing difficult PCI on patients in the East. With these synergies, PCI will definitely continue to thrive and help patients in the East and West alike.

A *good and useful* therapeutic modality for a common disease must be available to *all who need it*. PCI is such a therapy. Manufacturers of devices and adjunctive drugs necessary for PCI therapies must balance the cost and profit margins of their life saving products and make PCI widely available to all who need it in the Asia Pacific region.

Superimposition of the East West Pyramids

Western civilization evolves from biblical values dating from the era of the Roman Empire two milennia ago. Western values are like a normal pyramid, in my opinion, with a broad base; a bottom-up concept representing a democratic model with the people at the base electing the ruler at the top (*top-up model*). In contrast, Chinese civilization is like an inverted pyramid, a top-down Confucian model, with the power at the top and the insignificant individual at the bottom (*top-down model*). The Chinese pyramid has been hanging upside down much longer than the normal right-side-up pyramid of the West. The two will never and should never be aligned. To synergize the two pyramids, the two opposing pyramids should be superimposed on top of one another to produce a star. The overlapped hexagon in the center represents the area where the two cultures or civilizations should co-exist and co-evolve. The protruding six horns are insoluble differences that should be left alone (Fig. 65).

In the world today, there will always be the two pyramids, the two different halves of the world, the *have* versus the *have-not*, the East versus the West. Applying this to the practice of PCI, or any endeavor for that matter in the East and West, one should work synergistically in the common hexagonal area to move forward. The protruding '*horns*' representing differences in practice between the two worlds, should be left alone. I came across a review of the recently published autobiography of Henry Kissinger entitled *On China* in the May 14th 2011 issue of the *Herald Tribune* written by Maxwell Frankel. The author commented on Kissinger's view of how America and China could exist by co-evolution. To quote Mr. Frankel, '*Mr. Kissinger insists that the common interests the two [east & west] share should make possible a "co-evolution"…creating*

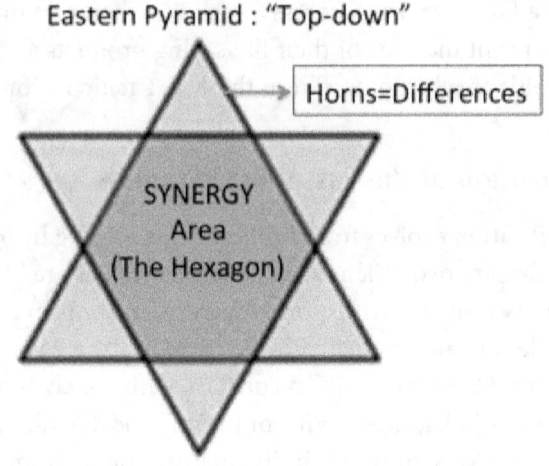

Fig. 65. Differences (horns) and synergies (Hexagon) between East and West.

a Pacific Community, comparable to the Atlantic Community...All Asian nations would then participate in a system perceived as a joint endeavor rather than a contest of rival [east & west] blocs'. Henry Kissinger had made more than 50 trips to China in his illustrious career as a top diplomat. We should heed his insightful advice on how the East and the West could work productively together in whatever field we choose to collaborate in. During my keynote lecture on 'Coronary Revascularization: Asia Pacific Perspectives', I suggested that the session on '*Cardiovascular Intervention: Intercontinental Crossfire*' in the Asia Pacific session at EuroPCR could be changed to '*Intercontinental Co-Evolution*' in future.

Clinical and coronary artery bypass surgical expertise are the strengths of western cardiology. This expertise is systematically transferred to developing countries through educational meetings, live demonstration courses and published scientific communications.

Basic research and large randomized clinical trials to find novel drugs and techniques to improve and refine existing cardiovascular therapies are conducted more often in the West than the East. International Good Clinical Practice (GCP) and Good Manufacturing Practice (GMP) for quality research and manufacturing are adhered to more in the West than the East. The large population pool, cheaper manufacturing cost and excellent basic bench research skills are strengths of the East. Cultural and financial constraints dictate certain clinical practice differences between the East and the West that have to be accepted. Coronary intervention skills are often pushed to the limits in the East due to lack of coronary bypass surgical skills. The positive impact of this eastern approach to coronary disease treatment has extended the feasibility and horizons of angioplasty to the benefit of many patients, sometimes to the bewilderment of their western counterparts. PCI workers in the East can absorb the labour of clinical scrutiny, research and educational benefits accumulated in the West. In turn the West can scrutinize, observe and learn the unique operative skills and clinical results accumulated from the lop-sided PCI treatment of the large number of patients in the East. A combined effort to compare the best surgical coronary revascularization therapy in the West with the best PCI therapy in the East for all categories of patients by a large randomized trial; 'SYNTAX East versus West' perhaps, is urgently needed to move coronary revascularization therapy forward.

Finally global multi-national medical and device companies should try to make their life-saving products affordable and accessible to all who need them, in both the East and the West. With these synergies, PCI will definitely continue to thrive and help patients in the East and West alike.

About six weeks after the conclusion of EuroPCR 2011 in Paris on July 4th, I received an encouraging email from an unknown PCI worker in Pakistan. In it, the spirit of cooperation between the East and the

West was described and the positive end result extolled. The email reads as follows:

> It was indeed a great pleasure and honour for me to sit on the same panel with you on the main arena on EuroPCR on 20th may 2011, and I am grateful to the Europcr faculty for giving me this opportunity. .... We in Pakistan look up to Europcr with great admiration and respect, as we feel that it is because of dedicated people like yourself that the field of interventional cardiology has mushroomed as it did. Pakistan owes a huge debt to EuroPCR for taking the interventional cardiology to this level where we in our limited capacity, are treating all patients in Pakistan, and not feeling the need to send our patients abroad for treatment. I think never before has the field of medicine witnessed this rapid growth and success, as intervention cardiology. I also feel that it was entirely because of people like you, that this great achievement has been accomplished, which has no doubt been phenomenal in easing the misery and mortality of humanity. Yours Sincerely, Dr S. Aziz, Rawalpindi, Pakistan 46000.

China's Contribution to the Treatment of Coronary Artery Disease

China boasts the largest PCI volume among the APSIC or Third Block in the global PCI community. China must therefore strive to demonstrate equivalent scientific standards as those of the western blocks. It must attain all three levels of the PCI Pyramid of Excellence. The first demands optimal PCI practice that requires both good clinical and technical skills. The patient must clearly benefit from the revascularization procedure compared to the standard conservative therapy. The interventional cardiologist must treat patients, not just lesions. Sadly, this is not always the case and treating lesions without considering the patients as a whole is common, not only in China but also worldwide. At this critical growth phase of PCI in China, the performance of PCI after careful clinical consideration will not only benefit the well-being of patients, but also the economic well-being of the country. It is heartening to see that PCI in China is well and truly in the second or 'New Knowledge' phase of the Pyramid of Excellence. At this level, China is well-suited to be excellent. China has a huge patient population ideal for conducting large randomized clinical trials to answer important clinical questions on interventional therapies. Drug coated stents using traditional Chinese herbal preparations are being investigated in Phase 2 and Phase 3 clinical trials. More and more large-scale clinical trials are being conducted to document the efficacy and safety of locally manufactured drug-coated stents. Clinical outcomes of treatment of severe coronary disease by angioplasty instead of surgery are being documented accurately and followed longitudinally. There are now sufficient good PCI centers in China to conduct large single-center clinical trials that will do the same job as the multi-center trials in the West. China alone can conduct the much needed SYNTAX East versus West randomized clinical trial in collaboration with the best surgical centers in the West. An international trial of coronary revascularization by PCI alone by the best operators in the East versus CABG by the best western operators is urgently needed to compare the efficacy of the two existing methods of treatment of coronary artery disease. If non-inferiority of the two techniques could be demonstrated, then China and the entire Third Block would have contributed significantly to the progress of the treatment of coronary artery disease by myocardial revascularization.

For data to be credible, clinical research in the Third Block must adhere strictly to international Good Clinical Practice (GCP) standards. Similarly, adherence to international Good Manufacturing Practice (GMP) in producing new local medical devices will allow China and other Asian countries to achieve international standards of medical practice. Finally, at the top of the Pyramid of Excellence, China is becoming a major player at the international level of Knowledge Exchange, in the same way the leaders in the West are today.

The Half-global Policy

I was asked to predict China's device market over the next decade in 1998. I said that China's interventional therapy was poised at the 'J' or takeoff point of an exponential growth curve then. A doubling in number annually would occur at the J curve until the linear growth phase or steady state could be reached. In 1995, the total number of PCI procedures performed throughout China was roughly 500. At the last estimate, the number of PCI procedures performed had reached the half million mark. This prediction of an exponential growth from 1998 turned out to be quite accurate and a more linear growth will soon occur when catheter laboratories providing PCI services can be scattered all over China.

In turn, I propose to the leaders of the global multi-national companies (MNCs) to adopt a 'half-global' policy for the manufacturing and sale of their life-saving medical devices. I have always believed there are two halves in this world, the *haves* (developed countries) and the *have-nots* (developing countries). Global or multinational companies therefore must have two, not one, policies for the distribution of their products: one for the developing countries and the other for developed countries. In my opinion, the world will never become one, all equally developed. The haves or the developed countries are mainly in the West, and the have-nots or the developing countries in the East. The haves commonly exploit the have-nots by obtaining cheaper labour and manufacturing costs for their products to maximize their profits. When I visited the manufacturing plants of some of major medical device companies in the United States, I observed that most of the factory workers were of Asian descent, for reasons of cheaper labour costs. Reducing production costs is perfectly reasonable but it must be accompanied by a comparable reduction in the price of the products. The same profit margin can be maintained with two different cost and price structures for a product manufactured in the two different halves of the world. One important constant must be preserved though, that is the quality of the two products manufactured in the two different halves of the world must be identical. A stent that cost 500 US dollars to manufacture in the United States can be sold with a four-fold profit for 2000 US dollars in the West. The same stent that could be manufactured for 500 RMB in China must be sold for 2000 RMB and not US dollars in the East, with exactly the same profit margin. The absolute cost and price of the product in the two worlds can be quite different and the profit margin and overall quality can still be the same. The net effect to the MNCs is the reduction in the size of their absolute profit. This crucial point must be agreed by global MNCs. The net lower price for the product in the developing world in turn will make the product more affordable to more patients who really need these life-saving drugs or devices. An effective therapy cannot be described as good when only a fraction of those who need it can afford it. This is the case for PCI therapy using stents. In developing countries all over the world today, only about 10% of coronary heart disease patients are getting coronary stent therapy. PCI using coronary stents can only really be good when all patients who need the therapy can afford and receive this therapy. This must be the ultimate goal of any novel life-saving drugs or devices. I have proposed this theory to the various MNCs in a short article, but to-date, no MNCs have adopted this proposed half-global policy.

8

East and West, Science and God

'Where Do You Really Come From?'

The Chinese translation of Massachusetts is *Mun Shan Ciu Se*, which, literally translated, means *Mountain full of Autumn Colours*. Autumn, or fall in American language, in Massachusetts is indeed colourful. The myriads of red, orange, yellow, green and gold all dancing against the clear blue sky is truly an inspiring sight to behold. When I was an overseas fellow at the Massachusetts General Hospital (MGH) for a year, I had only a simple camera and with it I tried my best to capture the magnificent autumn colours of Massachusetts. Most weekends during fall, we would drive to the White Mountain in New Hampshire and Maine to enjoy the mountain full of autumn colours. It was the autumn colours of New England that inspired me to take up photography. Photography is something of a hybrid of art and science. It is much less time consuming and known to be an art for 'instant gratification'. Being a busy cardiologist, photography quickly substituted for painting as the visual art form that satisfies my artistic creative instinct.

My so-called 'office' at the MGH was located in the basement of the Bulfinch Building, adjacent to the animal laboratory. The Bulfinch Building was named after its architect, Charles Bulfinch. It is a very historic building because it is the building where the famous Ether Dome is located. The Padua theatre under the dome of the Bulfinch Building was the place where ether anesthesia was first used on a patient for surgery in 1846. This sentinel event was hailed as the conqueror of pain in the history of medicine. Today, a large painting depicting this historic medical breakthrough hangs in the Windermere Library of Harvard University. As a matter of fact, a bitter court case erupted soon after the first use of ether anesthesia between Dr William Morton, a dentist, and Dr Charles Jackson, a surgeon, both claiming to be the discoverer of ether anesthesia. I am lucky to have in my collection, an autograph copy of one of the original papers on ether anesthesia published in 1848 by Charles Jackson.

Soon after starting work at MGH, my wife and I were invited to a welcome party organized by the Friends of MGH, a social club of Harvard University. At the party, a tall friendly American lady approached me and extended her welcome hand. After a warm handshake, we exchanged the following conversation:

'Hi, where do you come from?', she asked.
'Melbourne', I replied.
'Gee, that's like from the other side of the moon!', she quipped.
She then looked me straight in the eyes and asked,
'Where do you really come from?'
A little startled, and realizing that I don't really looked like a *dinky-di* Aussie, I replied *'Singapore'*.
With that she blurted,
'Which part of China is that?'

At that instant, I realised that no matter where I came from, my Chinese phenotype of yellow skin and black hair would betray my origin. The American lady would have asked no more questions if my answer to her first question was 'China'. The incident brought back memory of the time when Dr Howqua, with the best of intentions, presented us with the 'black and yellow' baby suit on the occasion to celebrate the first month of our son's birth. Many years later, when my son was about six years old, he returned home from school one day very stressed because his school mates had called him 'ching, chong, chang'. This term was derogatory and used for years with a racial connotation by native-born Australians to taunt Chinese migrants. He was quite baffled and defended himself very vigorously saying that he was born in Melbourne, the same as his classmates who were teasing him. Still sobbing, he asked his mother, '*Mum, I am not Chinese am I?*' This is typically the first of three phases of identity crisis that children of overseas Chinese immigrants would go through in their growing up in Australia or any other Caucasian society. The second identity crisis phase would come when they became teenagers in high school, the question they would ask then would be: '*Mum, what is my name in Chinese?*' Finally at university level, the third identity crisis phase question would be: '*Mum, how do I write my name in Chinese?*' I called these the three 'root seeking' questions for descendants of overseas Chinese in a Caucasian society.

I had to relate the story of the American lady at the Harvard MGH welcome party to my son when he was older. I sincerely told him that anyone of Chinese descent would always be recognised or assumed to be Chinese, no matter where one was born. His ancient Welsh name, Iefan, would not protect him from this fate.

When interviewed as an expatriate working in Singapore by the local newspaper, the *Straits Times,* the reporter wanted to know which country I really belonged to. I told him that in Singapore, I was looked upon as an Australian. In Australia, I am Chinese and in China, I am Singaporean. Now at 66, I really have an identity crisis having worked and lived in the three countries, each with its own distinct history and culture. Indeed, I have fallen into the clefts between the three. Friends try to console me by saying that I am a citizen of the world!

Rhythm of the East

Distinct differences in the way or rhythm of life between the East and the West can be appreciated in daily encounters. During my first visit to Beijing in the early eighties, the roads were congested with bicycles. For a visitor from the West, trying to cross Chang An Boulevard from my hotel, the Ming-zu Hotel, was a real challenge. The uninterrupted stream of cyclists gave one little chance of crossing from one side to the opposite of the 12-lane boulevard. Nevertheless, I could see how easily the locals were able to cross the wide boulevard, weaving through the on-coming cyclists effortlessly. Intrigued, I asked one of the local pedestrians what was the secret. He simply answered in Mandarin, '*Just walk, don't stop!*' More simply said than done, I thought. I then tried to cross as instructed when I saw a small gap in the on-coming cyclists. However, soon after commencing to cross, I estimated that I would be hit by one of oncoming cyclists if I were to continue to walk. I instinctively stopped. My sudden stop promptly disrupted the normal flow of all the cyclists. A number of them had to quickly adjust their tempo to avoid hitting one another and me! I realised then that I had upset the rhythm and flow of the cyclists by stopping. The consequence of not doing what I was told by the local pedestrian nearly ended up in disaster. Faced with a pedestrian crossing in front of them, cyclists in China would quickly adjust their speed, taking into account the walking speed of the pedestrian. The two rhythms would synchronize precisely to avoid a collision. From this simple daily life experience, I came to the conclusion that two very different rhythms exist in the East and the West. In the West, the pedestrian would only cross when there is no traffic. In the East, the pedestrian will cross despite the moving traffic. To be successful in the East, a westerner must understand the rhythm of the East. This rhythm is made up of its culture, philosophy and its value systems. This is the key to success for anyone wishing to do business in China.

'Wait and See'

Businesses in China in the early nineties were largely state-owned. Private enterprise was illegal until the economic reform introduced by Chairman Deng Xiao-ping was in full swing in the late 1990s. Many small private businesses started to emerge throughout China, mainly in the rural areas and to a lesser extent in the cities. One such private enterprise manufacturing safety pins in a northeast county was particularly successful and was planning to start a franchise. An envious rival company lodged a formal complaint to the relevant local authority accusing the successful company of running an 'illegal business'. At that time private enterprises were already widespread throughout the county. The county authorities did not know how to handle the complaint and referred it to higher authorities at the provincial government level. The provincial government too was at a loss and referred the complaint to the central government in Beijing. Eventually the complaint was brought to the attention of the Chairman, Deng Xiaoping. The complaint was a dilemma for the Chairman. If he were to overrule the complaint of illegality that was in fact true, private enterprise would flourish and the budding economic reform would receive a big booster. But he could not ignore the law and eventually after hearing the case out, he simply pronounced: *'leave this aside, wait and see!'*

In the West, his answer would be interpreted as 'put it on the next agenda'! But for the Chinese, the absence of a negative response would be interpreted as a positive response. The 'wait and see' decision of the Chairman was therefore interpreted as a positive nod by his subordinates at the various lower governmental levels and the franchise businesses went full steam ahead. Other private enterprises throughout China mushroomed as a result. The following year, when the Chairman enquired what had become of the case, he was told that his 'wait and see' decision had resulted in a boom of private enterprises in China. Shortly thereafter, private enterprise was legalised throughout China.

Similarly, in Singapore, the *U-Turn* sign is ubiquitous. One cannot make a U-turn unless there is a sign to indicate that one can do so. However, in Hong Kong, one can make a U-turn unless there is a sign forbidding it. Whether a glass is half full or half empty depends really on one's interpretation according to his cultural heritage and value system. The case of private enterprise in China described was more like the Hong Kong U-turn; one could turn unless there was a clear *No U-turn* sign.

The unwritten rule that in the absence of a 'no', 'yes' is taken for granted works most of the time in Asia, perhaps with the exception of Singapore. In Singapore, only do what the law tells you or you will be in trouble. In China, new initiatives usually start without official approval. Official approval is seldom granted until a project has been shown to be working reasonably smoothly and successfully. However, one must be pretty confident that a project will be successful before one dares to start a project without approval. Chinese officials will usually allow new initiatives to go ahead, at the same time advising the adventurer to 'not get into trouble'. 'Not getting into trouble' means that there should be no complaints. If problems or troubles were reported, one would surely be reminded that no official approval had ever been given. In contrast, in the West no one would dream of starting a project before official approval was obtained. For any westerner venturing into China, this 'Chinese way' of getting things started without official approval must be understood.

With my understanding of the two cultures and my practical working experiences in the East and West, I feel that I am in fact a conduit, much like the bypass graft used in coronary revascularization, connecting east and west, but with bi-directional flow. What flowed through the conduit, however, is not blood but the knowledge, tradition, culture and philosophy of the two ends.

Western and Eastern Learning

I received my early education in Singapore in the traditional Chinese way of learning, that is by memory retention and factual recall. This method of learning in the East has been exalted and perpetuated for more than 2000 years and used by generations of Confucian or *Ru* Scholars. Recitation of written texts was an essential part of the Chinese learning process and examination in the Chinese way of assessing success or failure of one's education. Lateral thinking was not encouraged and unilateral transfer of knowledge from the teacher to student was the norm. Learning Chinese calligraphy and painting by copying the old masters is the standard way of acquiring the art or technique. A beginner in Chinese painting or calligraphy learns by copying the composition and brush strokes of the masters to perfection. In fact, painting manuals such as the *Mustard Seed Garden Painting Manual* were published for this purpose. Learning by copying and recitation of retained facts or verses is the traditional way of learning in China, entrenched over the centuries.

When I arrived in Australia after completing my secondary education in Singapore, my tertiary education at Monash University in Australia was a whole new experience. I was enlightened to the huge difference in western and eastern learning methods. In a medical curriculum, the traditional Chinese learning method of committing facts to memory, worked very well for me in subjects such as anatomy and biochemistry where large amounts of factual knowledge need to be retained and regurgitated. When I undertook my driver's license examination, I recited my answers to all the road test questions asked by the testing officer, including punctuations. The Australian examiner was completely flabbergasted!

However, at group discussion sessions at the university, I quickly realised that my Australian colleagues out-performed me with less factual knowledge. The Asian students, including myself, were often speechless, when questions requiring flexible induction and deduction rather than factual recall were asked. The Australian students were much more articulate and capable of lateral thinking. They were able to work out the answers by reasoning using first principles rather than knowing factual answers. This western style of learning was very refreshing to me and impressed me deeply. One of my Australian classmates in particular intrigued me greatly with his learning style. He would skip most lectures that were boring. Walking out from classes was unthinkable in the way I was brought up in Singapore. I would take copious lecture notes and spend many more hours after each lecture, digesting, refining and summarizing all the lecture notes. Yet at examinations, the Australian student who skipped most lectures would always score better than me at examinations. I began to question the efficiency of my Chinese way of learning. Lateral thinking, deductive and inductive skills were central to western learning. Questioning teachers and even textbook knowledge was unthinkable for Asian students. These were food for thought and a totally new experience for me. My Australian way of education was thus the turning point for my education. I no longer would commit entire texts to memory, but would focus on important principles instead. However, retaining some essential factual knowledge to me is still very important, especially for scientific and medical pursuits. For a doctor, life could be at stake if wrong facts or no facts at all were at hand. A recent survey of the controversial 'tiger-mother' style of strict learning of the East and the more flexible and liberal learning technique of the West showed that the former appeared to yield better long-term outcomes. Nevertheless I believe a good combination of the two would be optimal. This is another good example for synergy in the hexagonal area in the superimposition of the eastern and western pyramids referred to earlier. One should never be tired of learning and Michelangelo's *'Ancora Imparo'* (*I am still learning*), adopted by Monash University as its motto in its coat-of-arms, must continue to inspire all serious students to learn in their own optimal way.

Traditional Chinese Medicine (TCM) and Western Medicine

Traditional Chinese Medicine (TCM) has been around for nearly three millennia. The *Yellow Emperor's Inner Canon* and the *Treatise of Disease of the Cold* by Zhang Zhong-jin are classics upon which TCM was founded. There is little doubt of the efficacy of some herbal remedies, acupuncture and other physical therapies of TCM. TCM is an empirical science unlike the inductive science of western medicine. In TCM, diseases are thought to be caused by an imbalance of the vital energies of the major organs in the body. The imbalance within the 'cold' and 'hot' organs, each with ill-defined energies, is thought to be the pathology of all kinds of ailment. Natural plants and animal parts, herbs and minerals, all with their distinctive heat or cold properties, can be used to supplement deficiencies of the hot or cold energies within the body that are the roots of all illnesses. A 'cold' deficiency illness can be treated with 'heaty' food or herbs and vice versa. Traditional Chinese prescriptions consist of a number of herbs, sometimes up to 20 plant or animal products. This 'poly-pharmacy' approach of TCM prescriptions is actually not too different to that used in western medicine where a combination of synergistic drugs are used to treat a certain illness. For example, the use of diuretics must be accompanied by the replacement of potassium loss as a result of diuresis. In a TCM herbal prescription, there is usually one principal or active ingredient, known as the 'emperor' herb. The action of the emperor herb is usually 'assisted' by a few other subsidiary or 'courtier' herbs. This delightful style of court operation of herbal therapy is known in Chinese as *jun chen zuo shi*, which literally translated means 'the collaboration of the king, knights and soldiers'. The entire 'pharmaceutical court' therefore has to work together to restore the balance of vital energies in the various hot and cold organs to return the body to its original balance and healthy state. This is the principle of TCM therapy in a nutshell. Western medicine in contrast, strives to understand the cause or mechanism of all disease processes on a cellular and now genetic and molecular level. Once the mechanism is understood, drugs, usually natural or synthetic, are then designed and manufactured to correct the dysfunction at a molecular level in the living cell. This is also the basis of modern individually tailored genetic pharmacotherapy. The pathologic concept of disease in TCM is therefore radically different to that in western medicine but the pharmacologic approach to disease therapy is actually quite similar for both. In TCM, the pathophysiology and treatment of diseases start at the organ level and move outward from the body towards the universe. The belief is that the environment through cosmic, etheric, astral and mental energies can heavily influence physical well-being by restoring the balance of energies in the organ and hence the entire body. The importance of external environmental influences on health is central in TCM. Conversely, western medicine concentrated on the organs initially to explain diseases and their cure but with the advent of modern science moves inwards into the cellular, nuclear, chromosomal and finally genetic spheres. Thus, western medicine and TCM essentially progress and move in opposite directions but together they cover the whole spectrum of the external and internal mechanisms and influences on health, from universe to genes. Therefore, in theory at least, to obtain the best outcomes in healthcare, it is logical that both intrinsic and extrinsic influences must be taken into account. The concept of psychosomatic illnesses and the concept of placebo or nocebo effects in western medicine resemble in some way the TCM approach to diseases. Interestingly, as western medicine delved deeper into the molecular and genetic realms, it began to invoke the use of energies in nature. An example of this can be found in the modern day theory of vitamin D deficiency in the etiology of diabetes mellitus. The sun is the most important natural source of vitamin D, and here the convergence of the two medicines can be seen. If one combines the external phenotypic emphasis of TCM and the intrinsic genotypic approach of western scientific medicine, one could eventually encompass the full spectrum of diseases and their cure and restore health in the most optimal way.

My incomplete comparison of the characteristics of TCM and western medicine is illustrated in the following table (Table 3):

Table 3. A comparison of western and traditional Chinese medicine.

Western Medicine	Traditional Chinese Medicine
Non-cultural	Cultural
Scientific	Empirical
Inductive	Deductive
Cause-Effect	Effect
Reductionist	Holistic
Structure	Process
Molecular	Organic
Physical	Energic

Not 'Mainstream Science'

In 2001, there were pockets of TCM research scattered in the various academic institutions of Singapore. I was given the task of developing TCM research as part of my role on the Executive Committee for Life Sciences initiatives of Singapore. A TCM Research Taskforce was convened with Dr Chiam Tao Soon as the chair and me as the deputy to come up with a proposal to start TCM research as part of the bioscience push for Singapore. One of the committee's first tasks was to register all of the on-going TCM research projects in Singapore. Concurrently, I led a delegation of health administrators and scientists to China to visit the leading TCM universities and research institutes in Beijing, Nanjing, Chengdu and a major herbal plantation in Kunming. The delegation also took into account the well-established TCM research institutes in Hong Kong and Taiwan to have a fuller picture of TCM research in Asia at that time (Fig. 66).

Fig. 66. Singapore Ministry for Health TCM Taskforce at the Central Bureau of TCM, Beijing 2001.

The TCM Research Taskforce submitted a paper entitled 'Report of the Traditional Chinese Medicine Taskforce' after six months of deliberation. I represented the Taskforce to present the paper at the Biomedical Sciences Executive Committee in January 2002. The taskforce recommended that a TCM Research Institute be established in Singapore in two phases. The first phase would involve the construction of an International Authentication and Reference Centre for TCM. Phase two would focus on the development of specific TCM research programs, especially in areas related to the elucidation of the mechanisms of action of traditional medicinal products. In addition, the taskforce recommended the establishment of a formal TCM education programme and a TCM Research Committee to provide a broad-based support to TCM research in Singapore.

When the report was presented to the international advisory panel of the Inter-Ministerial Executive Committee of Life Sciences of Singapore, one of its members, a Nobel Laureate and President of California Institute of Technology, cautioned against major investment on TCM research and made the following important remark: '*TCM is after all not mainstream science*'! I supported his comment wholeheartedly as the statement was both factual and pivotal to the reluctance to accept TCM by conventional western scientists. To me, the underlying reason for this reluctance is due to the lack of a common scientific communication 'language' between western science and TCM. By different language, I am not referring to the linguistic difference but the scientific methodology, evaluation and reporting of the two. Western drug or intervention research follows a standard protocol, is peer-reviewed, repeated for reproducibility and tested carefully for efficacy and safety in three standard trial phases. For any new pharmacotherapy to be applied clinically, positive results in Phase 1 or animal studies, Phase 2 First-in-man (FIM) human clinical trials and Phase 3 large controlled double-blinded randomized clinical trials must be confirmed. All scientific communications from animal studies, to case reports and large clinical trials are reported or presented in a common scientific protocol that is widely accepted and understood by the entire scientific community in the West.

In contrast, few TCM research results involving herbal or physical therapies are reported according to the above western scientific protocol. TCM research, when available, reports usually only positive evidence of the efficacy of a particular treatment or prescription. Negative results, sentinel adverse events, placebo effects and complications arising from therapies are often not reported. Details of therapies, herbs and other interventions are scanty and inclusion and exclusion criteria of population treated are usually not stated clearly. Results obtained are often not subjected to statistical analysis. Finally, Phase 2 or 3 clinical trials, if conducted at all, have not been randomized or double-blinded in accordance with international Good Clinical Practice (GCP) guidelines. Often herbal medicines that are in clinical use have not been manufactured in accordance with the international Good Manufacture Practice (GMP) standards either. Until research of TCM remedies can be conducted in the same manner as that of western pharmaceutical products and reported in similar peer reviewed manner, TCM will be regarded as 'not *mainstream science*'. It is imperative that TCM uses the same scientific language as western medicine. It is just as important for the west to make a genuine effort to understand TCM and help it to become mainstream science.

Western medical practitioners could partly blame exploitation of TCM by Shamanism and Taoism for their distrust of TCM. Three major concerns prevent the widespread acceptance of TCM by the western scientific community. The first relates to the inconsistency of the quality of the herbs used in TCM prescriptions, in particular, their sources, authentication and standardization processes. The second relates to variations in the methodologies for the preparation of the herbal prescriptions. Finally, the toxicities of some of the compounds, especially the content of heavy metals and poisonous contaminations, are never documented accurately. The latter are largely responsible for the serious adverse side effects of TCM, resulting in high incidence of kidney and liver complications.

I was invited to deliver one of the 2005 Dean's Lectures at the University of Melbourne; I chose 'Convergence of Western and Chinese Medicine' as the title of my lecture. I believe that the 'Fusion Point' that Joseph Needham postulated for different knowledge to merge could occur in the 21st century for western and Chinese medicine. This could happen with molecular biologic and genetic approaches to study Chinese herbal prescriptions. If modern scientific disciplines such as proteomics, genomics and bio-informatics can be introduced into TCM, the 'fusion point' of the two medicines might occur quicker. Concurrently, if some of the holistic approach of TCM could be accepted and adopted by western medicine, western healthcare standards would be lifted as well. TCM is already being regarded as an alternative medicine in the West and its popularity and acceptability is increasing day by day. Currently, about half the undergraduate curriculum of TCM universities in China is devoted to teaching western medicine. Graduates from these TCM universities are able to prescribe both western and Chinese medicines. In contrast, only 5% of the undergraduate medical curriculum in a western style medical school in China is devoted to the teaching of TCM. It is imperative for western medical education to incorporate some TCM teaching to improve healthcare overall in both the East and the West.

Between Painting and Poetry

My formal training in western painting was accomplished at NAFA in Singapore. My art teachers at NAFA belonged to the French impressionist and post-impressionist schools. They were strongly influenced by Fauvism, and pioneered a new style of art in South-East Asia known as *Nanyang* art. Leading the group were Cheong Soo Pieng, Chen Wen-xi and Georgette Chen. Cheong Soo Pieng taught only for a few years at NAFA and I was fortunate to have all three of them as my teachers during my three years at NAFA from 1959 to 1961. After graduation from NAFA, I held my first one-man art exhibition when I was a second-year medical student at Monash University in 1967. Two years later, a second one-man art exhibition was held at the Prahran Gallery to raise funds for the Queen Victoria Hospital when I was a PhD student at the hospital. It was difficult to paint without interruption when I started private cardiology practice. I turned to photography when I was in Boston and it gradually replaced painting as my main creative art medium. Ten years after starting photography, I held my first solo photographic exhibition at the Chinese Museum in Melbourne in 1992 to fund raise for the Epworth Medical Foundation. The exhibition was entitled *Between Painting and Poetry*. In photographic art, I was particularly inspired by the work of Peter Howard Emerson. Emerson was a British surgeon who gave up medicine for photography, soon after the invention of photography in the 1830s. Howard Emerson was a relative of the poet Ralph Waldo Emerson. He was a pioneer to champion photography as art. He was fondly remembered by his peers as '*a poet, whose silence is music to the eye*'. I love the tranquil and poetic nature of his photographs, not unlike my own. I paid a special tribute to P. H. Emerson's art by naming one of my favourite pictures *Music to the Eye*. This picture was taken at Hangzhou's Westlake. I love the motion and musical quality of this image of lotus stems in winter with the rippled reflections, created by holding the camera in one hand and throwing a pebble at the right spot in the water (Fig. 67).

At the opening of this exhibition in Melbourne, I was amused to overhear a discussion between an Aussie couple, discussing the photograph *Music to the Eye*:

> '*Isn't this a hybrid of Debussy and Fred Williams?*', said the lady,
> '*What a marvelous painting!*', said the man,
> '*It's a photograph, my dear!*', said the lady,
> '*It's a painting*', the man pronounced, after peering at the image closely.
> '*Don't be silly, dear, it's a photographic exhibition!*', the lady exclaimed.

Fig. 67. '*Music to the Eye*', photographed at Westlake, Hangzhou; a tribute to P H Emerson.

Photograph or painting, I was impressed by the sensitive and accurate analysis of the photograph. The poetic nature of the music of Debussy and the characteristic *dots and sticks* style of Fred Williams' Australian landscape painting are readily apparent in this image. Indeed I had these two artists in mind when I created this image. This commentary on the picture gave me great encouragement in my photographic art. The title I had chosen for this image was well-justified and Emerson would be proud of it as well. During the exhibition, I was deeply honoured when the late Albert Tucker, an important modern Australian artist and a fine photographer himself, came to the exhibition and actually purchased one of the exhibited pictures, more for charity and encouragement reasons than for inclusion in his collection. All 107 photographs were sold and the entire proceeds went to help refurbish the Epworth Hospital's Coronary Care Unit. In 1995, three years after my photographic exhibition, I published my first photographic art book entitled *Eastern Eye Western Light*.

Eastern Eye Western Light

Earlier, I have told the story of how I helped to resuscitate Albert Tucker's when I was a young doctor at the Alfred Hospital in 1978. When my photographic book was ready to be published in 1995, I thought it would be wonderful and a great honour to have the foreword of the book written by Albert Tucker. I had initially chosen the title "*Music to the Eye*" for the book. Albert Tucker was a softly spoken gentleman but an intellectual giant, quite unlike his usually angry and haunting paintings. He was also a very serious artist, a man of integrity and would not have his name associated with anything unworthy. When approached by me seeking a foreword from him for my book, his reply was surprisingly forthright: '*Show me the book and I'll see whether there is anything to write about!*' Bringing the completed draft of *Music to the Eye*, containing 100 original photographs, I arrived at his house in the Bohemian district of St. Kilda (Fig. 68). The meeting with the great artist that day was an unforgettable life experience and a highlight in my artistic career. I wish I had the encounter video-taped but I can remember every word that he uttered that day. He turned the pages of my book slowly from the cover, pausing to look at each image carefully without saying a word. After examining about half of the book, he closed the book and said to me, '*Music, I don't know much about, but you have a finely balanced eye between the East and the West, fifty-fifty on each side*'. He then reopened the book to point out the photographs to illustrate his assessment of my art. '*There, you see, you are obviously influenced by the impressionists.*' Pointing to another photograph, he said '*here is the eastern Zen composition, your Chinese influence*'. He was absolutely spot on because my photographs are greatly influenced by Bada Shanren, the Ming Dynasty artist whose use of space in his paintings — the so-called

Fig. 68. Albert Tucker examining the book '*Music to the Eye*' at St. Kilda, 1995.

'space-on-space' composition — had revolutionized Chinese painting. As for western influence, I am exquisitely sensitive to light, and all the famous 'light' artists in western art history, starting from Masaccio to Turner and Monet, have greatly inspired and influenced my photographic art. Tucker then continued to analyze many of my photographs for me, pointing out the oriental and western influence or a mixture of both in each of these images. At that time, I had already been engaged in photography for nearly 15 years but totally unaware of my own style. Prior to this, whenever I saw something worth photographing, I usually had in mind a painting by one of the great Chinese or western masters that I know. In fact, the reason for my photographic book was to try and show the reader what an artist sees when confronted with an emotion-provoking scene. Without examining the book further, Tucker concluded his examination of my art and said, '*Yes, there is something to write about, I will have the foreword delivered to you!*' I was beside myself and went home thinking about what he had said that afternoon for the next few weeks.

East and West, Science and God   267

A few days after my visit to Albert Tucker at his home, a yellow-lined foolscap paper with the foreword penciled in Tucker's original handwriting was dropped into my mailbox. This precious document was promptly framed and hung in a prominent spot in my home. The foreword helped me to define my photographic art. I then changed the title of my photographic book from *Music to the Eye* to *Eastern Eye Western Light* (Fig. 69). Tucker's foreword for my book is here quoted in full:

> *The first image in this book provides the underlying paradox in Yean Lim's imagery — two ducks going in opposite directions on the yellow river — which turns out to be Melbourne's Yarra River. Professor Yean Lim, a cardiologist and photographer of Chinese origin and an Australian citizen, is poised in a delicate balance between East and West. This combination gives him an exceptional degree of emotional and intellectual precision both in his profession and his love of photography — our present concern. Many of his images can be read in two*

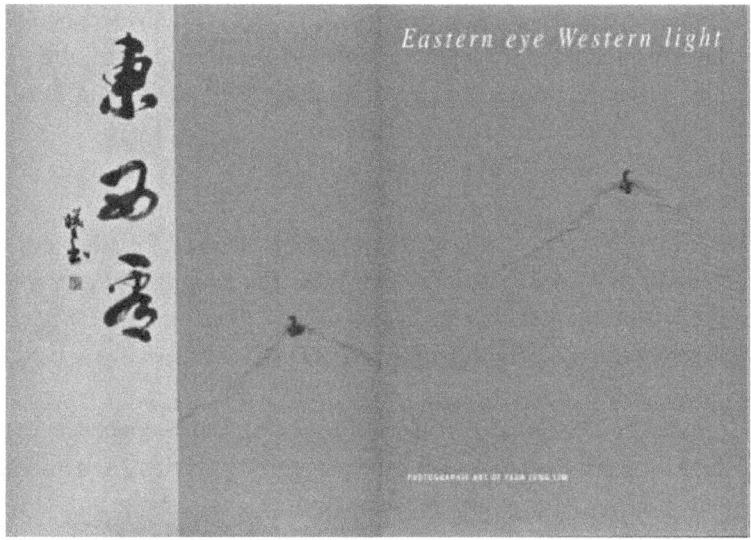

Fig. 69.   Photographic book *Eastern Eye Western Light*, published 1995.

ways — as calligraphic abstractions most evident in reeds and their reflections in a pond or as exquisite nature poetry and direct impressionist images. His surgical skills and discipline show in his micro-second responses to bird life and the evocation of moods created by transitory effects of light. I will leave the discovery of the visual pleasure of this book to you his audience. Albert Tucker

Convergence of Chinese and Western Painting

After its publication in Melbourne, *Eastern Eye Western Light* was listed among the top ten best sellers in the book review section of the *Age* newspaper. Mary Delahunty of the popular Sunday Afternoon arts programme on ABC television invited me to talk about the book on her programme. Mary Delahunty later became the Minister of the Arts, and then Minister of Education and Planning when the Labor Party won the Victorian State election. In my ten-minute interview, I summarized my personal view on the convergence of Chinese and Western paintings at the end of the 19th century. An expanded version entitled Convergence of Chinese and western painting was delivered as one of the keynote lectures to celebrate the 50th anniversary of the 1963 Catholic High School class reunion in 2013 at the school auditorium. The gist of the lecture is summarized below:

> J. Needham in 1970 stated that for a given realm of knowledge or practice, there comes a point when the differences vanished; i.e. when two forms of knowledge coalesced or converged. This point is referred to as the Fusion Point for that knowledge or practice. Trans-current Point, on the other hand, is when one knowledge overtakes the other.

Fusion points of various disciplines of human knowledge in the East and West have occurred over the past four centuries. In mathematics, astronomy and physics, the fusion and trans-current points were around the seventeenth century and in botany, the eighteenth century. The Fusion Point for painting occurred at the end of 19th century. In medicine, however, the Fusion Point for western and traditional Chinese medicine is yet to occur and could happen in the 21st century in my opinion.

Western painting was *descriptive* in the beginning. There was always a story, usually religious in nature, in the painting. Early western paintings were devoid of light and usually flat in nature or non-three-dimensional. The canvas was completely filled leaving no empty space. Light was not introduced into Western painting until the Quattrocento period of the Italian Renaissance. Artists such as Giotto, Masaccio and Fra Angelica transformed the flat Byzantine figures into three-dimensional portraits. Light is crucial in the development of western painting. The influence of light in western paintings became more prominent with the arrival of artists such as Leonardo da Vinci, Michelangelo and Raphael. The use of light in paintings was intensified by the Dutch painters, notably Vermeer and Rembrandt. The presentation of light in western paintings peaked with impressionism at the end of the 19th century, championed by Claude Monet and other artists in France and Europe. Artists in the West such as Vincent van Gogh, Cezanne and Matisse probably became aware of the vibrant-colors used in oriental art, in particular the Japanese Ukiyo-e woodblock prints of the Edo period by artists such as Hokusai, Hiroshige and Utamaro. One of Cezanne's watercolor paintings of melons demonstrates clearly the influence of oriental inkbrush on western painters (Fig. 70).

In contrast, traditional Chinese inkbrush paintings are by nature 'expressive', light is not a feature and abundance of empty space can be seen in Chinese paintings. The subject depicted in a Chinese painting does not always tell the full story intended by the artist; hence 'what you see is not always what you get'! The artist, if he feels inclined, will write a poem or a verse on the painting to indicate to the viewer his inner thoughts and feelings associated with that painting.

Fig. 70. Light introduced into Chinese painting (left: *Bamboo* by Xu Beihong; right: Watercolour *Melon* by P. Cezanne).

More often than not, the viewer is left to his own imagination. Chinese painting is therefore more *expressive* than descriptive, and even allegorical. For instance, horse represents success, pine tree longevity, fish forecasts abundance and so on. From the compositional point of view, the empty space in Chinese painting is very carefully planned and aesthetically balanced. Space is therefore as important or more important than the painted subjects. The use of space reached a zenith in the art of Bada Shenren, whose style has been described as the use of *space on space*.

Light was first introduced into Chinese inkbrush painting by artists such as Xu Beihong, who received formal training in western painting in Paris at the turn of the twentieth century. After his return to China, he revolutionized Chinese inkbrush painting by introducing light and perspective into Chinese painting, employing subtle shades of the black in the brush strokes to make the painted object three-dimensional. Bamboos painted by Xu Beihong were good example of the introduction of light into Chinese paintings (Fig. 70).

The incorporation of the effect of light in Chinese painting went a step further in the 20th century. Not only was direct light used in Chinese ink brush painting, but back-lit light, much the same as that used in photography, was also introduced into Chinese brush paintings. The example of the use of backlit light in Chinese paintings can be seen in the landscape paintings of Li Keran, especially in his famous series on the *Kweilin Li River*, painted in the mid 1970s (Fig. 71).

While light was being instilled into Chinese paintings in the beginning of 20th century, a quiet revolution in western painting was going on in Europe as well. Kandinsky coined the word *abstract* art in 1922 to explain his new painting style and western painting became 'expressive'. Abstract art, without clear subject or form, no longer tells a story. What you see is no longer what you get as it was in earlier western paintings.

Fig. 71. 'Back-lit light' introduced into Chinese painting (*Li River, Kweilin* by Li Keran).

Worse still, unlike the Chinese artist, a western artist does not inscribe any verse on the abstract painting to tell you the artist's feeling or emotion behind the work. Space was also introduced into western paintings with large areas of the canvas sometimes left blank. Interestingly, contemporary Chinese artists in the 21st century have returned to the traditional western style of light-filled, story-telling way of painting. Realism returned to the oil paintings of modern Chinese painters. The art of Lin Feng-mian and Wu Guan-zhong was heavily influenced by post-impressionism, fauvism and cubism. Artists such as Chen Yi-fei painted many Vermeer and Rembrandt-like portraits in the 20th century, a style that is very popular and emulated by many contemporary Chinese artists today.

Western and Chinese paintings have indeed converged at the end of the 19th and the beginning of the 20th century. The 'fusion point' in Chinese and western painting has occurred. I do not think there will be a 'trans-current point' in fine art or painting in particular. Art has no absolute value and, unlike scientific values, is difficult to measure and quantify. Art serves to enrich the soul and science to enrich the body, perhaps. However, I have attempted to use my scientific training to try to compare and contrast western and Chinese painting in an analytical and tabular fashion (Table 4).

Table 4. A comparison of western and Chinese painting.

Western Painting	Chinese Painting
Before the 20th Century	
Descriptive	Expressive
Light (3-dimensional)	No Light (2-dimensional)
No space	Space is part of painting
After the 20th Century	
Expressive (Abstract)	Descriptive, light-filled

Other important encounters in my artistic life included a meeting with maestros Wu Guang-zhong and Zhang Da-chian, two giants of 20th century Chinese art. I was fortunate to have met maestro Wu Guang-zhong in his Beijing home before he passed away and to have his original calligraphy for the title page of my next photographic book in progress, entitled *Window of the Heart* (Fig. 72).

The equivalent to Picasso in Chinese art in the 20th century was maestro Zhang Da-chian. Before going to Boston for my postgraduate studies in 1981, I visited the maestro at his studio '*mo ye jing se*' at the Double Creek district in the outskirt of Taipei. I was introduced to Maestro Zhang for professional reasons through his personal cardiologist, Dr Li Shi-hsuen, a personal friend at the Taiwan National Hospital. This visit was indeed a highlight in my life. I had earlier acquired a calligraphic couplet written by Zhang Da-chian on a topic related to botany and zoology. The couplet described the collection

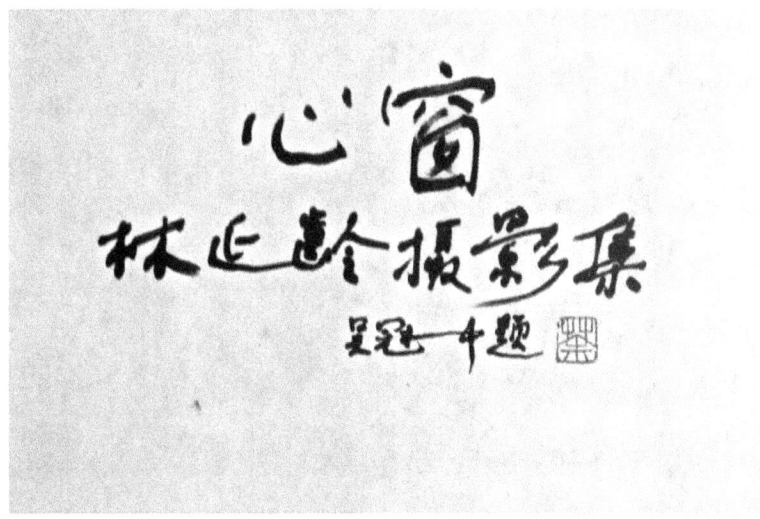

Fig. 72. Title page for second photographic book, entitled *Window of the Heart* (to be published); calligraphy by Wu Guang-zhong.

and illustration of plants in *Li-shou* and the depiction of plants and animals in *Er-ya*, two famous classic ancient Chinese texts. The two books could represent the study of and use of plants and animals in western and eastern pharmacopeia (Fig. 73), a subject close to my interests and heart.

Painting, Photography and Percutaneous Coronary Intervention

I am often asked whether my interest in art has helped me in my profession as an interventional cardiologist. The answer is definitely yes. The eye of a photographer has to be fast, decisive and accurate and so does the interventional cardiologist. In the same way, the mental planning and finger dexterity that one needs to write Chinese calligraphy, to create an artistic photograph and to perform a successful percutaneous

Fig. 73. At Zhang Da-chian's art studio '*Mo Ye Jing Se*', Taipei 1981 and couplet on the subjects of botany and zoology (From left back: YL, Joy, Mrs Zhang; seated: Zhang Dachian).

coronary intervention (PCI) procedure are very similar indeed. One of the greatest Chinese calligrapher who ever lived was Wang Xi-zhi. He had this to say about Chinese calligraphy:

> *Calmness is essential for calligraphy, plan strategically before applying the brush. The actual writing must not be rushed; it cannot be late either. It's like shooting arrow; one will miss the target if one hesitates.*

This sentiment could apply equally well to photography and coronary angioplasty. An interventional cardiologist has to take a carefully constructed and complete coronary angiogram. He must also be able to pinpoint the abnormalities instantaneously as soon as the X-ray image is taken. The abnormality can often be very subtle and a discerning and artistic eye would definitely have an advantage in picking out the slightest difference in size, shape, shade and density between normal and abnormal images. The similarity and synergy between art and medicine can be very well-illustrated by a series of photographs that I took during a winter vacation at Cradle Mountain in Tasmania. I was captivated by the images of currawongs (large crow-like birds native to Australia), perching on leafless branches of trees in winter. Images that I immediately identified with the classic composition and style of Bada Shan-ren. However, the greatest surprise came when I inverted two of the developed and printed photographs. The two upside-down images appeared uncannily like those of X-ray images of the human coronary arteries that I took every day in my professional work as an interventional cardiologist! One inverted image resembled that taken in the right oblique (RAO) view and the other in the left oblique (LAO) view of the human coronary angiogram (Fig. 74). These two inverted pictures made up the essential 'biplane' views of a human coronary angiogram that a cardiologist must obtain when performing routine coronary arteriography to diagnose coronary artery disease. Since the capture of these two photographs, I have always used them to illustrate the feasibility of combining art and medicine. I had these two photographs enlarged,

Fig. 74. Photographs of a bird on branches of a tree (left images) when inverted (middle images) resemble human coronary artery angiogram (right images).

framed and hung inverted on the wall in my office. Those who came into my office and commented that my pictures were upside-down were obviously not cardiologists!

I am yet to publish my second photographic book entitled *Window of the Heart*. I have in mind an eye coming from within the heart, especially apt for a cardiologist! The combination of the heart, the seat of all emotion, and the eye is essential in any creative art form. Photography is an art to 'let our eye be the vessel and the soul be filled'.

Emperor Qianlong's Mistake

Emperor Qianlong (1711–1799) ruled China for 60 years and during his long reign the Qing Dynasty was at its zenith. He was an exceptional poet and calligrapher and wrote over 10,000 poems. Qianlong was the eldest and favourite grandson of Emperor Kang-xi. Kang-xi was an all-round politician, scholar and patron of the arts who welcomed western scholars in his imperial court. He ruled China during the Enlightenment period in Europe. Kang-xi even promoted the Christian religion during his reign and often commanded edicts that were favorable to Christianity. Many Jesuit priests were guests or resident scholars in his court. These western scholars brought with them the most up-to-date western books, artwork and scientific instruments of the time. Thus, Kang-xi and his courtiers were quite informed about the scientific achievements of the West and western philosophy and culture in general. From a young age, Qianlong, being the eldest and favourite grandson, was brought up in a strict way by his grandfather Kang-xi. Emperor Kang-xi made sure that the future emperor Qianlong would receive the best education from teachers of both the East and the West. When the seventh son of Kang-xi, Yong-zheng, became Emperor, unlike his father he banished all foreign scholars from the Imperial Court. Contact with the West in the Qing imperial court was disrupted for many years. On the occasion of the 70th birthday of Emperor Qianlong, an English delegation led by Ambassador McCartney arrived at the Imperial Qing Court in Peking, bearing birthday presents for the Emperor from the King of England, and hoping to renew friendship with China. Among the gifts were the latest scientific discoveries in the West, including scientific chronometers, astrological instruments and the microscope. Emperor Qianlong, being a classical Chinese scholar and interested only in the humanities, was unimpressed by these gifts, thinking they were the same as those he had played with as a child. He failed to grasp the significant scientific progress that had occurred in the West in the short time between him and his grandfather Kang-xi. During his reign, Emperor Qianlong had spent all his time and resources collecting the best Chinese art and literature throughout China and paid no attention at all to the scientific revolution and the Enlightenment that were taking place in Europe.

In the traditional Confucian 'top-down' way, Emperor Qianlong ruled in an elitist and exclusivist manner. Around the time when Qianlong was Emperor in China, Catherine the Great was ruling Russia. Empress Catherine the Great was also a passionate patron of the arts. She had amassed the best of western art and her collection was equivalent in significance to that of Qianlong. Catherine decreed the construction of a public museum so that her collection could be viewed and enjoyed by the ordinary folk of Russia. This museum is now the famous Hermitage Museum in Leningrad, built in 1764. In contrast, ordinary Chinese citizens were forbidden access to Emperor Qianlong's private collection, housed in the Forbidden City. The best of China's art and cultural heritage was only collected for Qianlong's personal indulgence. In 1733 Qianlong ordered the edition of the penultimate 'Opus Magnum' of the Chinese literary collection, known as the *shi ku quan zu* or *The Complete Collection of the Four Treasuries*. For this project to be completed, Qianlong ordered the surrender of all books in public and private possession throughout China to the palace. A more sinister motive for this project was to eradicate any existing literary works that were deemed subversive to the Manchurian government at that time. The mega-project took a total of 4000 scholars and 19 years to complete. The entire collection of more than 151,700 volumes was locked up in four separate buildings that were part of the Forbidden City. Ordinary citizen scholars were forbidden access to these books. Just about this time, Denis Diderot, with the help of M. d'Alembert, successfully compiled the first encyclopedia in the western world, in France (Fig. 75). The encyclopedia was written with the goal of 'providing the public with knowledge necessary

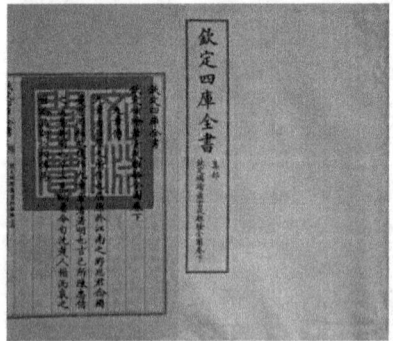 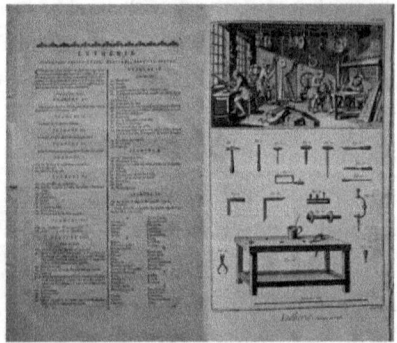

Fig. 75. One volume of the *shi ku qian zu*, commissioned by Emperor Qian-long (left) and a page from D. Diderot's first edition encyclopedia (right).

for self-improvement'. The French and European public in general benefited greatly from this gigantic literary effort, with contributions from ordinary citizens in society. The age of the knowledge-based economy had started in the 18th century in the West, but it has just begun in the East now. The progressive attitude of western rulers in the dissemination and sharing of knowledge contrasted strongly with the desire of the Chinese emperors to render their subjects ignorant so that they could be easily ruled. The self-indulgent attitude of the East compared to the egalitarian spirit of the West could explain why it is necessary today for students from the east to flock to the west for advanced learning. The knowledge-based economic gap explains the difference in scientific and technological advances between the East and the West. Over-indulging in the arts and neglecting the sciences was Emperor Qianlong's mistake; a mistake modern day Chinese citizens are still paying for today.

Mao's Last Musicians

Whenever I was painting as a child, I would play some classical music for inspiration. My family was poor and could not afford classical records or player. I borrowed a simple portable record player from my little uncle, my mother's younger brother, whose entire classical music collection consisted of two records, the 6th Symphony or *Pastoral Symphony* of Ludwig van Beethoven and the Violin Concerto of Peter Tchaikovsky played by Alfredo Campoli. I dreamt of owning my own record player and records from a young age. The dream came true when I won a scholarship to Melbourne to study medicine. I spent most of my savings on classical records and books. Now I have a large library and collection in the area of classical music, fine art, medicine and Christianity. The computerized electronic age has almost rendered my entire collection of classical records and CDs obsolete. The time I had spent creating a manual catalogue and index for my music collection appeared to have been wasted if not for the musical knowledge gained from creating such a catalogue. All the classical music that I want to listen to now can be stored in a pocket size electronic device called iPod. More amazingly, with this little gadget, I can now find and play a specific recording by a specific composer or artist, with a few clicks on the device, even when driving!

I have a wide circle of musician friends. Wang-hua Chu, one of the four composers of the famous *Yellow River Piano Concerto*, a neighbor in Melbourne, is among them. Chu's father, An-ping Chu, was a famous Chinese scholar who was persecuted, presumably to death, during the Cultural Revolution. The piano was considered a symbol of western decadence during the Cultural Revolution. Chu introduced the pianist Chen-zhong Yin, another of the four compsers of the Yellow River Concerto, to me when the latter visited Melbourne. During the Cultural Revolution, Yin had written many patriotic Communist songs known as *Red Songs*, with piano accompaniment in order to be able to continue playing the piano that was banned then. A particular series of red songs entitled *Red Lantern Story* had won the heart of Chairman Mao's wife, Jiang-qin, during a private performance. After this successful performance, Yin received an unexpected commission from Madam Mao to write '*a piece of music of revolutionary significance to celebrate the Chinese triumph over the Japanese occupation of China*'. Yin was the chairman of a small group of musicians appointed by the Ministry for Arts of the central government to compose the piece. Yin, a pianist, thought this was a golden opportunity to revive the piano and requested permission to compose a 'grand orchestral composition with piano accompaniment' (a piano concerto) from Madam Mao. Permission was granted and Yin quickly teamed up with Chu Wang-hua, the main composer, and two other assistants, Liu Juan and Shi Shu-chen, to compose the now famous *Yellow River Piano Concerto*. The mighty Yellow River has been a symbol of the immortal spirit of the Chinese people. Instead of the usual three movements of a western concerto, the final version of the *Yellow River Concerto for Piano* has four movements. My friend Chu told me the intriguing story behind the creation of this unusual four movement Chinese piano concerto.

The first private performance of the original version of the concerto in three movements took place at the Great Hall of the People for a small select group of high officials of the Communist Party, including Chairman Mao, his wife and Premier Zhou En-lai. At the end of the performance, Chairman Mao was very pleased with the piece but commanded that the popular revolutionary song 'The East Is Red' must somehow be incorporated into the concerto. With this direction, the composers went back to the drawing board and added the fourth movement based on the 'The East is Red' theme song. That's how the current familiar four-movement *Yellow River Concerto* was created.

I first met Yin Chen-zhong when he came to Melbourne to perform *The Yellow River Concerto* at the Melbourne Town Hall. Around that time, a popular book *Mao's Last Dancer* by Chen Chun-xi, a dancer of the Cultural Revolution, was being launched in Melbourne. After listening to the first-hand accounts of the persecution of pianists and the attempt to revive the piano with *The Yellow River Concerto*, I encouraged Yin and Chu to write a similar book on their many untold stories and call it *Mao's Last Pianists*.

Another of Mao's last musicians was Lim Kek Tjeng, a forgotten world-class Indonesian violinist of Chinese descent. His moving biography entitled *Beethoven of the Yellow Earth* could also be called *Mao's Last Violinist*. Lim together with Yehudi Menuhin was a pupil of George Enescu, the great Rumanian violinist. Lim met Chou En-lai in Paris and was invited by Chou to go China to set up a modern western orchestra in Beijing. Lim's wife, Elsie, was a world-class ballerina who later became the assistant director of the world-renowned *Cloud Gate Dance Group* in Taiwan. Together they responded to Chou En-lai's invitation and went to China voluntarily to start the Peking Radio Symphony Orchestra. However, not long after their arrival in Beijing, they were caught up in the Cultural Revolution and incarcerated for nine years. The personal sacrifice of Chu, Yin, Lim, Chen and so many other nameless ones to enhance the arts in China should be deeply admired and fondly remembered. They were all Mao's last artists.

One can see that the mistake of Qianlong did not end with him. For China to catch up with the western world, mistakes of Qianlong and the Cultural Revolution should never be repeated.

Chief Rabbi and the 'Wheat Kernel' Parable

The Chief Rabbi in Melbourne was a patient of mine. He had severe heart failure and could hardly walk without getting out of breath. One of his last wishes was to go to his synagogue one last time. The challenge for him was the walk to the synagogue two blocks away from his home. To fulfill his wish, I agreed to accompany him to walk to the synagogue. At snail's pace, starting and stopping every few steps, we managed to get to the synagogue without any mishap. After the service, the Chief Rabbi gave me a Jewish cap and jokingly made me an honorary Jew! My wife and I were invited home for dinner soon after his triumphant return to the synagogue. In the course of the dinner conversation, the Rabbi lamented the constant persecutions suffered by the Jews when I praised the Jews to be God's chosen race. He did not appear to be proud of this fact but instead lamented the senseless loss of six million innocent Jews during the holocaust in World War II. With trepidation, I tried to explain the will of the God of Abraham, Isaac and Jacob to a Jewish Chief Rabbi. It is almost sacrilegious for a Chinese Christian to try to explain the Jewish God to a rabbi. Nevertheless, knowing that rabbis do not accept Christ nor the New Testament, I gingerly quoted Christ to the Rabbi, from a verse in the New Testament, John 12:24 that says *'unless a kernel of wheat falls to the ground and dies, it remains only a single seed. But if it dies, it produces many seeds'*. I then told him the story of the seven young Cambridge Christians who went as missionaries to Africa in the mid-nineteenth century, and a few among them were martyred. Before their mission trip, an editorial of a London newspaper warned against the potential risk of losing their young and brilliant lives to their carnivorous audience in Africa. The warning by the newspaper was proven correct when some of them were indeed devoured. Another editorial soon followed to 'avoid further losses of young English Christians with blind faith'. In the ensuing two centuries, the Sudan Inland Mission (SIM) was established successfully in Africa. Today there are more than two million Christians in Africa as a result of the martyrdom of those early young English Christian missionaries. Unless a kernel falls to the ground and die, it will not produce many seeds. It is not always possible to understand why an apparently senseless event is allowed to happen in one's lifetime. But in the infinite time scale of God, the reason and purpose of God's action will be made clear. What appears to be right or wrong in one's lifetime may not be so in the history of time. It took nearly two centuries to see the reason for the sacrifice of the Cambridge missionaries. It might take a long time for the sacrifice of the six million innocent Jews to make sense to mere mortals but not to God. None of us living today is likely to be around to see the many seeds that are yet to come.

God's Business and Your Profession

In the late 18th century, the microscope had been invented and bacteria were identified as the cause of some deadly diseases. This was a major medical breakthrough and brought with it the idea that man could at last attain immortality. William Osler, the Christian doctor and the new brilliant professor at Johns Hopkins, was invited to deliver the prestigious annual Ingersoll Lecture, at Harvard University in 1908. The topic chosen for his lecture was 'Science and Immortality'. Instead of speaking on the tremendous scientific breakthroughs and how science would overcome mortality, Osler in his lecture advised going back to the Bible if one wishes to attain immortality. The intellectuals of Boston were not impressed. The editorial of the local newspaper, *The Globe*, was equally unflattering in its attack on the learned professor, saying *'that nothing new had been delivered at the Ingersoll lecture that year'*. I read the lecture a hundred years later, in the first edition. I agreed with Osler when he said that eternity could only be achieved through spiritual not physical means. Books can inform, but only the Bible can transform. Most believers tend to put their Bible on the shelf instead of in their hearts. As a medical scientist and a practising Christian, I am often asked: '*How can a scientist like yourself believe in God?*' The answer lies in the word 'believe'. Belief is a *spiritual* process, not an *intellectual* process. One can only believe in the Creation described in the Bible, not understand it. If one rejects the Creation, then one must accept that everything evolves from a void, the so-called 'Big Bang' theory. For there is nothing in between.

One day in 2008, I was asked to give a breakfast talk to the 'Business and Professional Group' of the Bible College of Victoria. I chose the title *God's Business and Your Profession* for my lecture to the many businessmen and professionals that were going to listen to me in the talk. As a Christian in any business or profession group, one should be able to defend one's faith. My profession is medicine and as a doctor scientist, I too have to defend my understanding of God and His Creation. I had read *The language of God* by Francis Collins, head of the Human Genome Project. Collins was an atheist and became a Christian. He could not use his knowledge in science and genetics to explain what he calls the 'Moral Law' or the knowledge of right and wrong. Being a geneticist, Collins was able to explain Darwinian evolution in genomic terms. Genomic evolution is far more precise than Darwinian evolution in explaining the changes observed within and across species, under the influence of changing environments. Although the substrates are different, the processes necessary for Darwinian or genomic evolution are almost identical. The tree of evolution that Darwin sketched a hundred years ago in his own hand and with the words *I think* was almost identical to the genomic tree of related species in the animal kingdom. Maybe in another hundred years, more gaps in the tree of life will be filled and evolution will be explained in even finer terms than chromosomes, genes and nucleic acids, the building blocks of life. Shakespeare wrote all his work with 26 English letters. Did God create a whole human being or just the basic building blocks of life and allow these to evolve?

Collins could not explain the so-called Moral Law, that instinctive comprehension of right and wrong, nor explain one's tendency to want to do the right thing, in genomic terms. This natural tendency to want to do good must have an origin. It is not genetically coded. Collins chose to conclude or *believe* that God must be the author of the Moral Law. I too chose the same: God rather than a void to arrive at the Moral Law. As a Christian, I have chosen to believe what is written in Genesis 1:26: '*let us make men in our image, in our likeness*'. This image of God carries with it the origin of 'good and right' or the so-called 'Moral Law' of Collins. With our understanding of science today, the *Theist-Evolutionist* or *Biologos* concept is acceptable, especially for men of science in the genome era.

Science deals with *extrinsic* or *relative* truth in the observed universe; whereas God holds the *intrinsic* or *absolute* truth. The opening verse of the Bible, a book written by God, '*In the beginning God created heaven and earth*', spells out this absolute truth. Our intellectual mind is incapable of comprehending any of the four terms in the opening verse of the Bible, namely '*beginning*', '*God*', '*Creation*', '*heaven and earth*' (or '*universe*'). Each of these four terms takes us beyond the boundary of our mind. Beyond the mind is the spiritual realm that requires the process of *believing* rather than *knowing*. To accept the concept of '*in the beginning, God, creation and universe*' is to accept God as the creator, the being beyond the boundary that separates mind from spirit. To an atheist, beyond the mind is void, but to a believer in the Creation, it is God. The answer to the age-old question of '*Where do we come from and where are we going?*' can only be found by faith through believing, not by knowing. A good and learned friend of mine, Lin Tze-ping, founder and editor of the Christian magazine '*Cosmic Light*', is a philosopher and a theologian in Taiwan. He elegantly explains the distinction between knowing and believing. '*Knowing*', he said, '*is seeing by sight and hearing by sound; whereas believing is seeing without sight and hearing without sound*'. I think there is great wisdom in his statement. Truth must be absolute and spiritual. According to the Bible, the fruits of the Holy or good Spirit are '*love, joy, peace, patience, kindness, goodness, faithfulness, gentleness and self-control*' (Galatians 5: 22). To me, these are absolute values.

Scientists are always seeking for the truth. But scientific truth is observed as relative truth. Relative truth changes with time, whereas absolute truth is timeless and immutable. Einstein's *Theory of Relativity* emphasizes this fact. Scientific truth or discovery, proven at one point in time, can often be disproven at another time. Scientific truth therefore is mutable. Science discovers but not invents. It can elicit relative truth. Scientific theories are based on observations of a universe already created, if one is a creationist. Science deals with what is already in existence. Science helps to explain the *how* but not the *why* of a phenomenon. Taxonomy, or the naming of objects created or discovered, is clearly described in the first book of the Bible when the created man was asked by God the Creator to name all other creatures: '*Whatever name the man called a creature brought before him, it shall be its name*' *(Genesis 2: 17)*. I conclude that science deals with the laws of the created, whereas creation follows the laws of the Creator. The laws of the Creator or God, for believers, are governed by the values of God and known through believing rather than knowing. In contrast, the laws of the created follow the nature of the created universe. My concept of Science versus Creation is summarized in the following table (Table 5).

Table 5. Science versus creation.

Science	Creation
Relative	Absolute
Finite	Infinite
Law of Creation	Law of Creator
Intellectual	Spiritual
Knowing	Believing
Seeing by sight	Seeing without sight
Hearing by sound	Hearing without sound

God's Words or Fairytales?

When I fractured my left leg after a fall in 1990, I was admitted to the cardiac ward of the Epworth Hospital where I normally worked, I received a very large *Get Well* card signed by all the nurses, who knew me well. On the front of the card was the message: '*Have a Break*'! The nurses thought this was the only way I could have a break (from work)! However, even as a patient, the nurses still gave me ECGs in the ward to report! I continued to give tutorials to medical students from my hospital bed, and in return they all signed my plaster cast. Before the leg accident, I was teaching adult Sunday school at church. My hectic schedule gave me little time to prepare my Sunday school lessons. Now immobilized in the hospital bed, my wife said: '*God has broken your leg so that you can adequately prepare your Sunday school lessons*'! I took her advice seriously and used the long break to prepare the subjects that I was going to teach when I recovered. As a result, a pile of biblical reference books surrounded my hospital bed.

One day, a Jewish cardiac surgical colleague came to visit me. Sitting beside me, he picked up the Bible on the bedside table and said: '*YL, how can you read this rubbish?*' I was startled by his remark and replied: '*this is a book of the Jewish God, the God of Abraham, Isaac and Jacob. Have you actually read the Bible, the Old Testament at least?*' '*Of course not*', he laughed. We worked at the same hospital and attended the weekly departmental journal club together. At the journal club, an assigned speaker for the week would present and critique a recently published journal article that could change current clinical practice. The presenter would have to read the article very carefully and critically. Using the journal club that both of us were familiar with as a reference, I asked my Jewish friend: '*How would you react if I were to conclude that a published scientific paper was rubbish without even reading it?*' He was silent. I then encouraged him to read the Bible first before we could have an informed debate to determine whether or not the Bible is rubbish.

The Bible is either the word of God or a 'fairytale' depending whether or not you believe in God. The two Chinese characters for fairytale are *shen hua*. The three Chinese characters to describe the Bible as words of God are *shen de hua*. The difference is subtle. To a non-believer, the Bible is like a fairytale (*shen hua*) book. However, to believers, it is *shen de hua*, a book of God's words that can change one's life. It is a living book that *transforms* rather than *informs*. Until one has read the Bible and been transformed by it, the Bible will always be a fairytale book.

'What's the Difference Between Me and the Homeless Man On the Street?'

Near the end of a farewell dinner for one of my Chinese fellows in Singapore, he suddenly asked:

> *Teacher, you have worked me very hard all year long and I have learnt much. But I often wonder what is the difference between a homeless person on the street and me? He sleeps all day doing precious little and here I have to work hard day and night?*

This is a soul-searching question that everyone should be asking himself or herself. Central to the question is the purpose of our existence. Who am I and where am I going? The lyric of a hymn entitled 'The content of life', written by a friend and colleague, answered the question aptly. '*Life is not measured by its length, but by its content*'. A brief but meaningful life beats a lengthy one with little content. If the content is full of love, care and support for the needy, the weak, the down trodden, the poor and the sick, then it will be a worthy life. What counts in life is not the mere fact that we have lived. It is what difference we have made to the lives of others that will determine the significance of the life we lived. A doctor's life is one that is meant to prolong the lives of others, to add value to others more than oneself. The young doctor had to work hard so that he would equip himself with delicate skills needed to help restore health to his patients when he returned home to Guangzhou. It is a much more noble existence than just sleeping all day long on the streets. All of us need to have a clear purpose for our existence and a life filled with worthy contents.

My Psalm 23

I was born into a Christian family. My maternal great grandmother migrated with her son to Singapore. As far as I know, she was the first member of our extended family to be baptized a Christian, in southern China in the late 19th century. She was undoubtedly the spiritual leader of the family until her death at the age of 81. My mother served as a deacon in the church that we all attended. I was educated from a kindergarten at a primary school run by the Presbyterian Church. I attended our church Sunday school class regularly with my parents. I knew many Bible stories from a young age and, as stated before, my private English tutor was a British missionary who had worked in Xiamen, the city of my roots in China. With all these early Christian influences, my faith in God, however, is not blind. I found truth in the Bible after deep personal thought, internal debate and soul searching. I am grateful to God for all the different gifts that He has given me to serve Him, especially choir conducting (Fig. 76).

In memory of my father and to follow in my mother's footstep, I have established a few scholarships, all named after my father: they are the Lim Koon Yaw scholarships, abbreviated to LKY, for students of music and Christian theological education. The LKY Music Travelling Scholarship of the Musical Society of Victoria (MSV) is awarded each year to enable a talented young Victorian musician of the Musical Society of Victoria, who aspires to become a concert artist, to study overseas. Three other scholarships for academic excellence are also awarded to graduates of the Chinese Department of the Melbourne School of Theology (MST-C) each year. Working with the Medical

Fig. 76.   Christmas caroling by the Combined Chinese Churches Choir, Melbourne, 1990.

Services International (MSI), a medical clinic was established in Zhoujie, a township high up in the mountainous area Da Liang Shan of Sichuan, China, to deliver basic healthcare to the minority people of the Yi tribe (Fig. 77).

In Hangzhou, a charitable medical clinic known initially as the Red Cross Pharmacy and now as the Bethesda Clinic was also established to provide free medicine and medical consultations to the poor. The Bethesda Clinic was staffed by a small group of dedicated voluntary retired Christian doctors and nurses (Fig. 78).

For many years prior to my involvement in medical missionary work in mainland China, I had already participated in the medical mission known as Chinese Christian Medical Mission (CCMM) in Taiwan. Our family of three would visit my in-laws and then serve as volunteers in the Christian Hospitals of Heng Chun and Pingtong in southern Taiwan. A number of young Christian doctors of CCMM also underwent clinical training with me at the Alfred and Epworth Hospitals in Melbourne in the early 1980s (Fig. 79).

Fig. 77.   Children of the Yi tribe, Da Liang Shan, Zhoujie, Sichuan, 2003.

My life can be reflected in the six verses of the 23rd Psalm of David in the Old Testament; the first verse, *'The Lord is my shepherd, I shall not want'* is fulfilled by the abundance that He has provided to our family till this day. Verse 2, *'He makes me lie down in green pastures, and leads me beside quiet waters'* reminds me of how the Lord had brought me to this 'lucky country' down-under, specifically to Melbourne, voted over and over again as the most livable city in the world. Not only have I had an excellent education; I have a loving wife and a son who has followed my footsteps to become an interventional cardiologist. The third verse, *'He restores my soul and guides me in paths of righteousness for His name's sake'* is the most instructive verse. The awakening of my soul to do good and right things in life has led me to work voluntar-

Fig. 78. Volunteer staff of the *Red Cross Pharmacy* (later renamed *Bethesda Clinic*), Hangzhou 1990.

Fig. 79. Co-workers of the Chinese Christian Medical Mission, 1984 (from left: Wang RT, Joy, YL, Chai MT, Jian CM, Chai CR, Wang LT).

ily in Australia, Singapore and China. The desire to train better doctors, in the end is motivated more by the awakening of the soul than the grief suffered after the loss of my father. A woken Christian soul would naturally want to help and love one's fellow men, especially the sick and the needy. I literally lived through verse 4 *'Even though I walk through the dark valley of the shadow of death, I will fear no evil, for you are with me, your rod and your staff, they comfort me'* when I had the car accident in a remote part of China. The fifth verse, *'You prepare a table before me in the presence of my enemies'* was realised when my workplace enemies were seated at the same table at my valedictory dinners. The final verse, *'You anoint my head with oil, my cup overflows. Surely goodness and mercy will follow me all the days of my life, and I will dwell in the house of the Lord forever'* allows me to count the countless blessings that God has bestowed upon my family and me.

On Wings like Eagles

People often ask me how I managed to cram so much into my life. The answer can again be found in the book of Isaiah in the Bible.

> *But those who hope in the Lord will renew their strength. They will soar on wings like eagles; they will run and not grow weary, they will walk and not be faint (Isaiah 40:31).*

I was fascinated to learn that eagles intermittently undergo a physical metamorphosis to renew their strength and energy. I also learnt that eagles are able to soar to great heights and fly with very little effort of their own. The secret of their effortless flight, however, lies in the interaction of their huge outstretched wings and the wind. The wind represents divine assistance, freely available to anyone who cares to interact with it. This is not only true for me but should be true for all Christians. If we relied only on our own efforts, we would fly like sparrows, flapping our wings endlessly to create the wind necessary to uplift us; we would be rapidly exhausted and fall to the ground dead, just like the demise of sparrows that caused the great famine of China in the Great Leap Forward era in China.

In the New Testament Bible, the parable of the talents has helped me to be humble. '*And unto one he gave five talents, to another two, and to another one; to every man according to his ability*' (Matthew 25:15). The important lesson here is not how many talents one has been given, but how one uses them: 'To be a profitable servant' is what the Master wants. In other words, we are expected to use the talents that each of us has been given wisely and diligently and to make profit for the Master who has entrusted us with these talents. Otherwise, we will be judged as 'wicked and lazy servants', and be cast into '*the darkness, where there will be weeping and gnashing of teeth*'.

Faced with something to accomplish, I always remind myself with the biblical verse documented in Chapter 4 Verse 6 of the book of

Zechariah: '*Not by might nor by power, but by my spirit, says the Lord Almighty*'. If one depends on people in powerful or influential positions to try to accomplish a task, one will invariably be let down. This is true for me in my various endeavors in the few countries that I have worked, Singapore in particular.

'God within You'

I will conclude my life story with a poem written by a patient, Kamala Devi Dhoraisingam, given to me shortly before she died. The poem, entitled 'God within you', was dedicated to all doctors and nurses, and published posthumously by her husband. There can be no greater satisfaction or reward for a doctor or a nurse who has given his or her life to caring for the sick, than to receive the following acknowledgement:

> *As you alleviate*
> *Pain, suffering*
> *May God be there with you*
> *Expressing Himself*
> *From within your thoughtful deeds*
> *So caringly done*
> *With love and kindness*
> *Failing never*
> *May He keep you*
> *Sparkling with wisdom*
> *Mind centered with vivid visions*
> *Built on clear thinking*
> *Keen understanding, good judgment.*
> *May God be enlightening you*
> *With happiness, with enthusiasm*
> *Elegant confidence and alertness*
> *Be cultivating within you*
> *Feeling of fulfillment*

While heightening, deepening
Your passion
Your dedication
Your chosen
Noble profession
Caring for the sick
Invoked by lively vibes that glow
From within your heart, mind, soul
May God be manifesting
Manifesting Himself all day
As you keep invoking Him
Invoking Him
With your vibes of love
Constant calmness
Enduring patience
Goodwill, joy, sincerity
Endless concern, compassion
Rising from the depths of your being

Rewards for Act of Love

Best work is achieved when it is done for the love of it, without hoping for any return. Love should more often be a verb, an act, and less often a noun, a feeling. Pride and self-centeredness are often the greatest resistance to the performance of acts of love, which require self-sacrifice. Adding value to oneself may be seen as success. However, adding value to other people's lives, instead of one's own, is significance, something greater than mere success. '*Do not do to others what one does not want done to oneself*'. This should be a universal value, even though first expressed by Confucius. It requires conscious learning. There are four recognised stages of learning: in the first, the beginner is both 'unaware and unable'. In the second stage, after acquiring some knowledge and skill, the learner is 'aware but still unable'. The third stage of learning is attained when one has acquired knowledge and skill and become 'consciously aware and technically able'. Finally, once aware and able, and with increasing age and experience, one becomes the Master, performing at one's best 'effortlessly and subconsciously'. This learning process applies to work of all kinds, intellectual or technical; but the pinnacle of all work is work for the love of it.

The reward of work out of love is not just *happiness* but *joy*. *Happiness* is a transient response to a pleasant event, but *joy* is the realisation of the real meaning of life and eternal truth. To attain Joy, one must first learn to love in a tangible way. To love oneself or to love something or someone that is lovely is easy and natural. To love someone who is repulsive and not lovely is unnatural and difficult. It requires great sacrificial learning. To love one's enemy is nearly impossible, to die for one's enemy can only be accomplished with the *no greater love* of Jesus Christ.

In any voluntary or involuntary service, whenever injustice appears to have been done and good work not rewarded, the response for a Christian should be different to that of a non-Christian. Using the standard cost-effective analysis model, one could chart a similar work-reward analysis of one's work, especially that out of love (Fig. 80):

The right lower quadrant represents an unexpected or unnatural situation where good work is not rewarded. In this quadrant, where injustice appears to have been done, the response for a Christian should be different to that of a non-Christian. A non-Christian would seek justice in a secular court of law. In contrast, a Christian should seek final judgment by God. Here also, the more one sacrifices, the more one gets in return. This return is joy in one's heart. This incorruptible or eternal reward comes with the understanding of the real meaning of love and life in general. The ultimate role model in this quadrant is Christ himself, with His sacrificial love, also known as *no greater love*.

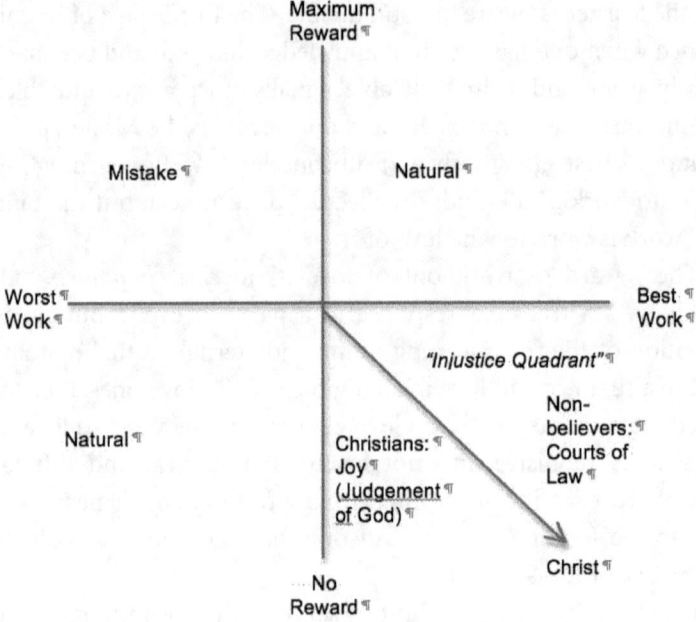

Fig. 80. Reward of *work out of love* is Joy everlasting.

In whatever endeavor, if one works constantly in this right lower quadrant one will be rewarded in the same way as the servants in Jesus' parable of the talents, where the master would say to his faithful servant:

Well done, thou good and faithful servant; thou hast been faithful over a few things; I will make thee rulers of many things. Enter thou into the Joy of thy Lord (Matthew 25: 21)

Epilogue

When I was younger and at the peak of my medical career, I wished that I could live longer than my father, who died at 43, and I could retire from my medical work at 65 years of age to pursue my other non-medical interests. As I write this epilogue on 19th January 2013, it marks my 65th birthday. Not only have my wishes been granted, I can hand over my medical practice to my only son, Iefan, who has turned out to be an interventional cardiologist. There is no greater satisfaction than this for any parent. Thirty years ago, I was inspired by the life of William Osler, told by his student Harvey Cushing. I sincerely hope the story told here will inspire ordinary young men and women who care to read it, to live a life that will make a difference to others.

My life was not significant compared to those who had inspired me. However, the last verse of the poem in the Coronary painting, *'to return to common folks goodness, not grief'*, could sum up my life's work as a doctor. By God's grace and planning, I have been able to act as a 'bypass graft conduit' between the East and the West, in medicine and other academic pursuits. This bypass conduit happens to connect a heart born in Singapore, nurtured in Australia and blossomed in China. What flows through this conduit is not oxygenated blood but love, for the sick and the poor, in both the East and the West.

Now in the winter of my life, I can also fully appreciate the final remarks of William Osler, at the end of a distinguished life:

> *I am a rich man, not in this world's goods, but rich in the goods which neither rust or moth has been able to corrupt, in treasures of friendship and good fellowship, and a fuller knowledge of men and manners.*

I will also treasure the friendships that I have and be grateful that I have not only a fuller knowledge of men and manners, but also the love of God. I shall therefore devote my remaining days to the healing of souls rather than of hearts.

When I was asked in an interview what would be my epitaph when the time comes, I replied *A healer of men and a servant of God* would be very nice, if I deserve it at all.

Chronology

1948 Born January 19th, Singapore
1952 Tao Nan (Chinese) Primary School, Radin Mas (English) Primary School
1954 First Prize, Singapore Open Children Art Exhibition
1956 First Prize, Annual Chinese Calligraphy Competition, Catholic High School
1961 Diploma of Fine Art (Dip. Fine Art), Nanyang Academy of Fine Art, Singapore
1962 Special Prize in Drawing, National Art Competition, Malaysia
1963 Secondary High School Certificate (Chinese), Catholic High School, Singapore
1965 Cambridge Higher School Certificate, St. Andrew's School, Singapore
1966 Colombo Plan Medical Undergraduate Scholarship to Australia
1967 First One-man Art Exhibition, Union Hall, Monash University
1968 Choir Master, Melbourne Overseas Christian Fellowship
1969 National Heart Foundation of Australia Research Scholarship
1970 Stawell Prize, Australian Medical Association
1970 Bachelor of Medical Science with Honours (BMedSc), Monash University

1971 Second One-man Art Exhibition, Prahran Gallery, in aid of the Queen Victoria Hospital Appeal Fund, Melbourne
1972 Bachelor of Medicine, Bachelor of Surgery with Honours (MBBS), Monash University
1972 Harriet Power Scholarship in Medicine, Alfred Hospital
1972 Robert Power Scholarship in Surgery, Alfred Hospital
1973 Married Wen Joy Ma of Taiwan
1974 Monash University Graduate Scholarship
1975 Hume Turnbull Scholarship for Research into Cardiovascular Diseases, Monash University
1976 National Health & Medical Research Council (NH&MRC) Postgraduate Research Scholarship, Australia
1976 Birth of son, Iefan
1977 Doctor of Philosophy (PhD), Monash University
1979 Research Fellowship, National Heart Foundation of Australia
1980 Fellow (FRACP), the Royal Australasian College of Physicians
1981 Friend of the Osler Library, McGill University, Montreal, Canada
1981 Gordon–Taylor Scholarship, University of Melbourne
1981 The Bushell Fellowship, Royal Australasian College of Physicians
1981 The Australasian College of Physicians (RACP) Traveling Fellowship
1981 Overseas Research Fellowship, National Heart Foundation of Australia
1981 Clinical and Research Fellow, Harvard University, Cardiac Unit, Massachusetts General Hospital, Boston, Cambridge, USA
1981 Choir Master, The Chinese Bible Church of Greater Boston, Woburn, Massachusetts, USA
1982 Fellow (FAMS), the Academy of Medicine, Singapore
1982 Member (CSANZ), the Australian and New Zealand Cardiac Society
1982 Member (FACR), the American Federation of Clinical Research

1982	Associate Director, Cardiovascular Unit, Epworth Hospital
1983	Chairman, Board of the Melbourne Chinese Christian Church
1984	Fellow (FACC), the American College of Cardiology
1984	Conductor, Combined Melbourne Chinese Churches
1985	Foundation Member, Chinese Medical Society of the Australian Medical Association
1986	Notable Graduate, Monash Medical Association
1986	27th Annual Exhibition of the A.M.A. Art Group, Victorian Art Society
1988	Senior Consultant, National Cardiovascular Technical Co-operation and Training Centre, Fu Wai Hospital, Beijing, China
1988	Foundation President, Chinese Sacred Music Society, Melbourne
1988	Member of the Board of Directors, Trans World Radio, Australia
1988	Adviser, Board of Directors, Melbourne Chinese Christian Association
1989	One-Man Photographic Exhibition, 'Between Painting and Poetry', Chinese Museum, Melbourne
1990	Director of Physician Training, Royal Australasian College of Physicians, Alfred Hospital, Melbourne
1991	Member, Editorial Committee, Journal of Chinese Medical Sciences, Chinese Academy of Medical Sciences, Beijing, China
1992	Foundation Member, Chairman, Board of the Chinese Ministry Department Bible College of Victoria
1993	Member, Board of the Chinese Writers' Association, Melbourne
1993	Inaugural Monash University Distinguished Alumni Award
1993	Foundation Director, Department of Cardiology, Box Hill Hospital, Melbourne
1993	Patron & Vice President, Board of the Musical Society of Victoria
1994	Guest Professor, Guangdong Cardiovascular Institute, Quangzhou, China
1994	Honorary Adviser, Quangdong Interventional Cardiology Society, Guangzhou, China

1994 Clinical Associate Professor, Department of Medicine, Faculty of Medicine, Monash University, Australia
1994 Visiting Cardiologist, The Heart Centre, Alfred Hospital, Melbourne
1995 Distinguished Overseas Affairs Award, Taiwan, Republic of China
1995 Patron. St. Edwards Art Society, St. Edwards Anglican Church Blackburn South, Victoria
1995 Photographic Book Launch *Eastern Eye Western Light*, Victorian Arts Centre
1995 Foundation Dean, Xiamen University Medical College, Fujian, China
1995 Honorary President, Zhejiang Provincial Hospital, Hangzhou, China
1995 Visiting Professor, Capital Medical University, Chaoyang Hospital, Beijing
1996 Associate Fellow (ARPS), Royal Photographic Society, United Kingdom
1996 Co-chairman, Great Wall International Symposium of Interventional Cardiology, Beijing, China
1997 Director, National Heart Centre, Singapore
1997 Chairman, National Committee on Cardiac Care, Ministry of Health, Singapore
1997 Director, Cardiovascular Institute, Xiamen, Fujian, China
1997 Member, International Editorial Committee, European Heart Journal
1997 Member (General Division), Order of Australia.
1998 Inaugural GWICC International PTCA Coach Award
1998 Honorary Professor, Monash University, Australia
1998 Consultant Professor, Shanghai Second Medical University
1998 Chairman, Cardiology Subspecialty Advisory Committee, Academy of Medicine, Singapore

1998 Visiting Professor, Dalian Medical University, China
1998 Visiting Professor, Liaoning Medical University, Shenyang, China
1998 Member, Society for Cardiovascular Magnetic Resonance (SCMR)
1999 Member, Editorial Board, Asian Annals of Cardiothoracic Surgery
1999 Chairman, Committee for Review of Medical Education, Ministry of Health, Singapore
1999 Vice-Chairman, Taskforce on Traditional Chinese Medicine Research, Singapore
2000 Chairman, National Medical Research Council, Singapore
2000 Member, Inter-Ministerial Life Science Executive Committee, Singapore
2001 Guest Professor, 4th Military Medical University, Xian, China
2001 Honorary Advisor, Anhui Heart Institute, Hefei, China
2001 Permanent Secretary, The Asia Pacific Society of Interventional Cardiology
2002 Visiting Professor, Peking Union Medical College, Beijing, China
2002 Visiting Professor, Institute of Cardiovascular Sciences, Peking University
2002 Chairman, Board of Directors, Nanyang Academy of Fine Arts, Singapore
2002 Member, Editorial Board, Experimental and Clinical Pharmacology and Physiology, Australia
2002 Foundation Director, Raffles Heart Centre, Raffles Hospital, Singapore
2003 Foundation Professor and Director, Centre for Cardiovascular Therapeutics, Western Health, Victoria, Australia
2003 Professorial Fellow, University of Melbourne
2004 Distinguished Personality, Chinese Medical Association, Victoria

2004   Deputy-Chairman, Board of the Chinese Theological Department, Bible College of Victoria
2004   Member, Board of MSI Professional Services, Australia
2005   Visiting Professor, Harbin Medical University, China
2005   Visiting Professor, Fudan University, Zhongshan Hospital, Shanghai
2005   Visiting Professor, Huaxi Clinical Medical Faculty, Sichuan University
2005   Honorary Director, Interventional Training Centre of Southwest China
2005   Fellow (FSCAI), the Society for Cardiovascular Angiography and Interventions, USA
2005   Dean's Lecture, Faculty of Medicine, Dentistry and Health Sciences, University of Melbourne
2006   Fellow (FESC), the European Cardiac Society
2006   Emeritus Fellow (FAPSIC), the Asia Pacific Society of Interventional Cardiology
2006   Fellow (FCSANZ), Cardiac Society of Australia & New Zealand
2006   Fellow of the Andreas Gruentzig Society
2006   Inaugural Garry Roubin Award, 2nd Asia Pacific Interventional Advances Conference (APIA)
2006   Vice-Chairman, Chinese Theological Department, Bible College of Victoria
2007   China Interventional Therapeutics (CIT) Special Contribution Award, Beijing
2007   Honorary Director, Heart Centre, 2nd Affiliated Hospital, Zhejiang University College of Medicine
2007   Inaugural Appreciation Plaque, Asia Pacific Society of Interventional Cardiology, Angioplasty Summit, Seoul, South Korea
2007   Visiting Professor, Wenzhou Medical University
2007   Significant Contribution Award, Chaoyang Hospital, Beijing

2008 Kasarn Jatigawanich Memorial Lecturer, Thailand Cardiac Society
2009 Life Achievement Award, 11th South China Congress of Cardiology, Guangzhou, China
2010 Honorary Director, Cardiology, No. 2 Affiliated Hospital, Zhejiang University, Hangzhou
2010 Honorary Professor, Tianjin Institute of Cardiology, Tianjin University, Tianjin
2010 Honorary President, Northern Guangdong People's Hospital, Shaoguan, Guangdong
2011 Leading Specialist, No. 7 People's Hospital, Zhenzhou, Henan
2011 Honorary President, Cardiovascular Institute, Henan Technological University, Luoyang, Henan
2011 Guest Professor, Department of Cardiology, Henan Provincial People's Hospital, Zhenzhou, Henan
2011 Honorary Director, Heart Centre of Henan Provincial Chest Hospital
2011 Special Contribution and Life Achievement Award, 5th Qianjiang Interventional Cardiology Congress, Hangzhou
2011 Special Contribution Award, 22nd Great Wall Cardiology Congress, Beijing
2012 Establishment of the Y.L.Lim Interventional Cardiology Fellowship at Western Health, Melbourne, Australia
2013 Chairman, Board of the Melbourne School of Theology, Chinese
2013 Visiting Professor, Qingdao University Hospital, Shangdong
2013 Visiting Professor, Qilu Medical University, Jinan, Shandong
2014 Honorary Director, Department of Cardiology, Chest Hospital, Tianjin
2014 Visiting Professor, Guangdong Cardiovascular Institute, Guangdong Pepoles' Provincial Hospital, Guangzhou

Index

A Walton, 70
A.E.Smith, 41
Agency for Science Technology
  and Research (A*STAR), 200
Albert Schweitzer, 94
Albert Tucker, 265
Alf Barnett, 50
Alfredo Campoli, 279
Aline Wong, 181
Ancora Imparo, 256
Andreas Gruentzig, 221
Andreas Gruentzig Society, 222
Antonio Colombo, 232
Anzhen Hospital, 136
Aquinas College, 27
Archibald McIntyre, 36
Arthur Boyd, 29
Arthur Lim, 154
Arthur Tan, 226
Asia Interventional Cardiovascular
  Therapeutics (AICT), 230

Asia Pacific Society of Cardiology
  (APSIC), 227
Aubrey Pitt, 57
Aunty Georgie, 31
Austin Hospital, 111
Australia China Indonesia
  Singapore Heart Foundation
  (ACIS), 112
Australian Labour Party, 51
Australian National Heart
  Foundation Overseas Research
  Fellowship, 63

Bada Shanren, 265
Baker International Diabetic
  Institute (Baker IDI), 201
Baker Medical Research Institute, 49
Bassett, 93
Beautiful China, 15
Bethesda Clinic, 290
Between Painting and Poetry, 263

bing-ren, 80
Biomedical Research Council (BMRC), 200
Biopolis, 201
Biosensor Company, 203
Box Hill Hospital, 100
Boyer's Block, 22
Brian Buxton, 108
Bruce Davis, 108
Bulfinch Building, 249

C J Officer-Brown Cardiothoracic Unit, 64
Cambridge Higher Certificate examination, 24
Cambridge University, 76
Cardiac Unit of MGH, 57
Caroline Street, South Yarra, 53
Catherine the Great, 277
Catherization and Cardiovascular Intervention (CCI), 230
Catholic High School, 9
Central Gippsland Hospital, 47
Centre for Cardiovascular Therapeutics, 69
Cezanne, 269
Chai Yuan Pei, 4
Changi General Hospital, 195
Charles Dotter, 224
Charles Toh, 175
Chen Yi-fei, 272
Chen Ai-jou, 204
Chen Chuan Hong, 173
Chen Chuan-rong, 124
Chen Hou-zu, 231

Chen Jiyan, 124
Chen Jun-zu, 115
Chen Wen-xi, 18
Chen-chang, 149
Cheng Hwee, 5
Chen-zhong Yin, 280
Cheong Soo Pieng, 18
Chia Boon Lok, 218
Chiam Tao Soon, 259
Chief Rabbi, 282
China Cardiovascular Interventional Forum (CCIF), 233
China Inland Mission (CIM), 95
China Interventional Cardiology Salon (CICS), 233
China Interventional Therapeutics (CIT), 228
Chinese Academy of Fine Art, 4
Chinese calligraphy, 11
Chinese Christian Medical Mission (CCMM), 290
Chinese Museum, 263
Chinese Technical Cooperation and Training Center of Cardiovascular Disease (CTCTCCD), 107
Chou En-lai, 281
chou tofu, 45
Christianity, 277
Cia Guo-liang, 170
Cia Shaobin, 140
Cindy, 31
Circulation, 57
Clifford Albutt, 76
Clifton Pugh, 62

Clinical Research Unit, 49
Collin Stevens, 163
Colombo Plan Scholarship, 21
Committee for the Review of Medical Education, 197
Complex Catheterization Therapeutics (CCT), 228
Coronary angiography, 108
Coronary artery bypass graft surgery (CABG), 108
Cradle Mountain, 275
Creation, 284
Cultural Revolution, 281
currawongs, 275

Dai Ji-zhong, 95
Dalian, 136
Dalian Medical University Hospital, 136
Darwinian evolution, 284
David Chesler, 57
David Fang, 118
Da-yi, 78
Da-yi jin chen, 82
Dean's Lectures, 262
Debussy, 264
Deng Xiao-ping, 252
Denis Diderot, 278
Devereaux, 41
Diagnostic Related Group (DRG), 193
Diao Yu Tai, 236
Ding Wen-chien, 113
Djeng Siew-lian, 231
Doctor of Philosophy, 55

Dolf Bachmann, 223
Donald Esmore, 109
Duke University, 198
Duncan Main, 116
Dunhuang, 139
durian, 43

Economic Development Board (EDB), 200
Eggleston & McDonald, 163
Electoral College, 189
encyclopedia, 278
Epping, 30
Epworth Cardiovascular Unit, 64
Epworth Eastern Hospital, 69
Epworth Medical Centre, 59
Epworth Medical Foundation, 110
Epworth-China connection, 111
Eric Chapman, 34
Eric Ferguson Glasgow, 35
Er-ya, 274
ESR Hughes, 50
Esther Holland, 116
Ether Dome, 250
Ethica Award, 237
Eugene von Guerard, 20
Eugenia Lumbers, 39
Europe Paris Course in Revascularization (EuroPCR), 227
Executive Committee for Life Sciences, 259

fair-dinkum, 30
fairytale, 288

Fang Qi, 106
Fellowship of the Asia Pacific
   Society of Cardiology (FPSIC), 229
Fok Yin Dong, 124
Forbidden City, 104
Foreign Exchange Notes (FEN), 101
Fourth Military Medical University, 141
FRACP, 56
Francis Collins, 284
Frank Balchin, 10
Frantisek Zivec, 40
Fred Williams, 264
Fu Wai Hospital, 106
Fujian, 1

George Stirling, 64
Georgette Chen, 18
Gerald Pohost, 57
Goh Chok Tong, 213
Good Clinical Practice (GCP), 243
Good Manufacturing Practice (GMP), 243
Gough Whitlam, 51
Grace Baker, 28
Graeme Sloman, 59
Great Wall Interventional
   Cardiology Congress (GWICC), 132
Guangdong Cardiovascular Institute, 123
Guangzhou Provincial Hospital, 123
Guo Jia-qiang, 106

Hangzhou, 113
Harriet Power Scholarship, 44
Harvard University, 57
Harvey Cushing, 75
He Guo-wei, 170
Heidelberg School, 66
Henry Kissinger, 241
Hermitage Museum, 278
Higher School Certificate, 21
Hippocratic Oath, 82
Hong Yong-shi, 154
Howitt Hall, 32
Hu Dayi, 132
Hu Jingtao, 85
Hua Tuo, 138
Huang Jie-fu, 187
Hui Bu, 4
Human Genome Project, 284

Iefan, 53
Ingersoll Lecture, 283
Inter-Ministerial Executive
   Committee for Life Sciences, 199
International Heart Forum (IHF), 233

J. Needham, 268
James Gobbo, 192
James Hudson Taylor, 94
James Hudson-Taylor III, 95
Jean Marco, 238
Jeff Kennett, 68
Jian Bao-dun, 115
Jiang-nan, 103

Jiang-qin, 280
Jin Fan, 113
John Balla, 69
John Jardine, 40
John Masterton, 50
John Singer Sargent, 160
Johns Hopkins Hospital, 89
Johns Hopkins Medical School, 160
Johor, 1
Joseph Dufresse, 12
joy, 297
Joyce Daws, 42
jun chen zuo shi, 257
Junbo Ge, 237
June Howqua, 41
June Pash, 42

Kalorama, 95
Kamala Devi Dhoraisingam, 295
Kang-xi, 276
Kiasu, 191
Kitty Smith, 41
Kokoura Live Course, 226
Krystal Bergin, 146
Kuala Lumpur, 19
kuan-xi, 110

Lancet, 39
Lau Eng Swan, 2
Lau Tek Jin, 3
Lee Foundation, 161
Lee Hsien Loong, 26
Lee Kong Chien, 161
Lee Kuan Yew, 33

Lee PS, 110
Lee Seng Gee, 210
Leonardo da Vinci, 94
Li Jiali, 123
Li Keran, 271
Li Lan-qing, 156
Li Shi-hsuen, 273
Lianhe zhaobo, 219
Lie Siong Tay, 112
Liem Sioe Leong, 112
Lim Boon Keng, 151
Lim Hak Tai, 16
Lim Kek Tjeng, 281
Lim Koon Yaw, 1
Lim Koon Yaw Memorial
  Scholarship, 26
Lim Nan San, 1
Lim's Ward Round, 88
Lin Ju-geng, 153
Lin Tze-ping, 285
Lin Zuguang, 124
Lingnan Congress of Cardiology,
  233
Li-shou, 274
Liu Chao-zhong, 139
Liu Jian, 235
Liu Kong-qian, 12
Liu Tai-ge, 216
Liu Zu-guo, 173
LKY Music Travelling Scholarship,
  289
Louis Ignarro, 145
Love, 296
Lu Shu-jen, 234

Lu Yan-shao, 113
Ludwig van Beethoven, 279

M. Nobuyoshi, 114
Ma Pu Yin, 45
Ma Wen Joy, 43
Mabel Brookes, 42
Mak Koon Hou, 226
Manolas E, 63
Ma Pu-yin, 45
Marco Polo, 139
Marie Tehan, 67
Marist Brothers, 9
Marjorie Roeder, 34
Mary Delahunty, 268
Mason Sones, 224
Massachusetts General Hospital (MGH), 57
Maxiang, 149
Mayo Clinic, 87
McGill University Medical School, 76
Medical Services International (MSI), 290
Melbourne Grammar School orchestra, 145
Melbourne School of Theology, 289
Meng-zi, 32
metabolic vascular intervention centres (MVIC), 73
Michael Kelly, 57
Michael Woolridge, 194
Michelle Yeoh, 217
Mingshasun, 140
Ministry for Health, 177

Miss Ma, 43
Mistri Wing, 203
Moktar Riady, 112
Monash University, 22
Moral Law, 284
Mount Elizabeth Hospital, 175
Mrs. Dalziel, 29
Murrumbeena, 29
Music to the Eye, 263
Musical Society of Victoria (MSV), 289

Nanyang Academy of Fine Art (NAFA), 16
Nanyang Technology University, 182
National Heart Centre, 24
National Heart Foundation of Australia, 57
National Heart Foundation Overseas Research Fellowship, 57
National Medical and Research Council (NMRC), 198
National Science and Technology Board (NSTB), 200
National University Hospital (NUH), 178
Nellie Shkolnikova, 145
Neuroscience Institute, 209
New Testament, 282
New Year resolution, 1
Ng Eik Chong, 112
Ngo So-Khim, 5
Ningxia People's Provincial Hospital, 140
Norman Bethune, 96

Northern interventional live course, 233
Northern Military Hospital, 137

Ocker, 30
Omega watch, 25
Organization for Economic Cooperation and Development (OECD), 85
Oriental Congress of Cardiology (OCC), 233
Osler Library, 76
Overseas Missionary Fellowship (OMF), 95
Overseas Union Bank, 3
Oxburgh Committee, 198
Oxford University, 76

Pan Shi-mao, 166
Paul Korner, 55
Paul Morawetz, 99
Peking Radio Symphony Orchestra, 281
Peking Union Medical College, 135
Peking University, 4
Percutaneous Transluminal Coronary Angioplasty (PTCA), 59
Peter Howard Emerson, 263
Peter Tchaikovsky, 279
Peter Wills Report, 199
Pharmaceutical Benefits (PBS) Scheme, 213
Philip Island, 53
Phoenix shrub, 14
poliomyelitis, 7

Prahran Gallery, 42
pregnancy hypertension, 55
Principle and Practice of Medicine, 66
Psalm of David, 291
Pudong, 101
Pyramid of Excellence, 188

Qi, 78
Qianjiang Interventional Cardiovascular Congress (QICC), 233
Qianlong, 276
Qing Dynasty, 3
Queen of Malaysia, 19
Queen Victoria Hospital, 36

Radin Mas, 10
Raffles Hospital, 208
Red Cross Chaoyang Hospital, 132
Red Cross Pharmacy, 290
Rediffusion Broadcasting Corporation, 5
Renji Hospital, 126
Renminbi, 101
Revision Notes in Clinical Medicine, 56
Richard Larkins, 199
Robert Porter, 37
Robert Power Scholarship, 44
Robert Whelan, 38
Rockefeller Medical Research Institute, 135
Rowan Walker, 48

Royal Australasian College of Physicians (RACP), 55
Royal College of Surgeons, 176
Run Run Shaw Hospital, 118

Sahu, 141
Saito, 237
Science, 285
Sha Meng-hai, 113
Shanghai, 101
Shaxi People's Provincial Hospital, 122
Shenyang, 137
shi ku quan zu, 278
Silk Road, 139
Simon Shorvon, 208
Singapore casemix, 195
Singapore Christian Home for the Aged, 5
Singapore General Hospital, 7
Singapore Heart Centre, 176
Singapore Heart Centre Live Demonstration Course, 226
Singapore Live Demonstration of Vascular Endo-therapy' (SingLIVE), 226
Singapore Polytechnic, 182
Singapore Story, 33
Singaporean Public Service Commission, 55
Sistine Chapel, 13
Society of Catheterization Angiography and Intervention (SCAI), 230
Southwest China Cardiovascular Symposium, 233

Special Economic Zone, 152
Special Prize for Drawing, 18
Spencer King III, 63
St. Andrew's School, 22
Stephen Lee, 232
Straits Times, 176
Student Research Scholarship, 41
Sudan Inland Mission (SIM), 283
Summer Palace, 105
Sun Xi-miao, 82
Sun Yat-sen, 151
Suzhou, 104
Swanston Street Church of Christ, 52
Sydney Opera House, 51
SYNTAX, 239

Taipei, 45
Taipei Imperial Palace Museum, 45
Tan Kah Kee, 150
Tang Shan, 130
Tanner Operation, 23
Tao Li Fen Fang, 144
Tao Shou-qi, 106
Tao-nan Primary School, 151
TCM Research Taskforce, 259
TCT-Asia Pacific, 228
Teaching Hospitals, 162
Teddy Chien, 236
The Alabama Student, 93
The New Yorker, 87
Thomas Linacre, 76
Thomas Sydenham, 76
Tin Hua, 5
Tiong Bahru, 7
To Live, 133
Toa Nan Primary School, 9

Tom Love, 30
Tong-an, 1
Tony Tan, 199
Traditional Chinese medicine (TCM), 256
Trans-Catheter-Therapeutics (TCT), 227
trans-current point, 272
Treatise of Disease of the Cold, 256
Tsing-hua University, 12
two pyramids, 241

Ukiyo-e, 269
Ulrich Sigwart, 232
University of Adelaide, 28
University of Hong Kong, 151

vascular intervention centre (VIC), 73
Vermeer, 272
Victor Chang, 111
Victor Kalff, 57
Victor Smorgon, 59
Victor Smorgon Fellowship in Cardiology, 61
Victorian casemix, 194

Wang Bing-yau, 126
Wang Jian-An, 119
Wang Li-min, 172
Wang Rong, 155
Wang Sin Ru, 172
Wang Xi-zhi, 275
Wangfujin, 135
Wang-hua Chu, 280
Weifeng Shen, 236

Wei-wei, 128
Wen Jen Building, 161
Werner Forssmann, 224
Western Hospital, 69
Whitehorse Gazette, 100
William A.W. Walters, 36
William Harvey, 76
William Osler, 75
World Health Organization, 87
Wu Guang-zhong, 273
Wu Jie-Ping, 157
Wuxi, 104

Xiamen City Emergency Centre, 154
Xiamen Eye Centre, 154
Xiamen Heart Centre, 154
Xiamen University, 150
xiao-kai, 12
Xijing Hospital, 114
Xu Beihong, 270
xue-tong, 17

Y L Lim Interventional Cardiology Fellowship, 71
Yan Kai-ran, 75
Yap family, 15
Yean Chuan, 6
Yean Kai, 6
Yean Leng, 7
Yean Teng, 5
Yee Choi, 128
Yehudi Menuhin, 281
Yellow Emperor's Inner Canon, 256
Yellow River Piano Concerto, 280
yi-jiang, 80

Yin Yin, 34
yi-shen, 80
yi-shi, 80
Yong Pang How, 206
Youth Male Chinese Association (YMCA), 3
Yunchuan, 140

Zhang Bei-mong, 166
Zhang Da-chian, 273
Zhang Shi-dian, 12
Zhang Yun, 173
Zhang Zhong-jin, 256
Zhejiang First Affiliated Hospital, 115
Zhejiang Hospital, 113
Zhejiang No 2 Affiliated Hospital, 119
Zhejiang People's Provincial Hospital, 120
Zhejiang University, 117
Zhen He Building, 165
Zheng Siew Lian, 114
Zhongshan Hospital, 162
Zhoujie, 290
Zhu Guo-ying, 170
zi cheng fu ye, 146
Zimei, 151
Zu Chuan-xi, 113
Zurich, 221

www.ingramcontent.com/pod-product-compliance
Lightning Source LLC
Chambersburg PA
CBHW051108230426
43667CB00014B/2491